D0636306

KEY MARKET
CONCEPTS

KEY MARKET CONCEPTS

BOB STEINER

REUTERS

An imprint of **Pearson Education**

London · New York · San Francisco · Toronto · Sydney · Tokyo · Singapore
Hong Kong · Cape Town · Madrid · Paris · Milan · Munich · Amsterdam

PEARSON EDUCATION LIMITED

Head Office:
Edinburgh Gate
Harlow CM20 2JE
Tel: +44 (0)1279 623623
Fax: +44 (0)1279 431059

London Office:
128 Long Acre
London WC2E 9AN
Tel: +44 (0)20 7447 2000
Fax: +44 (0)20 7240 5771
Website: www.business-minds.com

First published in Great Britain in 2001

ISBN 0 273 65040 8

British Library Cataloguing in Publication Data
A CIP catalogue record for this book can be obtained from the British Library.

10 9 8 7 6 5 4 3 2 1

Typeset by Pantek Arts Ltd, Maidstone, Kent.
Printed and bound in Great Britain by Redwood Books Ltd, Trowbridge, Wilts

The Publishers' policy is to use paper manufactured from sustainable forests.

TO MY WIFE,
BA

CONTENTS

RISK MANAGEMENT / 209

APPENDICES / 225

ABOUT THE AUTHOR

Bob Steiner is Managing Director of Markets International Ltd, an independent company specializing in training in a range of areas related to the international financial markets, treasury and banking. The company also provides advice to finance directors and treasurers of international companies on foreign exchange, money markets and other treasury matters. This ranges from written studies reviewing existing management policies and procedures, through the development of appropriate hedging strategies, to short-term market advice.

Bob was previously senior consultant with HongKong and Shanghai Banking Corporation, working in London and New York, in the dealing area, as a consultant to major US and European companies on treasury management. He has also been treasurer and fund manager of H P Bulmer Holdings plc and English and American Insurance Group plc, active in currency and interest rate management. He has thus been closely involved in treasury management as a consultant and a practitioner. He also worked in the Overseas Department of the Bank of England, and with the European Commission in Brussels.

Bob himself spends a considerable amount of time training bankers, systems staff, corporate staff and others involved in the financial markets. In particular, he personally runs courses for all the ACI exams – the ACI Diploma, the Dealing Certificate and the Settlement Certificate – as well as courses on Financial Calculations and Repos. He is the author of *Mastering Financial Calculations* and *Mastering Repo Markets*, published by FT Prentice Hall.

His academic background is an honours degree in mathematics from Cambridge University followed by further studies in economics with London University. He is a member of the ACI and of the Association of Corporate Treasurers.

TIME VALUE OF MONEY

SIMPLE INTEREST AND COMPOUND INTEREST

Definition

Simple interest is interest calculated on the assumption that there is no opportunity to re-invest the interest payments during the life of an investment and thereby earn extra income.

Compound interest is interest calculated on the assumption that interest amounts will be received periodically and can be re-invested (usually at the same rate).

HOW ARE THEY USED?

Simple interest

On short-term instruments, interest is usually 'simple' rather than 'compound'. Suppose, for example, that an investor places £1 on deposit at 8% per annum for 92 days. He expects to receive all the interest at the end of the period – in this case after 92 days. The 8% is however quoted per annum, so that the investor receives only a proportion of 8% – in this case $\frac{92}{365}$.

The total proceeds after 92 days are therefore the return of the principal, plus the interest:

$$£\left(1 + \left(0.08 \times \tfrac{92}{365}\right)\right)$$

Similarly, if the investor places £73 on deposit at 8% for 92 days, he will receive a total of:

$$£73 \times \left(1 + \left(0.08 \times \tfrac{92}{365}\right)\right)$$

Compound interest

Now consider an investment of £1 made for 2 years at 10% per annum with interest paid each year. At the end of the first year, the investor receives interest of £0.10. At the end of the second year, he receives interest of £0.10, plus the principal of £1. The total received is £0.10 + £0.10 + £1 = £1.20. However, the investor would in practice re-invest the £0.10 received at the end of the first year, for a further year. If he could do this also at 10%, he would receive an extra £0.01 (= 10% × £0.10) at the end of the second year, for a total of £1.21. The interest accumulated (excluding the £1 principal) is therefore £0.21. Similarly, if he invested £73 originally, he would achieve total proceeds at the end of two years of £73 × 1.21 = £88.33. The interest accumulated (excluding the £73 principal) is therefore £15.33.

These calculations assume that interest cashflows arising during an investment can be re-invested at the same original rate of interest (in this case 10%). Although this is frequently a very useful assumption, re-investment of such cashflows is in practice likely to be at different rates. Clearly if a different assumption is to be made, then in order to calculate the total proceeds accumulated by the end of an investment, account must be taken of the different rate paid on the interim cashflows – see the example below.

Sometimes interest is paid in several instalments even when the whole investment period is less than a year, or more frequently than annually when the whole investment period is longer than a year. In these cases, compounding must take account of each interest payment.

Related terminology

The *re-investment rate* is the rate at which interim interest cashflows can be re-invested – which may or may not be the same as the original investment rate.

⇨ *See also* effective rate, equivalent rate and continuously compounded rate.

FORMULAS

$$\text{interest calculated using simple interest} = \text{principal} \times \left(1 + \left(\text{interest rate} \times \frac{\text{days in period}}{\text{days in year}}\right)\right)$$

Note that 'days in year' can mean 365 (for example with a sterling deposit) or 360 (for example with a US dollar deposit) – see **money market basis**.

Assuming compound interest, with reinvestment at the original interest rate:

$$\text{interest accumulated after N years} = \text{principal} \times ((1 + \text{interest rate})^N - 1)$$

If the interest is paid in f instalments each year:

$$\text{interest accumulated after N years} = \text{principal} \times \left(\left(1 + \left(\frac{\text{interest rate}}{f}\right)\right)^{(f \times N)} - 1\right)$$

EXAMPLE 1

$843 is invested for 234 days at 6.5%, simple interest:

$$\text{interest amount} = \$843 \times 0.065 \times \frac{234}{360} = \$35.62$$

EXAMPLE 2

$843 is invested for 3 years at 6.5% (paid annually):

$$\text{interest amount} = \$843 \times (1.065^3 - 1) = \$175.30$$

EXAMPLE 3

$843 is invested for 3 years at 6.5% (paid quarterly):

$$\text{interest amount} = \$843 \times \left(\left(1 + \left(\frac{0.065}{4} \right) \right)^{(4 \times 3)} - 1 \right) = \$179.90$$

EXAMPLE 4

$843 is invested for 3 years at 6.5% (paid annually). By the end of the first year, interest rates for all periods have risen to 7.0% (paid annually). By the end of the second year, rates have risen to 7.5% (paid annually). Whenever an interest payment is received, it is re-invested to the end of the 3-year period. What are the total proceeds by the end of the third year?

The cashflows received from the original investment are:

end of year 1: $843 × 0.065 = $54.80
end of year 2: $843 × 0.065 = $54.80
end of year 3: $843 × 1.065 = $897.80

At the end of year 1, the $54.80 is reinvested at 7.0% to produce the following cashflows:

end of year 2: $54.80 × 0.07 = $3.84
end of year 3: $54.80 × 1.07 = $58.64

At the end of year 2, the $54.80 from the original investment plus the $3.84 arising from re-investment of the first year's interest is re-invested at 7.5% to produce the following cashflow:

end of year 3: $58.64 × 1.075 = $63.04

Total proceeds including the principal: $897.80 + $58.64 + $63.04 = $1,019.48

The result would be slightly different if the interest payments were re-invested only for one year at a time, and then rolled over, rather than re-invested to the maturity of the original investment.

EQUIVALENT RATE, EFFECTIVE RATE AND CONTINUOUSLY COMPOUNDED RATE

Definition

An **equivalent interest rate** is the rate which achieves the same total proceeds as another given interest rate (the nominal rate), but assuming a different frequency of compounding.

An **effective interest rate** is an equivalent interest rate, where the frequency of compounding is annual (i.e. 365 days).

A **continuously compounded interest rate** is an equivalent rate, where the frequency of compounding is infinite (i.e. the period of compounding is infinitesimally short).

HOW ARE THEY USED?

Nominal rates, equivalent rates and effective rates

Suppose bank A quotes 10% per annum (the *nominal rate*) for a 9-month (270 days) deposit, with all the interest paid at the end of 9 months. Bank B however quotes a lower nominal rate but pays the interest in quarterly instalments (2.5% each 3 months). Assuming that the interest instalments can be re-invested at this same rate, what nominal rate per annum must bank B quote so that, by the end of 270 days, the investor achieves exactly the same as if he had invested with bank A at 10%? The answer is called the quarterly equivalent of the 9-monthly rate. We could also ask the question the other way round – if we know the nominal rate quoted by bank B on a quarterly basis, what is the equivalent 9-monthly rate?

This idea can be extended for interest payments of any frequency – daily, 6-monthly (i.e. semi-annual), etc. In the particular case of interest paid each 365 days, and also calculated on the basis of a 365-day year (see **money market basis**), the equivalent rate is called the effective rate. To compare the nominal rate quoted for a 40-day investment with the nominal rate quoted for a 95-day investment – even though the investments will not last as long as a year – one approach is to calculate the effective rate in each case. We can also extend the idea to comparing interest paid with different frequencies on a long-term investment.

Continuous compounding

The effect of compounding increases with the frequency of interest payments, because there is an increasing opportunity to earn interest-on-interest. The annual rate is always greater than the semi-annual equivalent, which in turn is always greater than the monthly equivalent, etc.

In theory, the frequency could be increased indefinitely, with interest compounded each hour, or each minute, or ... . The limit is where the frequency is infinite – 'continuous compounding'. This can be used for converting all rates to continuously compounded equivalents for the purpose of comparison, as an alternative to effective rates. Continuously compounded rates are neat to work with mathematically and are used, for example, in option pricing models. They generally assume interest is calculated on a **bond basis** (effectively a 365-day year basis).

> Related terminology
>
> ⇨ *See* compound interest.

FORMULAS

In general, if a nominal interest rate per annum is quoted assuming interest is paid each d_1 days, what is the equivalent rate with interest paid each d_2 days?

$$\text{equivalent rate} = \left(\left(1 + \left(\text{nominal rate} \times \frac{d_1}{\text{days in year}}\right)\right)^{\left(\frac{d_2}{d_1}\right)} - 1\right) \times \frac{\text{days in year}}{d_2}$$

Note that 'days in year' can be 360 or 365 – see **money market basis**.

In particular:

$$\text{effective rate} = \left(1 + \left(\text{nominal rate} \times \frac{d_1}{\text{days in year}}\right)\right)^{\left(\frac{365}{d_1}\right)} - 1$$

$$\text{nominal rate} = \left((1 + \text{effective rate})^{\left(\frac{d_1}{365}\right)} - 1\right) \times \frac{\text{days in year}}{d_1}$$

Also:

$$\text{continuously compounded rate} = \frac{365}{d_1} \times LN \left(1 + \left(\text{nominal interest rate} \times \frac{d_1}{\text{days in year}}\right)\right)$$

or

$$\text{continuously compounded rate} = LN\,(1 + \text{effective interest rate})$$

$$\text{nominal interest rate} = \left(e^{\left(\text{continuously compounded rate} \times \frac{d_1}{365}\right)} - 1 \right) \times \frac{\text{days in year}}{d_1}$$

or

$$\text{effective interest rate} = e^{\text{continuously compounded rate}} - 1$$

'e', a number occurring in mathematical formulas, is approximately 2.7183. LN (…) means the logarithm (to base e) of a number. Both are found on financial and mathematical calculators.

EXAMPLE 1

The interest rate for a US dollar investment lasting 153 days is 6.51%.

$$\text{91-day equivalent rate} = \left(\left(1 + \left(0.0651 \times \frac{153}{360}\right)\right)^{\left(\frac{91}{153}\right)} - 1 \right) \times \frac{360}{91} = 0.0647 = 6.47\%$$

$$\text{effective rate} = \left(1 + \left(0.0651 \times \frac{153}{360}\right)\right)^{\left(\frac{365}{153}\right)} - 1 = 0.0673 = 6.73\%$$

$$\text{continuously compounded equivalent} = \frac{365}{153} \times \text{LN}\left(1 + \left(0.0651 \times \frac{153}{360}\right)\right)$$
$$= 0.0651 = 6.51\%$$

EXAMPLE 2

A 5-year investment has interest paid annually at 6.51% on a **bond basis** (effectively a 365-day year basis). Assume three months is an exact quarter of a year. Then:

$$\text{quarterly equivalent rate} = \left((1.0651)^{\left(\frac{1}{4}\right)} - 1\right) \times 4 = 0.0636 = 6.36\%$$

EXAMPLE 3

The effective rate for a US dollar investment lasting 91 days is 6.51%.

$$\text{nominal rate} = \left((1.0651)^{\left(\frac{91}{365}\right)} - 1\right) \times \frac{360}{91} = 0.0627 = 6.27\%$$

$$\text{continuously compounded rate} = \text{LN}(1.0651) = 0.0631 = 6.31\%$$

EXAMPLE 4

The continuously compounded equivalent for a US dollar 273-day investment is 6.51%.

$$\text{nominal interest rate} = \left(e^{\left(0.0651 \times \frac{273}{365}\right)} - 1\right) \times \frac{360}{273} = 0.0658 = 6.58\%$$

$$\text{effective rate} = e^{0.0651} - 1 = 0.0673 = 6.73\%$$

FUTURE VALUE (FV), PRESENT VALUE (PV), RATE OF DISCOUNT AND DISCOUNT FACTOR

Definition

The **future value** of an amount of money is the amount which can be achieved at a given date in the future by investing (or borrowing) the money at a given interest rate, assuming compound re-investment (or re-funding) of any interest payments received (or paid) before the end.

The **present value** of a future cashflow is the amount of money which needs to be invested (or borrowed) now at a given interest rate in order to achieve exactly that cashflow in the future, assuming compound re-investment (or re-funding) of any interest payments received (or paid) before the end.

A **rate of discount** is the interest rate which has been chosen for calculating a present value from a future amount.

A **discount factor** is the number by which you need to multiply a future cashflow, in order to calculate its present value.

HOW ARE THEY USED?

Short-term investments

If an investor deposits £100 for 98 days at 10% per annum, how much does he receive by the end? The answer (principal plus interest) is:

$$\text{£}100 \times \left(1 + \left(0.10 \times \frac{98}{365}\right)\right) = \text{£}102.68$$

£102.68 is said to be the future value (or 'accumulated value') after 98 days of £100 now. We can also ask the question in reverse: how much does an investor need to invest now to achieve £102.68 at the end of the 98-day period? We already know that the answer is £100, so that £100 is the present value of £102.68.

Therefore, if an investor is guaranteed to receive a particular amount of money in the future, how much money should he be willing to give up now in return? The answer is the present value of that future amount, because he knows that, by investing this present value, he can achieve the same future result. Therefore the value now, i.e. the price, of any investment is the present value of its future cash-flow(s). Any future cashflow, however arising, can be valued in this way.

As long as interest rates are not negative, any given amount of money is worth more sooner than it is later because, if you have it sooner, you can place it on deposit to earn interest on it. This is the 'time value of money'. The extent to which it is worthwhile having the money sooner depends on the interest rate and the time period involved.

Long-term investments

With long-term investments, interest is usually paid in instalments – often each year. The future amount achieved must therefore take account of compounding, i.e. earning more interest from re-investment of these interest payments. Future value and present value calculations for longer periods therefore take account of this.

Rate of discount and discount factor

The rate of discount is whatever interest rate has been chosen for making the present value/future value calculations. Depending on the exact purpose of the calculation, this might for example be a current market yield (for an investment) or a particular reference rate (for cashflow valuation).

A discount factor is a convenient way of arriving at a present value when you know the future value. Suppose, for example, that the 5-year discount factor for US dollars is 0.747258. The present value of $100 in 5 years' time is therefore:

$100 × 0.747258 = $74.73

Similarly, the present value of $579.84 in 5 years' time is:

$579.84 × 0.747258 = $433.29

The discount factor is in fact the present value of 1.

Related terminology

The calculation of a present value is sometimes known as *discounting* a future value to a present value.

⇨ *See also* compound interest, net present value (NPV) and internal rate of return (IRR).

FORMULAS

For investments not involving compounding (generally short-term investments):

$$\text{future value} = \text{present value} \times \left(1 + \left(\text{interest rate} \times \frac{\text{days in period}}{\text{days in year}}\right)\right)$$

$$\text{present value} = \frac{\text{future value}}{\left(1 + \left(\text{rate of discount} \times \frac{\text{days in period}}{\text{days in year}}\right)\right)}$$

$$\text{discount factor} = \frac{1}{\left(1 + \left(\text{rate of discount} \times \frac{\text{days in period}}{\text{days in year}}\right)\right)}$$

Note that 'days in year' can be 360 or 365 – see **money market basis.**

For investments over N years with interest compounded each year:

$$\text{future value} = \text{present value} \times ((1 + \text{interest rate})^N)$$

$$\text{present value} = \frac{\text{future value}}{((1 + \text{interest rate})^N)}$$

$$\text{discount factor} = \frac{1}{((1 + \text{interest rate})^N)}$$

Note that using a **continuously compounded interest rate**, the discount factor can be calculated as:

$$\text{discount factor} = e^{\left(-\text{continuously compounded rate} \times \frac{\text{days in period}}{365}\right)}$$

This way of expressing the discount factor is used commonly in option pricing formulas.

EXAMPLE 1

What is the future value in 92 days' time of $120 now, using 8% per annum?

$$\$120 \times \left(1 + \left(0.08 \times \frac{92}{360}\right)\right) = \$122.45$$

(Simple interest rate, because there is only one interest payment, at maturity.)

EXAMPLE 2

What is the 92-day sterling discount factor if the interest rate for the period is 7.8%?

What is the present value of £270 in 92 days' time?

$$\text{discount factor} = \frac{1}{\left(1 + \left(0.078 \times \frac{92}{365}\right)\right)} = 0.980719$$

present value = £270 × 0.980719 = £264.79

or:

$$\text{present value} = \frac{£270}{\left(1 + \left(0.078 \times \frac{92}{365}\right)\right)} = £264.79$$

(Simple interest rate, because there is only one interest payment, at maturity.)

EXAMPLE 3

What is the future value in 5 years' time of $120 now, using 8% per annum on a **bond basis** (effectively a 365-day year basis)?

$120 × ((1.08)^5) = $176.32

(The interest rate is compounded because interest is paid each year and can be re-invested.)

EXAMPLE 4

What is the 3-year discount factor based on a 3-year interest rate of 8.5% compounded annually?

What is the present value of £270 in 3 years' time?

$$\text{discount factor} = \frac{1}{((1.085)^3)} = 0.782908$$

present value = £270 × 0.782908 = £211.39

or:

$$\text{present value} = \frac{£270}{((1.085)^3)} = £211.39$$

(The interest rate is compounded because interest is paid each year and can be re-invested.)

EXAMPLE 5

What is the 92-day sterling discount factor if the continuously compounded interest rate for the period is 7.72%?

What is the present value of £270 in 92 days' time?

$$\text{discount factor} = e^{\left(-0.0772 \times \frac{92}{365}\right)} = 0.980729$$

present value = £270 × 0.980729 = £264.80

NET PRESENT VALUE (NPV) AND INTERNAL RATE OF RETURN (IRR)

Definition

A **net present value (NPV)** is the net total of several present values (arising from cashflows at different future dates) added together, some of which may be positive and some negative.

An **internal rate of return (IRR)** is the one single interest rate (**rate of discount**) which it is necessary to use when discounting a series of future values to achieve a given net present value or, equivalently, the interest rate which it is necessary to use when discounting a series of future values *including* an initial cashflow *now*, to achieve a *zero* net present value.

HOW ARE THEY USED?

NPV

Suppose that we have a series of future cashflows, some of which are positive and some negative. Each will have a present value, dependent on the time to that cashflow and the rate of discount used for that particular cashflow. The sum of all the positive and negative present values added together is the *net* present value or NPV. This gives a valuation of all the cashflows as a package – equivalent to a price now, for owning an investment which delivers these cashflows in the future, or the amount of money which it is worth spending now to achieve these cashflows in the future.

IRR

Suppose we have the following cashflows which might, for example, arise from some business project:

Now:	– $87
After 1 year:	+ $25
After 2 years:	– $40
After 3 years:	+ $60
After 4 years:	+ $60

What interest rate is needed to discount + $25, – $40, + $60 and + $60 back to a net present value of + $87? The answer is 5.6%. It can therefore be said that an initial investment of $87 produces a 5.6% internal rate of return, if it generates these subsequent cashflows (note that in this example one of these subsequent cashflows, after two years, is a further outflow rather than an inflow). This is equivalent to saying that, using 5.6%, the net present value of – $87, + $25, – $40, + $60 and + $60 is zero. Note that the sign of the cashflows represents the direction of flow (payment out or receipt).

The IRR measures the rate of return achieved by the cashflows irrespective of what might be considered as a current interest rate or market yield. If the flows above arose from an industrial project for example, the company involved would be achieving a 5.6% return on the project. If it believed that it could spend the initial $87 in a different way and achieve a significantly higher return than 5.6%, this might lead to rejection of the project.

Related terminology

⇨ *See also* **present value, rate of discount, discount factor, zero-coupon yield.**

FORMULAS

The cashflows can be discounted assuming **simple interest** or **compound interest** – see **present value**. Assuming compound interest, which would be appropriate for long-term cashflows, then:

$$NPV = \left(\frac{\text{first cashflow}}{(1 + \text{rate of discount})^{\text{years to first cashflow}}} \right) + \left(\frac{\text{second cashflow}}{(1 + \text{rate of discount})^{\text{years to second cashflow}}} \right) + \dots \text{etc.}$$

The rate of discount may be the same for each cashflow (for example calculating a bond price using the conventional **yield to maturity** as the rate of discount) or different (for example using a different **zero-coupon yield** for each cashflow).

It is not possible to write an explicit formula for an IRR. Rather, the same formula as above is used, with a zero NPV:

$$\text{initial cashflow} + \left(\frac{\text{first future cashflow}}{(1 + IRR)^{\text{years to first cashflow}}} \right) + \left(\frac{\text{second future cashflow}}{(1 + IRR)^{\text{years to second cashflow}}} \right) + \dots \text{etc.} = 0$$

Calculating an NPV is relatively simple: calculate each present value separately and add them together. Calculating an IRR, however, requires a repeated trial and error method ('iteration') and is therefore generally done using a specially programmed calculator. The calculator first makes a guess for the IRR and sees how close the result is to zero. On the basis of this, it makes a second guess and so on, until the result is acceptably accurate.

EXAMPLE 1

What is the NPV of the following future cashflows, discounting at a rate of 7.5% per annum on a **bond basis** (effectively a 365-day year basis)?

After 1 year:	+$83
After 2 years:	−$10
After 3 years:	+$150

$$\frac{\$83}{1.075} - \left(\frac{\$10}{(1.075^2)}\right) + \left(\frac{\$150}{(1.075^3)}\right) = \$189.30$$

EXAMPLE 2

What is the IRR of the following cashflows?

Now:	−$164
After 1 year:	+$45
After 2 years:	+$83
After 3 years:	+$75

Answer: 10.592%

To demonstrate this, use the IRR to work backwards to an NPV of zero:

$$-\$164 + \left(\frac{\$45}{1.10592}\right) + \left(\frac{\$83}{(1.10592^2)}\right) + \left(\frac{\$75}{(1.10592^3)}\right) = \$0$$

ANNUITY

Definition

An **annuity** is a regular stream of future cash receipts which can be purchased by an initial cash payment, or a regular stream of cash payments to repay an initial borrowing.

HOW IS IT USED?

An annuity is an investment designed to provide a regular stream of income rather than a lump sum at maturity. This would suit for example an investor's need to provide for a particular expense (such as school fees) over a number of years. A house mortgage structured with regular monthly payments over a number of years but no lump sum payment at maturity is similarly an annuity structure.

The regular payments are not necessarily equal. They can, for example, increase at a regular predetermined rate. This would be useful for an income stream designed to increase with forecast inflation.

The payment stream can also last indefinitely, in which case the annuity is known as a *perpetual*.

The size of the future cash amounts is determined by the *yield* appropriate to the investment. This is the same as the **internal rate of return** on all the cashflows (initial outflow and subsequent inflows).

A bond paying a fixed coupon rate can also be seen as a combination of an annuity (representing the coupon payments) plus a zero-coupon bond (representing the face value of the bond redeemed at maturity). This is one approach to interpreting the conventional formula for the price of a bond.

Related terminology

An annuity is also known as an *annuity certain*. When the payments are made at the end of each period, it is known as a *deferred annuity* and when they are at the beginning of each period, an *annuity due*.

⇨ *See also* **net present value** and **internal rate of return**.

FORMULAS

Annuity paying a constant amount at the end of each year

$$\text{initial cost} = \frac{\text{annual amount}}{\text{yield}} \times \left(1 - \left(\frac{1}{((1 + \text{yield})^{\text{number of years}})}\right)\right)$$

$$\text{annual amount} = \frac{\text{initial cost} \times \text{yield}}{\left(1 - \left(\frac{1}{((1 + \text{yield})^{\text{number of years}})}\right)\right)}$$

Annuity paying a constant amount at the beginning of each year

$$\text{initial cost} = \frac{\text{annual amount}}{\text{yield}} \times \left(1 + \text{yield} - \left(\frac{1}{((1 + \text{yield})^{(\text{number of years} - 1)})}\right)\right)$$

$$\text{monthly amount} = \frac{\text{initial cost} \times \text{yield}}{\left(1 + \text{yield} - \left(\frac{1}{((1 + \text{yield})^{(\text{number of years} - 1)})}\right)\right)}$$

Annuity paying a constant amount at the end of each month

The monthly formulas given here assume that the yield is quoted on the basis of monthly interest payments rather than as an annual equivalent rate (i.e. **effective rate**). If the rate is quoted as an effective rate, it can be converted to a monthly **equivalent rate** first.

$$\text{initial cost} = \frac{12 \times \text{monthly amount}}{\text{yield}} \times \left(1 - \left(\frac{1}{\left(\left(1 + \left(\frac{\text{yield}}{2}\right)\right)^{(12 \times \text{number of years})}\right)}\right)\right)$$

$$\text{monthly amount} = \frac{\text{initial cost} \times \text{yield}}{\left(12 - \left(\frac{12}{\left(\left(1 + \left(\frac{\text{yield}}{12}\right)\right)^{(12 \times \text{number of years})}\right)}\right)\right)}$$

Annuity paying a constant amount at the beginning of each month

$$\text{initial cost} = \frac{12 \times \text{monthly amount}}{\text{yield}} \times \left(1 + \frac{\text{yield}}{12} - \left(\frac{1}{\left(\left(1 + \left(\frac{\text{yield}}{12}\right)\right)^{(12 \times \text{number of years} - 1)}\right)}\right)\right)$$

$$\text{monthly amount} = \frac{\text{initial cost} \times \text{yield}}{\left(12 + \text{yield} - \left(\frac{12}{\left(\left(1 + \left(\frac{\text{yield}}{12}\right)\right)^{(12 \times \text{number of years} - 1)}\right)}\right)\right)}$$

Annuity paying an amount at the end of each year which increases each year at a constant growth rate

$$\text{initial cost} = \frac{\text{first annual amount}}{(\text{yield} - \text{growth rate})} \times \left(1 - \left(\left(\frac{(1 + \text{growth rate})}{(1 + \text{yield})}\right)^{\text{number of years}}\right)\right)$$

$$\text{first annual amount} = \frac{\text{initial cost} \times (\text{yield} - \text{growth rate})}{\left(1 - \left(\left(\frac{(1 + \text{growth rate})}{(1 + \text{yield})}\right)^{\text{number of years}}\right)\right)}$$

Perpetual annuity paying a constant amount at the end of each year

$$\text{initial cost} = \frac{\text{annual amount}}{\text{yield}}$$

$$\text{annual amount} = \text{initial cost} \times \text{yield}$$

Perpetual annuity paying an amount at the end of each year which increases each year at a constant growth rate

$$\text{initial cost} = \frac{\text{first annual amount}}{(\text{yield} - \text{growth rate})}$$

$$\text{first annual amount} = \text{initial cost} \times (\text{yield} - \text{growth rate})$$

All the following examples assume that yields are quoted on a **bond basis** (effectively a 365-day year basis), rather than a **money-market basis** (effectively a 360-day year basis).

EXAMPLE 1

What is the cost of a 10-year annuity paying $5,000 at the end of each year and yielding 6%?

$$\text{initial cost} = \frac{\$5,000}{0.06} \times \left(1 - \left(\frac{1}{(1.06^{10})}\right)\right) = \$36,800.44$$

EXAMPLE 2

How much is payable at the end of each year on a 7-year annuity yielding 6%, if the initial investment is $60,000?

$$\text{annual amount} = \frac{\$60,000 \times 0.06}{\left(1 - \left(\frac{1}{(1.06^{7})}\right)\right)} = \$10,748.10$$

EXAMPLE 3

What is the cost of a 10-year annuity paying $5,000 at the beginning of each year and yielding 6%?

$$\text{initial cost} = \frac{\$5,000}{0.06} \times \left(1.06 - \left(\frac{1}{(1.06^9)}\right)\right) = \$39,008.46$$

EXAMPLE 4

A 25-year mortgage of £100,000 is structured with equal payments at the beginning of each month and no lump sum paid at maturity. The interest rate is 7.5% per annum (monthly basis).

$$\text{monthly payment} = \frac{£100,000 \times 0.075}{\left(12.075 - \left(\frac{12}{\left(\left(1 + \left(\frac{0.075}{12}\right)\right)^{(12 \times 25 - 1)}\right)}\right)\right)} = £734.40$$

EXAMPLE 5

What is the cost of a 10-year annuity, yielding 6% and paying $10,000 at the end of the first year and subsequent amounts which increase by 3% each year (i.e. $10,300 at the end of the second year, $10,609 at the end of the third year, etc.)?

$$\text{initial cost} = \frac{\$10,000}{(0.06 - 0.03)} \times \left(1 - \left(\left(\frac{1.03}{1.06}\right)^{10}\right)\right) = \$83,188.04$$

EXAMPLE 6

What is the cost of a perpetual annuity paying $5,000 at the end of each year and yielding 6%?

$$\text{initial cost} = \frac{\$5,000}{0.06} = \$83,333.33$$

EXAMPLE 7

An investor has $250,000 to place in a perpetual annuity yielding 6% and paying an amount at the end of each year which increases each year by 4%. What would the first annual payment be?

$$\text{first annual amount} = \$250,000 \times (0.06 - 0.04) = \$5,000$$

ZERO-COUPON YIELD AND YIELD CURVE

ZERO-COUPON YIELD, THE SPOT YIELD CURVE AND BOOTSTRAPPING

Definition

A **zero-coupon yield** is the actual or theoretical *yield* earned on an instrument where there are no cashflows other than at the start and at maturity.

The **spot yield curve** shows zero-coupon yields against time to maturity.

Bootstrapping is a process of building up a theoretical spot yield curve by calculating zero-coupon yields for successively longer maturities from those for shorter maturities.

HOW ARE THEY USED?

Zero-coupon bond

A zero-coupon instrument is one which pays no coupon. For example, a company might issue a 5-year bond with a face value of 100 but no coupon. Clearly an investor would not pay 100 for this; he would pay considerably less to allow for the fact that alternative investments would earn him interest. The investor might find such an investment useful because a zero-coupon bond provides certainty of return. With a coupon-bearing bond, the investor is at risk to the rate at which he will be able to re-invest the coupons as they arise during the life of the bond; the **yield to maturity** on the bond assumes (by definition) that the coupons can be re-invested at the same yield to maturity throughout, which is, of course, very unlikely in practice. With a zero-coupon bond, there is no such reinvestment risk; the investor knows exactly how much he will have accumulated by maturity. This can be particularly important for investors such as, say, pension funds with specific liabilities which need to be matched by assets. Investors in zero-coupon bonds can also sometimes be attracted by differences between tax rates on coupons and tax rates on capital gains.

Zero-coupon yield

A zero-coupon yield is the **compound** yield earned on such an instrument; it is the interest rate per annum which it is necessary to use to *discount* the **future value** of the instrument (i.e. its face value) to the price paid for it now. This is the same as the **internal rate of return (IRR)** on the instrument. This interest rate is always given as the decompounded rate, not the simple annual rate (with a 5-year zero-coupon bond for example, it is not sufficient just to take the difference between face value and purchase price, as a proportion of the purchase price, and divide it by 5).

For many markets and maturities, there might be no zero-coupon instrument available. There will nevertheless be theoretical zero-coupon yields which are consistent with the 'usual' yields available in the market – that is, the yields on coupon-bearing instruments.

Bootstrapping

One method of calculating these theoretical zero-coupon yields is to build up synthetic zero-coupon structures by combining a series of actual coupon-bearing instruments in such a way that all the cashflows net to zero except for the first and the last. A convenient way of doing this is first to construct a 2-year zero-coupon structure, then a 3-year structure, then a 4-year structure etc. This process is known as bootstrapping.

In the example below, we use three bonds as our starting point, none of which is priced at *par* (i.e. 100). We could instead use bonds priced at par, or time deposits (which also return the same original principal amount at maturity). In the case of **interest rate swaps (IRS)** for example, we would indeed expect to have par swap rates as our starting point to calculate the corresponding theoretical zero-coupon swap yields. The bootstrapping process is exactly the same, with initial cashflows of 100 each instead of the non-par prices used in the example below.

If all market prices and yields are consistent, it will not matter which actual coupon-bearing instruments we use to construct the zero-coupon yields. In practice however they will not be exactly consistent and it is generally preferable to use instruments priced as closely as possible to par.

Bond and cashflow valuation

A zero-coupon yield is unambiguous: it is a measure of the relationship between a single future value and its present value. We can therefore value any future cashflow if we know the market's view of the zero-coupon yield to that future time. An interest rate swap trader for example might have many unrelated cashflows on his trading book. The entire book can be valued by valuing each cashflow separately with the appropriate zero-coupon yield to give their total **net present value (NPV)**. Similarly, we can calculate the NPV of a series of bond cashflows by discounting each cashflow at the zero-coupon yield for that particular period. The result will be the price for that bond exactly consistent with the zero-coupon curve. A single yield – the internal rate of return – can then be calculated which would arrive at this same price; this single yield is the usual **yield to maturity** quoted for the bond.

The resulting price and yield might in practice be slightly different from the actual market price. The investor then needs to decide whether, if the theoretical price is lower, he considers the bond over-priced. Conversely, if the theoretical price is higher than the market price, he might consider the bond a relatively cheap investment.

Generally, there is no exact *arbitrage* to bring the market price precisely in line with this theoretical price, because there are often no exactly corresponding zero-coupon instruments. It is therefore often more a question of using zero-coupon yields to compare different bonds, to see which is better value at current market prices. In the case of government securities where **strips**, i.e. zero-coupon bonds, can be traded however, a direct comparison can be made between the price of the bond and the prices of its stripped components, so that the arbitrage is possible.

When valuing future cashflows, it is common to multiply by a **discount factor**, rather than discount using a zero-coupon yield. This is simpler but mathematically equivalent, because the discount factor has already taken into account the necessary compounding of the zero-coupon yield.

There is, of course, more than one spot yield curve. In the same way that in each currency there is a yield curve for government bonds, a different curve for AA-rated bonds, a different curve for interest rate swaps, etc., so there is a different spot curve for each also. Valuation of cashflows requires the use of whichever zero-coupon yields or discount factors are appropriate in that particular case.

Curve fitting

For bond yields, it is not generally possible in practice to find a series of existing bonds with the most convenient maturities – say 1 year, 2 years, 3 years, 4 years, etc. – from which we can construct the zero-coupon rates by bootstrapping. Instead, we must use what are actually available, which will be a variety of maturities which are not whole numbers of years. We therefore need to draw a curve to **interpolate** between existing yields in order to establish rates for all possible maturities. This is a relatively complex operation, requiring assumptions to be made about the mathematical nature of the curve and some degree of compromise in order to make the curve smooth.

Related terminology

The spot yield curve is also known simply as the zero-coupon yield curve.

⇨ *See also* **par yield curve**, **discount factor** and **net present value (NPV)**.

CALCULATION METHOD

Bootstrapping

Construct a synthetic 2-year zero-coupon investment from a 2-year coupon-bearing investment and a 1-year borrowing. The amount of the 1-year borrowing is chosen so that the total repayment amount offsets exactly the 1-year coupon of the 2-year investment. The 2-year zero-coupon yield is then:

$$\left(\frac{\text{2-year cashflow}}{\text{initial cashflow}} \right)^{\left(\frac{1}{2}\right)} - 1$$

Then construct a synthetic 3-year zero-coupon investment from a 3-year coupon-bearing investment, a 2-year zero-coupon borrowing and a 1-year borrowing. The amount of the 2-year zero-coupon borrowing (at the rate that has just been calculated) is chosen so that the total repayment amount offsets exactly the 2-year coupon of the 3-year investment. The amount of the 1-year borrowing is chosen so that the total repayment amount offsets exactly the 1-year coupon of the 3-year investment. The 3-year zero-coupon yield is then:

$$\left(\frac{\text{3-year cashflow}}{\text{initial cashflow}} \right)^{\left(\frac{1}{3}\right)} - 1$$

This process can be continued as long as necessary.

Cashflow valuation

value now of a cashflow in N years' time = cashflow $\times$ discount factor for N years

where:

$$\text{discount factor} = \frac{1}{(1 + \text{zero-coupon yield})^N}$$

A 'fair' value for any coupon-bearing bond is the NPV of all the bond's cashflows, using zero-coupon discount factors. The bond's yield to maturity can then be calculated from this **dirty price** (see **yield to maturity** for this calculation).

EXAMPLE 1

Suppose that the 1-year interest rate is 10% and that a series of bonds is currently priced as follows:

	Price	Coupon	Maturity
bond A	97.409	9%	2 years
bond B	85.256	5%	3 years
bond C	104.651	13%	4 years

Consider a 2-year investment of 97.409 to purchase 100 face value of bond A and a 1-year borrowing of 8.182 at 10.0%. The cashflows are:

Year				Net Cashflows
0	− 97.409	+ 8.182		− 89.227
1	+ 9.000	− 9.000		
2	− 109.000			+ 109.000

In this way, we have constructed what is in effect a synthetic 2-year zero-coupon instrument, because there are no cashflows between now and maturity. The amount of 8.182 was calculated as the amount necessary to achieve 9.000 after 1 year – that is, the present value of 9.000 after 1 year.

$$\text{The 2-year zero-coupon rate is therefore } \left(\frac{109.00}{89.227}\right)^{\left(\frac{1}{2}\right)} - 1 = 0.10526 = 10.526\%$$

Next, consider a 3-year investment of 85.256 to purchase 100 face value of bond B, a 1-year borrowing of 4.545 at 10.0% and a 2-year zero-coupon borrowing of 4.093 at 10.526%. The cashflows are:

Year				Net Cashflows
0	− 85.256	+ 4.545	+ 4.093	− 76.618
1	+ 5.000	− 5.000		
2	+ 5.000		− 5.000	
3	− 105.000			+ 105.000

Again, 4.545 is the present value of 5.000 after 1 year; 4.093 is the present value of 5.000 after 2 years.

$$\text{The 3-year zero-coupon rate is } \left(\frac{105.00}{76.618}\right)^{\left(\frac{1}{3}\right)} - 1 = 0.11076 = 11.076\%$$

Finally, consider a 4-year investment of 104.651 to purchase 100 face value of bond C, a 1-year borrowing of 11.818 at 10%, a 2-year zero-coupon borrowing of 10.642 at 10.526% and a 3-year zero-coupon borrowing of 9.486 at 11.076%. The cashflows are:

Year					Net Cashflows
0	– 104.651	+ 11.818	+ 10.642	+ 9.486	– 72.705
1	+ 13.000	– 13.000			
2	+ 13.000		– 13.000		
3	+ 13.000			– 13.000	
4	+113.000				+ 113.000

The 4-year zero-coupon rate is $\left(\dfrac{113.000}{72.705}\right)^{\left(\frac{1}{4}\right)} - 1 = 0.11655 = 11.655\%$

EXAMPLE 2

Using the same zero-coupon yield structure as developed in example 1, what are the fair prices and yields to maturity of:

(i) a 4-year 5% coupon bond?
(ii) a 4-year 11.5% coupon bond?
(iii) a 4-year 13% coupon bond?

The zero-coupon yields are as above:

1-year: 10.000%
2-year: 10.526%
3-year: 11.076%
4-year: 11.655%

The zero-coupon discount factors are therefore:

1-year: $\dfrac{1}{(1.1)} = 0.90909$

2-year: $\dfrac{1}{(1.10526)^2} = 0.81860$

3-year: $\dfrac{1}{(1.11076)^3} = 0.72969$

4-year: $\dfrac{1}{(1.11655)^4} = 0.64341$

(i)   The cashflows of the first bond are 5 (coupon after 1 year), 5 (coupon after 2 years), 5 (coupon after 3 years) and 105 (coupon plus principal redeemed after 4 years).

Price = $(5 \times 0.90909) + (5 \times 0.81860) + (5 \times 0.72969) + (105 \times 0.64341) = 79.84$. Yield to maturity = 11.58% (see **yield to maturity** for this calculation).

(ii) Price = $(11.5 \times 0.90909) + (11.5 \times 0.81860) + (11.5 \times 0.72969) + (111.5 \times 0.64341) = 100.00$. Yield to maturity = 11.50%.

(iii) Price = $(13 \times 0.90909) + (13 \times 0.81860) + (13 \times 0.72969) + (113 \times 0.64341) = 104.65$. Yield to maturity = 11.49%.

THE PAR YIELD CURVE

Definition

The **par yield curve** shows *yield* against time to maturity for theoretical bonds which would be priced at *par* to be consistent with the yields of actual instruments available in the market.

HOW IS IT USED?

A par yield is the yield to maturity of a *coupon*-bearing bond priced at par. Clearly, it is very unlikely at any one time that there will be a bond priced exactly at par for any particular maturity. Therefore, such a bond is generally theoretical. The reason for considering such a theoretical bond, rather than yields of existing coupon-bearing bonds, is that anything else would be arbitrary. We could for example consider a range of existing five-year bonds – one with a 3% coupon, one with a 7% coupon and one with a 12% coupon. Even assuming the same issuer for all the bonds and no tax or other hidden effects, we would not expect the market **yield to maturity** to be exactly the same for the three bonds. The cashflows are on average rather further in the future in the case of the 3% coupon bond than in the case of the 12% coupon bond; if longer-term yields are higher than shorter-term yields, for example, the later cashflows should be reflected by a higher yield than the early cashflows, so that the 3% coupon bond should have a slightly higher yield than the 12% coupon bond. The 7% coupon bond's yield should lie between the other two. Rather than choose one of these arbitrarily, we therefore choose a bond priced at par to be representative of coupon-bearing yields for that particular maturity. On a coupon date, this is a bond whose coupon is the same as its yield.

In order to construct the yields of these theoretical par bonds, we use theoretical **zero-coupon yields**, which in turn are constructed from a series of existing bonds (generally non-par) in the market. We use these zero-coupon yields (or the equivalent discount factors) to construct theoretical bonds whose price – calculated as their net present value (NPV) – would be par. There is of course not only one par yield curve and its associated zero-coupon yield curve. Rather, there are as many par yield curves as there are issuers. Government bond yields will generally be lower than corporate bond yields or **interest rate swap (IRS)** yields for example.

A par yield curve tends to be exaggerated by the corresponding zero-coupon curve. That is, a positive par yield curve is reflected by a higher zero-coupon curve and a negative par yield curve by a lower zero-coupon curve (see Figure 1).

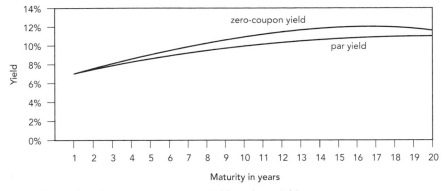

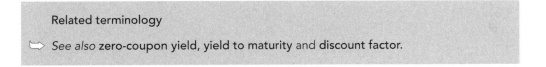

FIGURE 1 Comparison between zero-coupon yields and par yields

Related terminology

⇨ *See also* **zero-coupon yield**, **yield to maturity** and **discount factor.**

FORMULAS

$$\text{par yield for N years} = \frac{1 - \text{the discount factor for year N}}{\text{the sum of the discount factors for all years from 1 to N}}$$

where:

$$\text{discount factor for year N} = \frac{1}{(1 + \text{zero-coupon yield for year N})^N}$$

This can also be expressed as:

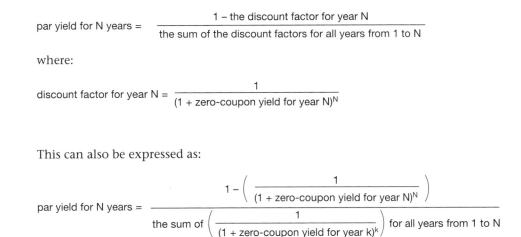

$$\text{par yield for N years} = \frac{1 - \left(\dfrac{1}{(1 + \text{zero-coupon yield for year N})^N} \right)}{\text{the sum of} \left(\dfrac{1}{(1 + \text{zero-coupon yield for year k})^k} \right) \text{for all years from 1 to N}}$$

EXAMPLE

What is the par yield curve, based on the following zero-coupon yields?

1-year: 10.000%
2-year: 10.526%
3-year: 11.076%
4-year: 11.655%

The zero-coupon discount factors are:

1-year: $\dfrac{1}{(1.1)} = 0.90909$

2-year: $\dfrac{1}{(1.10526)^2} = 0.81860$

3-year: $\dfrac{1}{(1.11076)^3} = 0.72969$

4-year: $\dfrac{1}{(1.11655)^4} = 0.64341$

The 1-year par yield is the same as the 1-year zero-coupon yield.

$$\text{2-year par yield} = \frac{1 - 0.81860}{(0.90909 + 0.81860)} = 0.1050 = 10.50\%$$

$$\text{3-year par yield} = \frac{1 - 0.72969}{(0.90909 + 0.81860 + 0.72969)} = 0.1100 = 11.00\%$$

$$\text{4-year par yield} = \frac{1 - 0.64341}{(0.90909 + 0.81860 + 0.72969 + 0.64341)} = 0.1150 = 11.50\%$$

THE FORWARD-FORWARD YIELD CURVE

Definition

The **forward-forward yield curve** shows **zero-coupon yields** against time to maturity for forward periods of a particular length, often one year, starting on one forward date and ending on another forward date.

HOW IS IT USED?

In theory, a forward-forward interest rate is the rate at which someone can borrow or lend money, from one forward date to another. When such forward periods last 3 months, the instrument typically used to underlie such a transaction is an interest rate **futures** contract. For forward periods lasting longer than three months, several consecutive futures contracts can be used together in a **strip**. Such forward-forward interest rates should be in line with what the market expects cash market rates will be when that future time arrives – if not, then market participants would either borrow or lend (or deal in equivalent instruments such as futures, **forward rate agreements (FRAs)** and **interest rate swaps (IRS)**) so that supply and demand would move the forward-forward rate closer to the expected rate.

Even if there is not a practical market in forward-forward borrowing and investing, the question still arises, 'What does the market expect interest rates to be in the future?' In practice, the rates quoted in the capital markets (i.e. for instruments with a maturity generally longer than one year) are usually not forward-forward rates. This contrasts with the money markets (i.e. for instruments with a maturity or period generally up to one year), where instruments such as futures are frequently quoted. Nevertheless, the rates actually quoted – such as bond yields and swap yields for a variety of maturities – should still be broadly consistent with where the market believes that longer-term yields will be in the future. It is therefore possible to construct from a 'usual' yield curve – for example, a yield curve of government bonds from 1 year onwards, or a yield curve of swap rates from 1 year onwards – what the corresponding theoretical forward-forward yields would be, consistent with these existing market yields. In cases where futures contracts are available, it is also possible to construct forward-forward yields from a strip of futures.

Because the forward-forward yield curve reflects expectations, it is a useful guide to the structure of the market. Clearly forward-forwards for any period could be chosen as representative of these expectations, but typical periods to consider could be 1 year (a yield curve showing forward-forwards from 1 year to 2 years, 2 years to 3 years, 3 years to 4 years, etc.) or 3 months (showing forward-forwards from 1 year to 15 months, 24 months to 27 months, 36 months to 39 months, etc.). In the case of 3-month periods, the curve would be consistent with the implied yields of futures contracts.

In practice, a forward-forward yield curve (for example, a series of 1-year forward-forward yields) can be constructed from zero-coupon yields, which themselves can be constructed by **bootstrapping** from existing market yields. This process is circular: it is equally possible to begin with forward-forward yields or market expectations of future yields and create from them a consistent zero-coupon yield curve.

A forward-forward period of 1 year starting, for example, 2 years from now and ending 3 years from now is known as a '2 years v. 3 years', etc.

A par yield curve tends to be exaggerated by the corresponding zero-coupon curve. The forward-forward curve tends to exaggerate further a change in shape of the zero-coupon curve (see Figure 2).

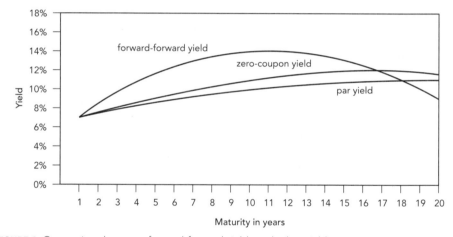

FIGURE 2 Comparison between forward-forward yields and other yields

Related terminology

⇨ *See also* zero-coupon yield, discount factor, forward-forward interest rate and strip.

FORMULAS

forward-forward yield from k years to (k + 1) years

$$= \frac{(1 + \text{zero-coupon yield for } (k + 1) \text{ years})^{(k + 1)}}{\left((1 + \text{zero-coupon yield for } k \text{ years})^{k}\right)} - 1$$

This can also be expressed as:

forward-forward yield from k years to (k + 1) years

$$= \frac{\text{zero-coupon discount factor for } k \text{ years}}{\text{zero-coupon discount factor for } (k + 1) \text{ years}} - 1$$

Alternatively, constructing from futures prices:

forward-forward yield from k years to (k + 1) years

Note that 'days in period' means the number of days in the 3-month period and 'days in year' can mean 365 (for example with sterling) or 360 (for example with US dollars) – see **money market basis**.

Conversely:

zero-coupon yield for k years

$$= \left(\begin{array}{l} (1 + \text{cash interest rate for 1 year}) \times (1 + \text{forward-forward rate from 1 year to 2 years}) \\ \times (1 + \text{forward-forward rate from 2 years to 3 years}) \times \ldots \\ \ldots \times (1 + \text{forward-forward rate from } (k - 1) \text{ years to } k \text{ years}) \end{array} \right)^{\frac{1}{k}} - 1$$

EXAMPLE 1

What are the 1-year v. 2-year forward-forward yield, the 2-year v. 3-year forward-forward yield and the 3-year v. 4-year forward-forward yield, given the following zero-coupon yields?

1-year:	10.000%
2-year:	10.526%
3-year:	11.076%
4-year:	11.655%

The zero-coupon discount factors are:

1-year: $\dfrac{1}{1.1} = 0.90909$

2-year: $\dfrac{1}{1.10526^2} = 0.81860$

3-year: $\dfrac{1}{1.11076^3} = 0.72969$

4-year: $\dfrac{1}{1.11655^4} = 0.64341$

1-year v. 2-year yield $= \dfrac{0.90909}{0.81860} - 1 = 0.1105 = 11.05\%$

2-year v. 3-year yield $= \dfrac{0.81860}{0.72969} - 1 = 0.1218 = 12.18\%$

3-year v. 4-year yield $= \dfrac{0.72969}{0.64341} - 1 = 0.1341 = 13.41\%$

EXAMPLE 2

The 1-year interest rate is now 10%. The market expects the 1-year cash market rate to rise to 11% after 1 year and to 12% after a further year. What would you expect the current 2-year and 3-year zero-coupon yields to be, consistent with these expectations?

2-year zero-coupon yield $= (1.10 \times 1.11)^{\left(\frac{1}{2}\right)} - 1 = 0.1050 = 10.50\%$

3-year zero-coupon yield $= (1.10 \times 1.11 \times 11.12)^{\left(\frac{1}{3}\right)} - 1 = 0.1133 = 11.33\%$

THE MONEY MARKETS

TRUE YIELD AND DISCOUNT RATE

Definition

The **true yield** (or simply *yield*) on a short-term investment is the income earned on it as a proportion of the principal amount invested, generally expressed as a rate per annum. It is the rate currently quoted by the market at any given time, or implied by the current market price for the investment – as opposed to the *coupon* paid by the issuer for the investment, which is based on the coupon rate and the *face value*.

A **discount rate** is an alternative method of market quotation used for certain *securities* (US and UK treasury bills for example). It expresses the income earned on the security as a proportion of the face value of the security received at maturity, instead of as a proportion of the amount invested at the beginning.

HOW ARE THEY USED?

Coupon-bearing instruments v. discount instruments

Some investment instruments, such as a *certificate of deposit*, are issued with a coupon. This means that the issuer promises to repay the face value of the instrument (i.e. the amount invested at the beginning) plus an amount to represent interest, according to a fixed rate (the 'coupon rate'), or according to some other reference method, determined when the instrument is issued.

Other instruments are issued without any such coupon. These are known as 'discount' instruments or **zero-coupon** instruments. This means that only the face value of the instrument is paid at maturity, without a coupon. In order for the economic effect of this to be the same as with a coupon-bearing instrument, the investor pays a smaller amount for this investment initially. Treasury bills for example are generally discount instruments.

Consider, for example, a sterling Treasury bill with a face value of £10 million, issued for 91 days. At maturity, the investor receives only the face value of £10 million. If the yield on the bill is 10%, the price the investor will be willing to pay now for the bill is its **present value** calculated at 10%:

$$\text{value} = \frac{£10 \text{ million}}{\left(1 + \left(0.10 \times \frac{91}{365}\right)\right)} = £9{,}756{,}749.53$$

Discount/true yield

In the US and the UK, a further complication arises in the way the interest rate is quoted on certain specific discount instruments – as a discount rate instead of a yield. If an investor invests £98.436 in sterling commercial paper at a yield of 10% for 58 days, he expects to receive the £98.436 back at the end of 58 days, together with an amount representing his yield as follows:

$$£98.436 \times 0.10 \times \frac{58}{365} = £1.564$$

In this case, the total proceeds at the end of 58 days – principal plus interest – are:

£98.436 + £1.564 = £100.00

If an economically identical investment were made in a sterling Treasury bill, the face value of the instrument would still be £100 and the initial amount invested would still be £98.436, but the difference of £1.564 is called the *amount of discount* and conventionally is subtracted from the £100 to arrive at the £98.436, rather than the other way round. The discount rate is then the amount of discount expressed as an annualized percentage of the face value, rather than as an annualized percentage of the original amount paid. The discount rate in this case works out to be 9.84%, so that:

$$£100 \times 0.0984 \times \frac{58}{365} = £1.564$$

The discount rate (9.84% in this example) is always less than the corresponding yield (10% in this example). As they imply the same thing, it is of course possible to convert from one to the other.

This can perhaps be understood intuitively, by considering that because the discount amount is received at the beginning of the period whereas the equivalent yield is received at the end, the discount rate should be the 'present value of the yield', which it is (see the formula below).

Instruments quoted on a discount rate in the US and UK include domestic currency treasury bills and trade bills, while a yield basis is used for loans, deposits and certificates of deposit. Domestic commercial paper in the US is also quoted on a discount rate basis, while international commercial paper ('Eurocommercial paper') and sterling commercial paper are quoted on a yield basis. Note however that while the sterling Treasury bills issued by the UK government are quoted on a discount rate, the Treasury bills it issues denominated in euros are quoted on a true yield, as are other international instruments denominated in euros.

Instruments quoted on a discount rate

US	UK
Treasury bill	sterling Treasury bill
bankers' acceptance	bankers' acceptance
domestic commercial paper	

Related terminology

Confusingly, expressions such as *rate of discount* or 'discounting at a rate of' used in the following way refer to a yield and not a discount rate: 'The **present value** of 100 in 3 years' time, using a rate of discount of 10% per annum, is 75.13' or 'the present value of 100 in 3 years' time, discounting at a rate of 10% per annum, is 75.13'.

FORMULAS

In general:

secondary market value of a short-term security

= present value of the security's value at maturity

$$= \frac{\text{maturity proceeds}}{\left(1 + \left(\text{current market yield} \times \frac{\text{days left to maturity}}{\text{days in year}}\right)\right)}$$

Note that 'days in year' can mean 365 (for example with a sterling security) or 360 (for example with a US dollar security) – see **money market basis**.

Therefore:

For a coupon-bearing instrument:

$$\text{secondary market value} = \frac{\text{face value} \times \left(1 + \left(\text{coupon rate} \times \frac{\text{original days to maturity}}{\text{days in year}}\right)\right)}{\left(1 + \left(\text{current market yield} \times \frac{\text{days left to maturity}}{\text{days in year}}\right)\right)}$$

For a discount instrument (i.e. a non-coupon-bearing instrument) traded on a yield:

$$\text{secondary market value} = \frac{\text{face value}}{\left(1 + \left(\text{current market yield} \times \frac{\text{days left to maturity}}{\text{days in year}}\right)\right)}$$

For a discount instrument (i.e. a non-coupon-bearing instrument) traded on a discount rate:

$$\text{amount of discount} = \text{face value} \times \text{discount rate} \times \frac{\text{days to maturity}}{\text{days in year}}$$

$$\text{secondary market value} = \text{face value} - \text{discount amount}$$

$$= \text{face value} \times \left(1 - \left(\text{discount rate} \times \frac{\text{days left to maturity}}{\text{days in year}}\right)\right)$$

$$\text{rate of true yield} = \frac{\text{discount rate}}{\left(1 - \left(\text{discount rate} \times \frac{\text{days left to maturity}}{\text{days in year}}\right)\right)}$$

$$\text{discount rate} = \frac{\text{rate of true yield}}{\left(1 + \left(\text{yield} \times \frac{\text{days left to maturity}}{\text{days in year}}\right)\right)}$$

EXAMPLE 1

A certificate of deposit with face value €1 million and a coupon of 5% was issued on 15 March with a maturity of 15 September (184 days). What is its value on 15 April (153 days left to maturity) if the market yield is now 5.3%?

$$\text{secondary market value} = \frac{€1,000,000 \times \left(1 + \left(0.05 \times \frac{184}{360}\right)\right)}{\left(1 + \left(0.053 \times \frac{153}{360}\right)\right)} = €1,002,963.80$$

EXAMPLE 2

Commercial paper with face value €1 million was issued on 15 March with a maturity of 15 September (184 days). What is its value on 15 April (153 days left to maturity) if the market yield is now 5.3%?

$$\text{secondary market value} = \frac{€1,000,000}{\left(1 + \left(0.053 \times \frac{153}{360}\right)\right)} = €977,971.20$$

EXAMPLE 3

A US Treasury bill with face value $1 million was issued on 15 March with a maturity of 15 September (184 days). On 15 April (153 days left to maturity), the discount rate is 5.3%.

$$\text{amount of discount} = \$1,000,000 \times 0.053 \times \frac{153}{360} = \$22,525.00$$

$$\text{secondary market value} = \$1,000,000.00 - \$22,525.00 = \$977,475.00$$

$$\text{rate of true yield} = \frac{0.053}{\left(1 - \left(0.053 \times \frac{153}{360}\right)\right)} = 0.0542 = 5.42\%$$

EXAMPLE 4

A US Treasury bill with 153 days left to maturity has a yield of 5.3%. What is the equivalent discount rate?

$$\text{discount rate} = \frac{0.053}{\left(1 + \left(0.053 \times \frac{153}{360}\right)\right)} = 0.0518 = 5.18\%$$

VALUE DATES, INTERPOLATION AND EXTRAPOLATION

Definition

The **value date** of a money market transaction is the date on which the transaction is consummated, i.e. delivery takes place.

Interpolation is the process of estimating a price or rate for value on a particular date by comparing the prices actually quoted for value dates earlier and later than the date required.

Extrapolation is the process of estimating a price or rate for value on a particular date, from other known prices, when the value date required lies outside the period covered by the known prices.

HOW ARE THEY USED?

In many transactions, there is a delay, of one day or more, between agreeing on a transaction with the counterparty and actually transferring the cash and/or securities. This allows time for settlement instructions to be generated and effected. In the international foreign exchange and money markets for example, the standard value date (*spot* value date) is two working days after transaction date ('T+2'). In this case, value dates for forward settlement are based on this spot date, rather than on the transaction date.

Foreign exchange prices and money market rates are normally quoted for regular forward dates, for example 1, 2, 3, 6 and 12 months forward after the spot date. This means that the 1-month price, for example, is quoted for one calendar month after the current spot date. If the current spot date is 21 April, the 1-month forward date will be 21 May. If the forward delivery date falls on a weekend or holiday, the value date becomes the next working day. No adjustment in the forward value date is made for any weekends or public holidays between the spot date and the forward delivery date.

One exception to these rules is when the spot value date is at or close to the end of the month. Suppose that the spot value date is earlier than the last working day of the month, but the forward value date would fall on a non-working day. If necessary, the forward value date is brought *back* to the nearest previous business day in order to stay in the same calendar month, rather than moved forward to the beginning of the next month. This is known as the *modified following* convention.

Another exception arises if the spot value date is the last working day of a month. In this case, the forward value date is the last working day of the corresponding forward month. This is referred to as dealing *end/end*.

Interpolation and extrapolation

A deal may in fact be arranged for value on any working day (or any day which is a working day in both currencies for foreign exchange). Dates which do not fit in with calendar month dates are called *broken dates* or *odd dates*. The prices for these dates are generally calculated by assuming that a straight line can be drawn between the rates already known for the nearest whole month dates on either side – 'straight-line' interpolation.

Suppose for example that the 1-month rate (30 days) is 8.0% and that the 2-month rate (61 days) is 8.5%. The rate for 1 month and 9 days (39 days) assumes that interest rates increase steadily from the 1-month rate to the 2-month rate – a straight-line interpolation. The increase from 30 days to 39 days will therefore be a $\frac{9}{31}$ proportion of the increase from 30 days to 61 days. The 39-day rate is therefore as shown in Figure 3:

$$8.0\% + ((8.5\% - 8.0\%)) \times \tfrac{9}{31} = 8.15\%$$

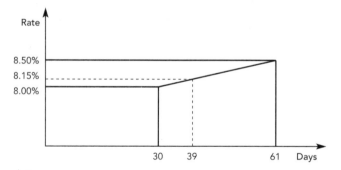

FIGURE 3 Interpolation

If the broken date required is just before or just after the known periods, rather than between them, the same principle can be applied (in this case extrapolation rather than interpolation). If, for example, we wanted the 63-day rate, based on the same information as above, we would arrive at (as shown in Figure 4):

$$8.0\% + ((8.5\% - 8.0\%) \times \tfrac{33}{31}) = 8.53\%$$

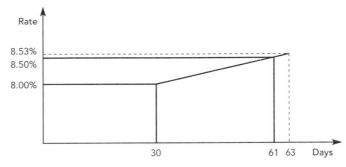

FIGURE 4 Extrapolation

Related terminology

Value date is sometimes known as *settlement date*. In some bond markets however there can be a difference between the date on which the cash/bond delivery takes place (*settlement date*) and the date to which accrued coupon is calculated (*value date*).

If a bank deals in any month that is not a regularly quoted date – for example for 4 or 5 months' maturity – this is called an 'in-between' month because it is between the regular dates.

For a better estimate of interpolated and extrapolated rates, a series of known rates can be joined by a curve rather than a straight line. This is known as *curve fitting*.

FORMULA

For straight-line interpolation or extrapolation:

the rate required

$$= \text{the first known rate} + \left(\frac{\text{(the second known rate – the first known rate)}}{\text{(the second known date – the first known date)}} \times \text{(the date required – the first known date)} \right)$$

EXAMPLE 1

Ordinary Run

Dealing date: Friday 14 April

Spot date: Tuesday 18 April (2 working days forward)

1 month: Thursday 18 May

2 months: Monday 19 June (18 June is a Sunday)

3 months: Tuesday 18 July

4 months: Friday 18 August

EXAMPLE 2

Dealing date: Tuesday 28 August

Spot date: Thursday 30 August (not the last working day of the month)

1 month: Friday 28 September (30 September is a Sunday but Monday
                  1 October would be in the following month)

2 months: Tuesday 30 October

EXAMPLE 3

End/End

Dealing date: Wednesday 26 June

Spot date: Friday 28 June (last working day of June)

1 month: Wednesday 31 July (last working day of July)

2 months: Friday 30 August (last working day of August)

EXAMPLE 4

The 2-month (61 days) rate is 7.5% and the 3-month (92 days) rate is 7.6%. What are the 73-day rate and the 93-day rate, using straight-line interpolation?

$$73\text{-day rate} = 7.5\% + \left(\frac{(7.6\% - 7.5\%)}{(92 - 61)} \times (73 - 61) \right) = 7.539\%$$

$$93\text{-day rate} = 7.5\% + \left(\frac{(7.6\% - 7.5\%)}{(92 - 61)} \times (93 - 61) \right) = 7.603\%$$

FORWARD-FORWARDS, FRAS AND FUTURES

FORWARD-FORWARD INTEREST RATE

Definition

A **forward-forward** interest rate is the rate for a cash borrowing or lending which starts on one forward date and ends on another forward date, with the term, amount and interest rate all fixed in advance.

HOW IS IT USED?

Someone who expects to borrow cash in the future has a risk that interest rates will by then have risen. A forward-forward removes this risk by fixing the rate in advance. Similarly, an investor who will be depositing cash in the future can fix the rate in advance to protect against any possible fall in rates.

A forward-forward starting, for example, 2 months from now and ending 5 months from now – a period of 3 months – is known as a 2 v 5 or 2 x 5 or sometimes 2/5.

The theoretical forward-forward formula below assumes that the bank quoting the forward-forward rate is constructing it and hedging it from the cash market. In other words, if a bank agrees to lend money to a customer forward-forward 2 v 5, for example, that it would itself take a 5-month borrowing from the market (at the 5-month *offer* rate) and place a 2-month deposit (at the 2-month *bid* rate), in order to have funds available from 2 months to 5 months to lend to the customer. Similarly, if the bank agrees to take a deposit from a customer forward-forward 2 v 5, then it would itself place a 5-month deposit in the market (at the 5-month bid rate) and borrow for 2 months (at the 2-month offer rate), and thus be ready to re-finance itself using the customer's deposit from 2 months to 5 months.

In practice, this would be cumbersome and expensive because of the bid-offer spreads, transaction costs, credit line utilization, balance sheet management and **capital adequacy** constraints. In developed markets where a liquid **futures** market exists, a bank is therefore more likely to hedge a forward-forward by using futures contracts. In this case, the forward-forward rate will be based on the interest rates implied by the futures prices. The possibility of *arbitrage* however means that this rate cannot move far from the theoretical forward-forward rate as calculated below.

Related terminology

Forward rate agreements (FRAs) and **futures** are both *contracts for differences* which can be used with an economic effect similar to a forward-forward.

In the foreign exchange market, a **forward-forward** is a **forward swap** from one forward date to another forward date.

FORMULA

theoretical forward-forward interest rate

$$
= \left(\frac{\left(1 + \left(\text{interest rate to second date} \times \dfrac{\text{days until second date}}{\text{days in year}}\right)\right)}{\left(1 + \left(\text{interest rate to first date} \times \dfrac{\text{days until first date}}{\text{days in year}}\right)\right)} - 1 \right)
$$

$$
\times \frac{\text{days in year}}{\text{days in forward-forward period}}
$$

'Interest rate to first (second) date' means the interest rate for a cash borrowing or lending from now until that date.

The bid rate for the forward-forward rate is calculated using the bid rate of the cash interest rate to the second date and the offer rate to the first date. The offer rate for the forward-forward uses the offer rate and bid rate respectively.

Note that 'days in year' can mean 365 (for example with sterling) or 360 (for example with US dollars) – see **money market basis**.

Note also that this construction of a theoretical forward-forward rate applies only for periods up to one year. A money market deposit for longer than one year typically pays interim interest each year (or each 6 months) and at maturity. This extra cashflow must be taken into account in the forward-forward structure. The most straightforward approach to this is using **zero-coupon** yields.

EXAMPLE

The US dollar interest rate for 2 months (61 days) is 5.7%/5.8%. The rate for 5 months (153 days) is 5.5%/5.6%. What is the 2 v 5 forward-forward rate for the 92-day period from 2 months to 5 months?

$$\left(\frac{\left(1 + \left(0.055 \times \dfrac{153}{360}\right)\right)}{\left(1 + \left(0.058 \times \dfrac{61}{360}\right)\right)} - 1\right) \times \frac{360}{92} = 0.0525 = 5.25\%$$

$$\left(\frac{\left(1 + \left(0.056 \times \dfrac{153}{360}\right)\right)}{\left(1 + \left(0.057 \times \dfrac{61}{360}\right)\right)} - 1\right) \times \frac{360}{92} = 0.0548 = 5.48\%$$

Therefore the 2 v 5 forward-forward is 5.25%/5.48%.

FORWARD RATE AGREEMENT (FRA)

Definition

An **FRA** is an agreement to pay or receive, on an agreed future date, the difference between a fixed interest rate, agreed at the outset, and a reference interest rate actually prevailing on a given future date for a given period. A net cash settlement is made, calculated on the length of the agreed future period and an agreed notional principal amount. The reference rate taken for the interest rate in the future is generally the interbank *offer* rate at that time, such as *LIBOR*.

HOW IS IT USED?

As with most instruments, an FRA can be used for *hedging*, *speculation* or *arbitrage*, depending on whether it is used to offset an existing underlying position or taken as a new position.

Hedging

An FRA is an *off-balance-sheet* instrument which can achieve the same economic effect as a **forward-forward**. For example, someone who expects to borrow cash in the future can buy an FRA to fix, in advance, the interest rate on the borrowing. When the time to borrow arrives, he borrows the cash in the usual way at LIBOR, or some margin over LIBOR. Under the FRA, which remains quite separate, he receives or pays the difference between LIBOR and the FRA rate, so that he achieves the same net effect as with a forward-forward borrowing (see Figure 5).

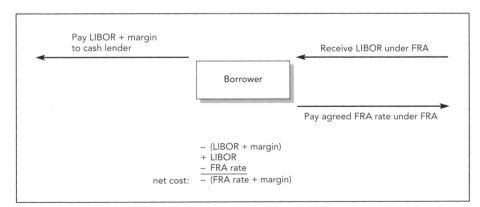

FIGURE 5 Interest flows with an FRA plus underlying borrowing

The FRA net settlement is conventionally not paid at the end of the future period covered by the FRA (as the underlying interest would be), but rather at the beginning of that period. To allow for this timing difference, the FRA settlement amount is discounted to a **present value** when it is paid. This is taken into account in the FRA settlement formula below.

As with a forward-forward, an FRA covering a period starting, for example, 2 months from now and ending 5 months from now – a period of 3 months – is known as a 2 v 5 or 2 × 5 or sometimes 2/5.

The party to an FRA which is paying the agreed fixed FRA interest rate and receiving LIBOR is known conventionally as the buyer of the FRA. The other party is the seller. In the case of a customer wishing to protect the interest rate earned on a future deposit from falling, for example, the customer would be the seller and the bank providing the FRA would be the buyer. In this case, the reference rate used is still LIBOR, regardless of whether the customer is likely to receive *LIBID* or some other rate on his actual deposit in the future (see Figure 6).

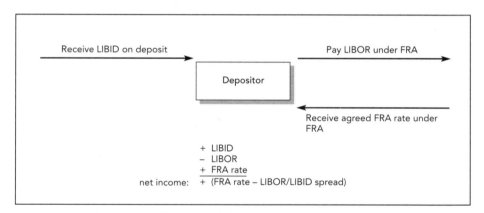

FIGURE 6 Interest flows with an FRA plus underlying deposit

Speculation

The basic trading strategy is to use an FRA to speculate on whether the cash interest rate when the FRA period begins will be higher or lower than the fixed FRA rate agreed. If the trader expects interest rates to be higher, he buys an FRA; if he expects rates to be lower, he sells an FRA.

Another strategy is a **spread**, to buy one FRA and sell another for a different period, speculating that there will be a change in the steepness of the *yield curve*.

Arbitrage

An FRA is an *over-the-counter* equivalent of a **futures** contract. Theoretical FRA prices and futures prices should both be in line with forward-forward prices and hence with each other. In practice, they may sometimes be out of line with each other, giving scope for arbitrage, for example by buying an FRA and buying a futures contract at the same time for the same period, to lock in a profit.

Related terminology

➪ *See also* **forward-forward** and **STIR futures.**

FORMULAS

As with forward-forwards, FRA rates in developed markets are generally hedged and priced from interest rate futures. If this is not practicable, the theoretical FRA rate can be calculated as follows:

theoretical FRA rate

$$= \left(\frac{\left(1 + \left(\text{LIBOR to second date} \times \dfrac{\text{days until second date}}{\text{days in year}}\right)\right)}{\left(1 + \left(\text{LIBOR to first date} \times \dfrac{\text{days until first date}}{\text{days in year}}\right)\right)} - 1 \right) \times \frac{\text{days in year}}{\text{days in FRA period}}$$

'LIBOR' in this theoretical FRA rate means the interbank offer rate for the period to the first or second date, current at the time of quoting the rate, rather than any particular reference LIBOR rate. An alternative is to use *LIMEAN* instead of LIBOR and then to add a typical LIBOR–LIMEAN spread to the result (see example 1 below).

Having established this theoretical FRA price, a dealer would then build a bid/offer spread round it before quoting.

$$\text{FRA settlement amount} = \text{notional principal} \times \frac{(\text{FRA rate} - \text{LIBOR}) \times \dfrac{\text{days in FRA period}}{\text{days in year}}}{\left(1 + \left(\text{LIBOR} \times \dfrac{\text{days in FRA period}}{\text{days in year}}\right)\right)}$$

'LIBOR' in the FRA settlement amount is the LIBOR reference rate at the beginning of the FRA period – or in the case of a *Eurocurrency* FRA, LIBOR 2 working days before the beginning of the FRA period.

The net settlement amount as expressed here is paid from buyer to seller if it is positive, or from seller to buyer if it is negative.

EXAMPLE 1

The US dollar interest rate for 2 months (61 days) is 5.7%/5.8%. The rate for 5 months (153 days) is 5.5%/5.6%. What is the theoretical 2 v 5 FRA rate for the 92-day period from 2 months to 5 months?

Either:

$$\left(\frac{\left(1 + \left(0.056 \times \frac{153}{360}\right)\right)}{\left(1 + \left(0.058 \times \frac{61}{360}\right)\right)} - 1\right) \times \frac{360}{92} = 0.05414 = 5.414\%$$

Or:

$$\left(\frac{\left(1 + \left(0.0555 \times \frac{153}{360}\right)\right)}{\left(1 + \left(0.0575 \times \frac{61}{360}\right)\right)} - 1\right) \times \frac{360}{92} = 0.05365 = 5.365\%$$

5.365% + typical LIBOR–LIMEAN spread of, say, 0.05% = 5.415%

The dealer will then put a bid/offer spread around this price and quote, say, 5.39%/5.44%.

EXAMPLE 2

A company expects to deposit $2,000,000 for 6 months (183 days), starting in 2 weeks' time and fears that interest rates may fall. The company therefore sells a 2-weeks v $6\frac{1}{2}$ months FRA. The FRA is quoted as 6.75%/6.80%, so the company deals at 6.75%. Two weeks later, the cash market 6-month rate is 6.90%/6.95% and the company actually places the deposit at LIBID (6.90%). The result is approximately as follows:

company receives	6.90%		from deposit
company receives	6.75%		under FRA
company pays	6.95%	(LIBOR)	under FRA
net income	6.70%		(FRA rate less the LIBOR–LIBID spread)

In this case, the company would have been better off if it had not sold the FRA, but the FRA did nevertheless provide the protection required against a potential fall in rates.

The exact FRA settlement amount is as follows:

$$\$2,000,000 \times \frac{(0.0675 - 0.0695) \times \dfrac{183}{360}}{\left(1 + \left(0.0695 \times \dfrac{183}{360}\right)\right)} = -\$1,963.95$$

$1,963.95 is therefore paid from the company to the bank at the beginning of the 6-month period.

Note that because this settlement amount involves discounting the difference between 6.75% and 6.95% at LIBOR (i.e. 6.95%) but the company in fact deposits at only LIBID (i.e. 6.90%), the net income is very slightly different from 6.70% (slightly higher in this case).

STIR FUTURES CONTRACT AND MARGIN

Definition

A **STIR (short-term interest rate) futures contract** is an agreement on a recognized futures exchange to deposit a *notional* standard principal amount, at an agreed interest rate, for a standard period starting on a standard future date. The deposit is non-deliverable and cash settlements are made instead, calculated on the standard period and the notional standard principal amount.

Variation margin, which is settled daily between the counterparties, is the profit or loss arising on a futures position between the close of business one day and the close of business the next day.

Initial margin is collateral lodged with the exchange clearing house or the broker before trading a futures contract, to protect it against default in the event of variation margin subsequently being called but not being paid.

HOW ARE THEY USED?

In general, a futures contract is effectively equivalent to a *forward* transaction. The important mechanical differences between the two arise in several ways. First, a futures contract is traded on a particular exchange (although two or more exchanges might trade identically specified contracts). A forward however, which is also a deal for settlement on a future date, is dealt *over the counter* (OTC) – a deal made between any two parties, not on an exchange.

Second, futures contracts are standardized, while forwards are not. The specifications of each futures contract are laid down by the relevant exchange.

Third, some futures contracts – including interest rate futures – do not allow for the underlying instrument or commodity to be delivered. A trader buying a STIR futures contract cannot insist that, on the future delivery date, his counterparty makes arrangements for him to have a deposit from then onwards at the interest rate agreed. Rather, he must reverse his futures contract at or before delivery, thereby taking a cash profit or loss. Allowing for these differences, interest rate futures are an exchange-traded equivalent of **forward rate agreements (FRAs)**.

Contract specifications

Each futures contract is based on a standard amount, which varies between contracts. For example a euro interest rate futures contract is based on a notional principal of €1 million. The period is also standardized. This is typically 3 months although, as for example with the euro contract, a 1-month contract is also sometimes available.

The notional start date of the future period is also standardized and is typically the third Wednesday of any of the available delivery months (typically the next 3 months following dealing and March, June, September and December thereafter).

The price is quoted as an index rather than an interest rate. This is expressed as 100 minus the implied interest rate. Thus a price of 93.52 implies an interest rate of 6.48% (100 − 93.52 = 6.48).

All contracts are completely *fungible* – that is, once a purchase of a certain quantity of a particular contract is added to an existing holding of the same contract, there is no distinction between the two purchases; they simply become a single, larger holding of the contract. When a *long* or *short* position is offset by a subsequent sale or purchase, this closes the position, rather than leaving two offsetting positions.

By the close of trading for each contract (which is at, or shortly before, the start of the futures period), the exchange declares an *exchange delivery settlement price* (EDSP), which is the closing price at which any contracts still outstanding will be automatically reversed. This is typically 100 minus the official fixing for the *interbank offer* interest rate.

Margin

Following confirmation of a transaction on the exchange, the clearing house substitutes itself for each counterparty, becoming the seller to every buyer and the buyer to every seller.

Members of the exchange who have traded are debited or credited each day with variation margin which reflects the day's loss or profit on contracts held. This valuation (*marking to market*) measures the difference between the closing price each day and the closing price the previous day. By the time the contract is closed, there is therefore no further settlement to be made other than the final day's variation margin.

These variation margin payments – which add up to the total profit or loss – are not calculated on the actual number of days in the future period to which the EDSP will relate (which might for example be 92 days for a 3-month futures contract). Instead, the calculation is based on a round number of months out of a year. Variation margin is therefore based on exactly three-twelfths of a year and exactly one-twelfth of a year for 3-month and 1-month futures respectively.

In order to protect the clearing house for the short period until a position can be revalued and variation margin called for if necessary, clearing members are also required to place collateral with it before each deal is transacted. This collateral is called initial margin. As variation margin is paid each day, the initial margin is relatively small in relation to the potential price movements over a longer period. Depending on the size of initial margin, and the exchange's current rules, variation margin may not be called for below a certain level.

Customers, in turn, are required to pay initial margin and variation margin to the member through whom they have cleared their deal.

Comparison with FRAs

It may be helpful to compare futures with FRAs:

- Futures prices are quoted as an index, while FRAs are quoted as an interest rate.

- Futures and FRAs are in 'opposite directions'. A buyer of an FRA profits if interest rates rise. A buyer of a futures contract profits if interest rates fall.

- The amount, start date and period are standardized for a futures contract but entirely flexible for an FRA.

- The initial and variation margin system makes the clearing house virtually risk-free as a counterparty and should make all dealing less of a credit risk than OTC dealing based on credit lines.

- The FRA settlement is calculated on the exact number of days in the future period. The futures settlement (variation margin) is calculated on a notional period of exactly three-twelfths (or one-twelfth) of a year.

- FRA settlement is made at the beginning of the future period and is discounted to a present value. Settlement on a futures contract is made even earlier, through variation margin, but is not discounted.

- In developed markets, standardization and transparency generally ensure a liquid market in futures contracts, with narrower buy/sell spreads than in FRAs. In minor currencies, this is not always so.

As with an FRA, a futures contract can be used for *hedging*, *speculation* or *arbitrage*, depending on whether it is taken to offset an existing underlying position or taken as a new position.

Hedging

A futures contract is an *off-balance-sheet* instrument which can achieve the same economic effect as a **forward-forward**. For example, someone who expects to borrow cash in the future can sell futures, to fix in advance the interest rate on the borrowing. When the time to borrow arrives, he borrows the cash in the usual way at LIBOR, or some margin over LIBOR. He then reverses the futures, which remain quite separate, by which time he has received or paid settlements via variation margin, so that he achieves the same net effect as with a forward-forward borrowing (see Figure 7). Because the futures will be based on standard dates, periods and amounts, rather than exactly matching his borrowing, the hedge is unlikely to be a very precise one – there will be **basis risk**.

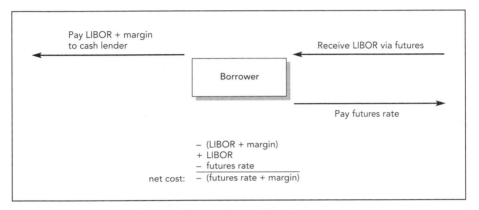

FIGURE 7 Effective interest flows with futures plus underlying borrowing

In the same way, a trader selling an FRA to a customer, or buying one from him, can hedge his position by selling or buying futures.

Speculation

The basic trading strategy is to use futures to speculate on whether the cash interest rate when the futures period begins will be higher or lower than the rate implied by the futures now. If the trader expects interest rates to be higher, he sells futures; if he expects rates to be lower, he buys futures. He does not need to wait until the beginning of the futures period to capture the effect, as he can reverse his position at any time up to then.

Another strategy is a **spread**, to buy one futures contract and sell another, speculating that there will be a change in the steepness of the *yield curve*.

Arbitrage

Theoretical FRA prices and futures prices should both be in line with forward-forward prices and hence with each other. In practice, they may sometimes be out of line with each other, giving scope for arbitrage, for example by buying an FRA and buying a futures contract at the same time for the same period, to lock in a profit.

> Related terminology
>
> ⤳ *See also* **forward rate agreement (FRA)**, which is an *over-the-counter* (OTC) equivalent of a futures contract, and **forward-forward.**
>
> A **futures** contract is referred to by the beginning of the future period. Thus a March 3-month futures is a notional deposit beginning in March and ending in June.
>
> The smallest change in price allowed by the exchange for a particular futures contract is called a *tick* (for example 0.005, i.e. half a basis point, is the smallest price change for euro futures). *Tick value* is the profit or loss on a contract arising from a one-tick change in price (i.e. €12.50 is the tick value for euro futures).

FORMULAS

profit/loss on long position in 1 futures contract

$$= \text{notional contract size} \times \frac{(\text{sale price} - \text{purchase price})}{100} \times \frac{\text{length of contract in months}}{12}$$

In developed markets, the interest rate implied by the futures price is effectively the 'raw material' of the market, rather than something which can be derived by formula. That is, the futures interest rate is simply the market's expectation of where the cash market interest rate will be in the future, and other rates are derived from this futures rate. The argument is circular however, as the futures price must be in line with any cash market rates so generated, or arbitrage will eventually cause some rate or rates to change. To the extent therefore that futures prices are derived from cash market rates:

theoretical futures price = 100 − (theoretical forward-forward interest rate × 100)

where:

theoretical forward-forward rate

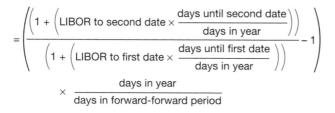

$$= \left(\frac{\left(1 + \left(\text{LIBOR to second date} \times \frac{\text{days until second date}}{\text{days in year}}\right)\right)}{\left(1 + \left(\text{LIBOR to first date} \times \frac{\text{days until first date}}{\text{days in year}}\right)\right)} - 1 \right) \times \frac{\text{days in year}}{\text{days in forward-forward period}}$$

'First date' and 'second date' mean the beginning and end of the futures period to which the EDSP will apply. *LIBOR* in this theoretical forward-forward rate means the interbank offer rate for the period to the first or second date, current at the time of quoting the rate, rather than any particular reference LIBOR rate. An alternative is to use *LIMEAN* instead of LIBOR and then to add a typical LIBOR–LIMEAN spread to the result.

EXAMPLE 1

It is now January and a company expects to borrow $1,000,000 for 3 months (92 days), starting in May, at LIBOR plus a margin of 0.25%. It fears that interest rates may rise and therefore sells a June futures contract at 92.68. It therefore expects to achieve a borrowing cost of 7.57% (the implied futures rate of 7.32%, plus the 0.25% margin). In May, the company borrows $1,000,000 at 7.48%, which is the LIBOR then prevailing, plus a margin of 0.25%, giving a total of 7.73%. At the same time, it closes out its June futures contract at 92.58, which is the price then available.

Through variation margin, the company has made a profit of 0.10% (92.68 − 92.58 = 0.10). Combined with the actual borrowing cost of 7.73%, this gives the company a net cost of 7.63%. This is more than the 7.57% anticipated, because the implied June futures interest rate of 7.42% (100 − 92.58 = 7.42) at which the company closed its position in May is not the same as 3-month LIBOR (7.48%) at that time. Nevertheless, in this case, it was better than if the company had not hedged at all. The all-in cost of 7.63% is not precise because of the unknown timing of the variation margin cashflows.

EXAMPLE 2

The June 3-month euro futures price is 92.67/92.68 and a trader believes that implied future interest rates will fall. He therefore buys the futures at 92.68. A week later, rates have fallen by 12 basis points and the futures price is 92.79/92.80. He closes out his position by selling the contract at 92.79. His profit, received through variation margin over the week, is:

$$€1,000,000 \times 0.0011 \times \frac{3}{12} = €275$$

EXAMPLE 3

Market prices are currently as follows for the euro. The futures delivery date is in 2 months' time:

2 v 5 FRA	7.22 / 7.27%
3-month futures	92.67 / 92.68

A trader can arbitrage between these two prices by dealing at 7.27% in the FRA and at 92.68 in the futures market. He buys the FRA and is therefore effectively paying an agreed 7.27% (and receiving LIBOR) in 2 months' time. He also buys the futures contract and is therefore effectively receiving (100 – 92.68)% = 7.32% (and paying LIBOR) in 2 months' time. He has therefore locked in a profit of 5 basis points.

In practice, this example will be complicated by several factors.

First, the FRA settlement is discounted but the futures settlement is not. The trader needs to increase slightly the notional amount of the FRA traded, to adjust for this. As we do not know the discount factor in advance, we need to estimate it – for example, by using the FRA rate itself.

Second, the period of the 2 v 5 FRA might be, for example, 92 days, while the futures variation margin settlement is based on exactly three-twelfths of a year (effectively 90 days for a currency where the money market convention is ACT/360). The trader needs to increase slightly the number of futures contracts traded to adjust for this.

Combining these two points, we could make an adjustment as follows:

notional amount of FRA traded

$$= \text{notional amount of futures contracts} \times \left(1 + \left(\text{FRA rate} \times \tfrac{92}{360}\right)\right) \times \frac{90}{92}$$

BASIS RISK

Definition

In general, **basis risk** is the risk that the price or rate of one instrument or position might not move exactly in line with the price or rate of another instrument or position which is being used to hedge it.

HOW IS IT USED?

A trader's position is often hedged with a related but different instrument. For example, when a trader sells an FRA to a customer and is not willing to leave this position open, he could simply close his position by buying an identical FRA from another bank. However he might very well instead hedge the position by selling futures contracts. The advantage would be that, in developed markets, futures markets are generally very *liquid* and the *bid/offer spread* is very fine. The disadvantage would be that the profit or loss incurred on the futures contract or contracts would almost certainly not move exactly in line with the loss or profit on the FRA. He thus has a basis risk.

Related terminology

Basis or *simple basis* is the difference between the actual futures price trading in the market and (100 – the current cash interest rate).

Value basis is the difference between the actual futures price trading in the market and the theoretical futures price which can be calculated according to the underlying cash market prices.

Theoretical basis is the difference between the theoretical futures price which can be calculated according to the underlying cash market prices and (100 – the current cash interest rate).

These differences tend towards zero on the last trading day for the futures contract.

A spread position taken by a trader is effectively a position which deliberately establishes a basis risk, because the trader believes that the difference between the two instruments will change in his favour.

EXAMPLE 1

Example 1 of the section on **STIR futures contract and margin** involves a company hedging an expected future borrowing by using a futures contract. The risk which the company is trying to hedge is what 3-month LIBOR will be in mid-May. The instrument being used to hedge this risk is a June futures contract, which represents the market's expectation of what the 3-month rate will be in June. Although between January and May, these two rates will move approximately in line, they are not exactly the same by the time May arrives.

EXAMPLE 2

On 1 April a futures trader sells a 1 v 4 FRA to a customer which will settle on 4 May and he hedges this by selling futures contracts for delivery on 18 June. The trader cannot be perfectly hedged because by 4 May the cash market 3-month LIBOR against which the FRA will be settled will not necessarily have moved since 1 April to the same extent as the futures price. He thus has a basis risk.

SPREAD

Definition

In general, a **spread** is any trading strategy in which a trader buys one instrument and sells another, related instrument, with a view to profiting from a change in the price difference between the two. In particular, a futures spread is the purchase of one futures contract and the sale of another; an FRA spread is the purchase of an FRA for one forward-forward period and the sale of an FRA for a different period.

HOW IS IT USED?

Calendar spread

Suppose that a trader expects the forward *yield curve* to become more positive (or less negative) but has no view on whether the whole forward curve will move up or down. This means he expects shorter-term interest rates to fall relative to longer-term rates. A strategy which will benefit from such a change is a spread to buy nearer-dated futures and sell later-dated futures, for example to buy a June futures contract and sell the following September contract. This strategy is unaffected by an absolute move up or down in all forward rates, because it involves a simultaneous purchase and sale, which would be affected in an equal but opposite way by such an absolute move. An equivalent strategy would be to sell a near-dated FRA such as a 3 v 6 and buy a later-dated FRA such as a 6 v 9. If the trader expects the yield curve to become less positive or more negative, he would trade the spread the other way round.

Another spread strategy known as a 'boomerang' involves buying a **strip** of futures and simultaneously selling the same number of contracts all in the nearest date. Traded this way round, it will make a profit, for example, if a negative yield curve becomes more negative.

In euro interest rate futures, for example, both 1-month and 3-month futures are traded. A trader expecting 1-month rates to rise relative to 3-month rates can therefore also sell 1-month futures and buy 3-month futures for the same future month. The size of the 3-month futures contract is €1,000,000 but the size of the 1-month contract is €3,000,000, thereby giving the same *tick value* for the two contracts and facilitating a spread between the two (see example 2 below).

Cross-market spread

A spread can similarly be taken on the difference between two markets. For example if sterling interest rates are above dollar rates and a trader believes that the difference between them will narrow, he could buy sterling futures and sell dollar futures for the same future month.

Similarly, a trader might expect the difference between 3-month dollar interbank rates and US Treasury bill rates to widen, and therefore buy US Treasury bill futures and sell Eurodollar interest rate futures (based on LIBOR). This is known as buying a *TED spread*.

A longer-term spread can be taken if a trader has a view on short-term yields compared with bond yields – for example a spread between 3-month Eurodollar futures and long-term USD bond futures. In this case an adjustment has to be made for the difference in maturity of the underlying instrument. Settlement on the short-term futures is based on 90 days, while settlement on the bond futures relates to a notional bond of at least 15 years' maturity. For a given change in yield therefore, there will be a far greater profit or loss on the bond futures than on the short-term futures. To balance this, the trader would buy or sell a much smaller notional amount of the bond futures than of the short-term futures.

Related terminology

Buying a futures contract for a particular month and selling a contract for a later month is considered to be 'buying' the spread; selling the nearer contract and buying the later contract is 'selling' the spread.

A bond spread is a long position in one bond coupled with a short position in another bond, expecting a relative increase in the price of the first compared with the second.

EXAMPLE 1

On 19 June, USD rates are as follows and a trader expects that the yield curve will become even more negative:

3-month LIBOR:	6.375%
6-month LIBOR:	6.0625%
9-month LIBOR:	5.75%
September 3-month futures price:	94.34
December 3-month futures price:	95.03

If longer-term rates fall relative to shorter-term ones as expected, the December futures price will rise relative to the September futures price. The trader therefore sells September and buys December futures. Suppose, after 1 month, the prices are as follows:

2-month LIBOR:	6.75%
5-month LIBOR:	6.35%
8-month LIBOR:	5.87%
September futures price:	93.98
December futures price:	95.05

The trader can now reverse his position, having made the following profit on the two trades:

September contract:	+ 36 basis points (94.34 − 93.98 = 0.36)
December contract:	+ 2 basis points (95.05 − 95.03 = 0.02)
total profit:	+ 38 basis points

$$\text{cash profit per contract} = \$1{,}000{,}000 \times 0.0038 \times \frac{3}{12} = \$950$$

The spread was successful because there was a shift in the yield curve as expected.

EXAMPLE 2

EUR rates are as follows and a trader expects that the yield curve will flatten:

September 1-month futures price:	94.44 (implied rate: 5.56%)
September 3-month futures price:	94.29 (implied rate: 5.71%)

The trader sells a 1-month contract and buys a 3-month contract. The yield curve then rises and flattens, with the futures prices changing as follows:

September 1-month futures price:	94.19 (implied rate: 5.81%)
September 3-month futures price:	94.15 (implied rate: 5.85%)

The trader can now reverse his position, having made the following profit and loss on the two trades:

1-month contract:	+ 25 basis points (94.44 − 94.19 = 0.25)
3-month contract:	− 14 basis points (94.15 − 94.29 = −0.14)
total profit:	+ 11 basis points

The value of a 1 basis point movement is €25 on both the 1-month contract and the 3-month contract:

$$€3{,}000{,}000 \times 0.0001 \times \frac{1}{12} = €25 \qquad\qquad €1{,}000{,}000 \times 0.0001 \times \frac{3}{12} = €25$$

Therefore:

$$\text{cash profit on the spread per contract} = 11 \times €25 = €275$$

The spread was successful because there was a flattening of the yield curve as expected.

STRIP

Definition

A **strip** is the purchase or sale of a series of consecutive interest rate **futures** contracts or **forward rate agreements (FRAs)**.

HOW IS IT USED?

A futures contract typically covers a 3-month period. If a trader wishes to cover a period of say 6 months, 9 months or 12 months, he can use a series of consecutive contracts to cover the whole period. Each individual contract implies an interest rate for that 3-month period due at the end of that period (despite the fact that the mechanics of futures do not result in a payment at the end of the period). The implied interest rates for each futures contract period must therefore be compounded together to calculate the overall rate achieved.

A strip constructed in this way can be used to *hedge* or *arbitrage* against a longer-term instrument. If a trader for example sells a June futures and a September futures at the same time, he can hedge against an FRA he has sold to a customer for the period from June to December.

Strips can be created like this for as long a period as futures are available. **Interest rate swaps (IRS)** for example can also be priced and hedged from a strip of futures.

> **Related terminology**
>
> ⇨ *See also* **forward rate agreement (FRA)** and **futures** contract.
> A bond **strip** is, confusingly, not a related term.

FORMULA

the interest rate for a longer period up to one year

$$= \left(\left(1 + \left(i_1 \times \frac{d_1}{\text{days in year}} \right) \right) \times \left(1 + \left(i_2 \times \frac{d_2}{\text{days in year}} \right) \right) \times \left(1 + \left(i_3 \times \frac{d_3}{\text{days in year}} \right) \right) \times \ldots - 1 \right)$$
$$\times \frac{\text{days in year}}{(d_1 + d_2 + d_3 + \ldots)}$$

where i_1 is the cash interest rate for the first d_1 days and i_2, i_3, ... are the forward interest rates for the subsequent periods lasting d_2, d_3, ... days.

Note that 'days in year' can mean 365 (for example with sterling) or 360 (for example with US dollars) – see **money market basis**.

For periods beyond one year, this formula gives a non-annualized version of a **zero-coupon** rate, rather than a rate as usually quoted.

EXAMPLE 1

Suppose that it is now January and that the following USD rates are available. At what cost can a fixed-rate borrowing for 9 months be constructed?

3-month LIBOR:	8.5% (92 days)
3 v 6 FRA:	8.6% (91 days)
6 v 9 FRA:	8.7% (91 days)

(i) Borrow cash now for 3 months.

(ii) Buy a 3 v 6 FRA now based on the total repayment amount in April (principal plus interest).

(iii) Re-finance this total amount in April at the 3-month LIBOR in April.

(iv) Buy a 6 v 9 FRA now based on the total repayment amount in July (principal plus interest calculated at the 3 v 6 FRA rate now).

(v) Re-finance this amount in July at the 3-month LIBOR in July.

Suppose that in April when the first FRA settles, 3-month LIBOR is 9.0% and that in July when the second FRA settles, 3-month LIBOR is 9.5%. Although market practice is for the FRA settlements to be made at the beginning of the relevant period discounted at LIBOR, the economic effect is the same as if the settlement were at the end of the period but not discounted – assuming that the discounted settlement amount could simply be invested or borrowed at LIBOR for the period. For clarity, we will therefore assume that the FRA settlements are at the ends of the periods and not discounted.

This gives the following cashflows based on a borrowing of 1:

January: + 1

April: $- \left(1 + \left(0.085 \times \frac{92}{360}\right)\right)$ [repayment]

$+ \left(1 + \left(0.085 \times \frac{92}{360}\right)\right)$ [refinancing]

July: $- \left(1 + \left(0.085 \times \frac{92}{360}\right)\right) \times \left(1 + \left(0.09 \times \frac{91}{360}\right)\right)$ [repayment]

$+ \left(1 + \left(0.085 \times \frac{92}{360}\right)\right) \times \left(0.09 - 0.086\right) \times \frac{91}{360}$ [FRA settlement]

$+ \left(1 + \left(0.085 \times \frac{92}{360}\right)\right) \times \left(1 + \left(0.086 \times \frac{91}{360}\right)\right)$ [refinancing]

October: $- \left(1 + \left(0.085 \times \frac{92}{360}\right)\right) \times \left(1 + \left(0.086 \times \frac{91}{360}\right)\right) \times \left(1 + \left(0.095 \times \frac{91}{360}\right)\right)$ [repayment]

$+ \left(1 + \left(0.085 \times \frac{92}{360}\right)\right) \times \left(1 + \left(0.086 \times \frac{91}{360}\right)\right) \times \left(0.095 - 0.087\right) \times \frac{91}{360}$ [FRA settlement]

Most of these flows offset each other, leaving the following net flows:

January: $+ 1$

October: $- \left(1 + \left(0.085 \times \frac{92}{360}\right)\right) \times \left(1 + \left(0.086 \times \frac{91}{360}\right)\right) \times \left(1 + \left(0.087 \times \frac{91}{360}\right)\right) = -1.066891$

The cost of funding for 9 months thus depends only on the original cash interest rate for 3 months and the FRA rates, compounded together. The cost per annum is:

$$(1.066891 - 1) \times \frac{360}{274} = 0.0879 = 8.79\%$$

EXAMPLE 2

A dealer expects to borrow €10 million for six months from 19 June and wishes to lock in a future borrowing rate.

Date:	17 March
Amount:	€10 million
June futures price:	91.75 (implied interest rate: 8.25%)
September futures price:	91.50 (implied interest rate: 8.50%)

To hedge the borrowing, the dealer sells 10 June and 10 September euro futures. Three months later, the rates are as follows:

Date:	17 June
3-month LIBOR:	9.00%
6-month LIBOR:	9.50%
June futures EDSP:	91.00
September futures price:	90.22

The dealer now reverses the futures contracts and has the following profits:

June contract:	75 basis points (91.75 – 91.00 = 0.75)
September contract:	128 basis points (91.50 – 90.22 = 1.28)
total profit:	203 basis points

The total profit on the June/September strip is 203 basis points, in 3-month interest rate terms. This is equivalent to 1.015% in 6-month interest rate terms. This profit is received in June, but could be invested (say at LIBOR) until December when the borrowing matures. This would give a profit of:

$$1.015\% \times (1 + (0.095 \times \tfrac{183}{360})) = 0.01064 = 1.064\%$$

Therefore:

$$\text{effective borrowing rate} = \text{6-month LIBOR} - \text{futures profit}$$
$$= 9.50\% - 1.064\% = 8.436\%$$

THE BOND AND REPO MARKETS

ACCRUED INTEREST, CLEAN PRICE AND DIRTY PRICE

Definition

The **accrued interest** on a bond is the proportion of the bond's coupon which has been accrued, or 'earned but not yet paid', since the last coupon payment.

The **clean price** of a bond is the price of the bond excluding any accrued interest and, in most but not all markets, is the price quoted and dealt in the market. It is usually expressed as the clean price of 100 units of the bond's face value.

The **dirty price** of a bond is the price of the bond including any accrued interest. This is the all-in price actually paid for the bond.

HOW ARE THEY USED?

Accrued interest

The issuer of a bond makes regular coupon payments – usually annually, semi-annually or quarterly – to each bondholder. Apart from the first coupon period or the last coupon period, which may be irregular, coupons are generally paid on regular dates. Thus semi-annual coupons on a bond maturing on 17 February 2015 would typically be paid on 17 August and 17 February each year. If a semi-annual bond pays one coupon on 30 April, for example (that is, at month-end), the other coupon might be either on 31 October (also month-end) as with a US *Treasury bond*, or on 30 October as with a UK *gilt*.

The accrued interest is that part of the coupon which the bond has 'earned' so far since the last coupon date and corresponds to the proportion of the current coupon period which has already passed. If a bondholder sells the bond, he feels he is entitled to this portion of the coupon and therefore requires that the buyer of the bond pays it to him.

Even though the previous coupon may have been delayed, for example the coupon date was a Sunday so the coupon was paid the following day, the accrual calculation is taken from the regular scheduled date, not the actual payment date. Also, the accrued interest is calculated up to a **value date** which in some markets can sometimes be slightly different from the *settlement date* for the transaction. This does not affect the total dirty price paid. In some markets, if the scheduled coupon payment date is a Saturday, the payment is actually made on the previous working day, rather than on the next working day, as is the more usual convention.

Ex-dividend

The issuer of the bond often needs several days to change the records in order to make a note of the new owner. When a bond is sold shortly before a coupon date, if there is not enough time to make this administrative change, the coupon will still be paid to the previous owner.

The length of time taken varies widely. The issuer pays the coupon to the holder registered on a date known as the *record date*. This is therefore the last date on which a bond transaction can be settled in order for the new owner to be recorded in time as entitled to the coupon, and a bond sold up to this date is said to be sold *cum-dividend*. A bond sold for settlement after this date is said to be sold *ex-dividend* or *ex-coupon*. In some cases it is possible to sell a bond ex-dividend before the normal ex-dividend period.

If a bond sale is ex-dividend, the seller, rather than needing to receive accrued interest from the buyer, will need to pay it to the buyer. The final days of the coupon period which 'belong' to the buyer will in fact be paid to the seller by the issuer. At the ex-dividend point, therefore, the accrued interest becomes negative. In this case, the accrued interest is calculated from value date to the next scheduled coupon date (rather than the next actual coupon payment date if that is different because of a non-working day).

Dirty price and clean price

The concept of valuing a bond is the same concept used for pricing other financial instruments. The total price paid for a bond should be the **net present value (NPV)** of all the future cashflows which arise from holding the bond. This net present value is known as the dirty price of the bond and is conventionally expressed as the price for 100 units of the bond's face value.

This all-in price which the buyer is prepared to pay should therefore not be affected by the amount of accrued interest. To reconcile this to the concept of accrued interest, the total cash dirty price is effectively considered as two separate amounts – the clean price and the accrued interest. The price quoted in the market is the clean price, which is equal to dirty price minus the accrued coupon.

A reason for this convention is that, even if the bond's yield remains constant, the value of the bond (the dirty price) changes significantly as the next coupon date is approached, whereas the clean price changes only slightly from day to day. The clean price can therefore give a clearer idea of the change in the market (see Figure 8).

Related terminology

Accrued interest is also known as *accrued coupon*.

⇨ *See also* net present value (NPV).

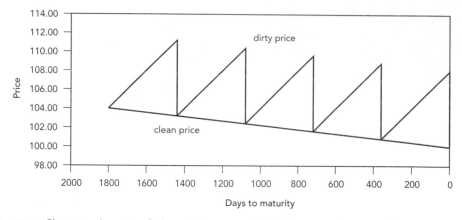

FIGURE 8 Change in the price of a bond (8% coupon, 7% yield) as maturity approaches

FORMULAS

Accrued interest, dirty price and clean price are all often expressed as for 100 units of the bond's face value.

Accrued interest

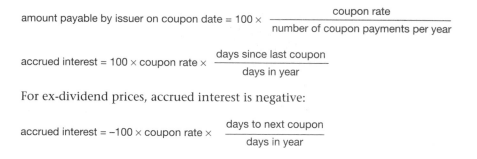

$$\text{amount payable by issuer on coupon date} = 100 \times \frac{\text{coupon rate}}{\text{number of coupon payments per year}}$$

$$\text{accrued interest} = 100 \times \text{coupon rate} \times \frac{\text{days since last coupon}}{\text{days in year}}$$

For ex-dividend prices, accrued interest is negative:

$$\text{accrued interest} = -100 \times \text{coupon rate} \times \frac{\text{days to next coupon}}{\text{days in year}}$$

Theoretical price

In general, for a given **yield to maturity**, the theoretical all-in value of a straight-forward bond with no **puts** or **calls** involved in it is given by the following:

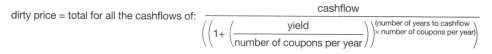

$$\text{dirty price} = \text{total for all the cashflows of: } \frac{\text{cashflow}}{\left(\left(1 + \left(\frac{\text{yield}}{\text{number of coupons per year}}\right)\right)^{\left(\substack{\text{number of years to cashflow} \\ \times \text{ number of coupons per year}}\right)}\right)}$$

In practice, certain assumptions are generally used when calculating the dirty price corresponding to a given **yield to maturity**:

- It is often assumed that coupon payments are made on the regular scheduled dates, regardless of whether these are non-working days, and that the time periods between them are round amounts – exactly half a year, 1 year etc., rather than an odd number of actual calendar days.

- The number of days until each cashflow and the number of days in a year are calculated according to conventions, which differ between different bond markets – see **bond basis**.

Given these assumptions, the general formula above can be expressed as the following conventional formula:

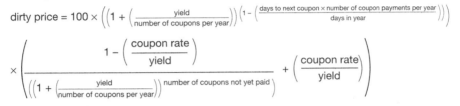

$$\text{dirty price} = 100 \times \left(\left(1 + \left(\frac{\text{yield}}{\text{number of coupons per year}} \right) \right) \left(1 - \left(\frac{\text{days to next coupon} \times \text{number of coupon payments per year}}{\text{days in year}} \right) \right) \right)$$

$$\times \left(\frac{1 - \left(\dfrac{\text{coupon rate}}{\text{yield}} \right)}{\left(\left(1 + \left(\dfrac{\text{yield}}{\text{number of coupons per year}} \right) \right) \right) \text{number of coupons not yet paid}} + \left(\frac{\text{coupon rate}}{\text{yield}} \right) \right)$$

Adjustments to this formula are necessary if there are different cashflows to be discounted, for example an unusual first coupon period which gives an odd first coupon payment, early partial redemptions of the bond, or changes in the coupon rate during the bond's life.

Other approaches are also used. In the UK gilt market for example, some market participants quote yields taking into account the exact number of days between the actual cashflows. Some also use a 'year' of $365\frac{1}{4}$ days to allow for the average effect of leap years.

It then follows that:

clean price = dirty price – accrued coupon

Dirty price actually settled

As far as market settlement is concerned, once a clean price has been transacted, the dirty price used for settlement will be:

dirty price = clean price + accrued coupon

EXAMPLE 1

A bond pays a 9% coupon semi-annually. Maturity is on 15 August 2006. The current market yield (also semi-annual) for the bond is 8%. Interest is calculated on a 30/360 basis (see **bond basis**). What are the accrued interest, dirty price and clean price for settlement on 12 June 2001?

Time from 15 February 2001 (the last coupon date) to 12 June 2001 is 117 days on a 30/360 basis.

$$\text{accrued interest} = 9 \times \frac{117}{360} = 2.925$$

Time from 12 June 2001 to 15 August 2001 (the next coupon date) is 63 days on a 30/360 basis.

$$\text{dirty price} = 100 \times \left(1.04^{\left(1 - \left(\frac{126}{360}\right)\right)}\right) \times \left(\frac{1 - \left(\frac{0.09}{0.08}\right)}{(1.04^{11})} + \left(\frac{0.09}{0.08}\right)\right) = 107.075$$

$$\text{clean price} = 107.075 - 2.925 = 104.15$$

EXAMPLE 2

A bond with an annual coupon of 7.3% and maturity 17 August 2005 is purchased for settlement on 13 August 2001 at a price of 98.45. The record date is 7 working days before the coupon date. Accrual is on an ACT/365 basis (see bond basis).

$$\text{accrued interest} = -\frac{4}{365} \times 7.3 = -0.08$$

$$\text{dirty price to be paid} = 98.45 - 0.08 = 98.37$$

MONEY MARKET BASIS AND BOND BASIS

Definition

Money market basis refers to the calculation of interest on the basis that there are exactly 360 days in each year; this is the market convention in the majority of money markets and is generally used also for certain long-term instruments such as *floating rate notes* and medium-term *CDs*.

Bond basis refers to the calculation of interest on the basis of a 'bond' year. This is less precise because, as described below, there is more than one way of calculating a year in the bond markets. In general however, bond basis approximates to the assumption that there are exactly 365 days in each year. Bond basis is used for some money markets as well as for fixed-rate bonds.

HOW ARE THEY USED?

Although there are 365 or 366 days in each calendar year, interest rates are generally quoted in the markets according to a fixed convention for the number of days in a year, and the convention varies between markets. In the US dollar money market, for example, interest is quoted and calculated on the assumption that there are only 360 days in each interest year. Thus in a full calendar year (say from 15 June, one year, to 15 June, the next year), a depositor earning interest which has been quoted at 10% will in fact earn more than 10%, because he will earn 10% for each 360 days but, as his investment lasts 365 days, he is actually due 365 days' worth of interest. In a leap year, he would be due even more (366 days' worth of interest). This is the money market basis calculation. It does not mean that he gains a bonus, but rather that the person quoting the rate of 10% is doing so on the basis that he knows it conventionally refers to only 360 days, and will therefore quote a lower rate than he would have done if it referred to 365 days.

In the sterling money market, on the other hand, interest is quoted and calculated on the assumption that there are 365 days in each year, regardless of whether 29 February is involved. Thus in a normal full calendar year, a depositor earning interest which has been quoted at 10% will in fact earn exactly 10%. In a leap year, he would again be due slightly more. Exactly this method is also used in some bond markets, and is therefore known as a bond basis method.

In both these cases, the depositor earns interest for each 'actual' (calendar) day that he holds the deposit, but the interest 'year' is either 360 or 365 days long. In the fixed-interest bond markets however, the situation is more complex. The coupon amount actually paid on a coupon date is generally a round fraction of the coupon rate: for semi-annual coupons, exactly half the coupon rate is paid each 6 months, etc. For the purpose of **accrued interest** and **dirty price** calculation however, there are several different conventions used for calculating fractions of a coupon period. Both the length of the interest year and the number of days in the period are based on convention rather than precisely on the calendar, as detailed below.

In the appendix, we have given a list of the conventions used in several important markets.

CALCULATION METHODS

In each case, the actual interest paid, or interest accrued, is calculated as:

$$\text{interest amount} = \text{principal} \times \text{interest rate} \times \frac{\text{days in period}}{\text{days in year}}$$

The following are the common methods for calculating the fraction $\frac{\text{days in period}}{\text{days in year}}$:

Money market basis: ACT/360

Divide the actual number of calendar days in the period by a year of 360 days (as in the US dollar money market).

Bond basis: ACT/365

Divide the actual number of calendar days in the period by a year of 365 days (as in the sterling money market). This is also known sometimes as ACT/365-F or ACT/365-Fixed.

Bond basis: 30(E)/360

This is the 'Eurobond/European' version of 30/360. There are 360 days in each year. Each month is assumed to have exactly 30 days, regardless of the month and regardless of leap years. This is also known sometimes as 360/360.

To calculate the number of days from $\text{day}_1/\text{month}_1/\text{year}_1$ until $\text{day}_2/\text{month}_2/\text{year}_2$, first make the following adjustments:

if either day_1 or day_2 is 31, change it to 30

The number of days in the period is then given by:

$$((\text{year}_2 - \text{year}_1) \times 360) + ((\text{month}_2 - \text{month}_1) \times 30) + (\text{day}_2 - \text{day}_1)$$

Bond basis: 30(A)/360

This is the 'American' version of 30/360. It is the same as 30(E)/360 with the following exception:

if day_1 is 31 and day_2 is not 30 or 31, do not change day_1 to 30

Bond basis: ACT/ACT

The investment period is taken as the actual number of calendar days in the period. The year is taken as the number of actual calendar days in the bond's current coupon period multiplied by the number of coupon payments per year.

A variation on this is used in *ISDA* documentation for **interest rate swaps (IRS)**: the year is taken as 365 for that part of the period falling in a normal year and 366 for that part falling in a leap year. In this context, this method is also known as ACT/365.

In general, conversion between any two methods is as follows:

$$i_2 = i_1 \times \frac{days_1}{year_1} \times \frac{year_2}{days_2}$$

where:

i_1	=	interest rate quoted on the first basis
$days_1$	=	days in the period according to the first basis
$year_1$	=	days in the year according to the first basis
i_2	=	interest rate quoted on the second basis
$days_2$	=	days in the period according to the second basis
$year_2$	=	days in the year according to the second basis.

EXAMPLE 1

The interest paid, or accrued, from 15 December 2000 until various dates, for each of the various methods, is calculated on the basis of the fraction shown below. The ACT/ACT bond basis assumes a semi-annual coupon period from 15 December to 15 June (182 days).

	ACT/360	ACT/365	30(E)/360	30(A)/360	ACT/ACT (bond)	ACT/ACT (ISDA)
30 May 2001	$\dfrac{166}{360}$	$\dfrac{166}{365}$	$\dfrac{165}{360}$	$\dfrac{165}{360}$	$\dfrac{166}{364}$	$\left(\dfrac{17}{366} + \dfrac{149}{365}\right)$
31 May 2001	$\dfrac{167}{360}$	$\dfrac{167}{365}$	$\dfrac{165}{360}$	$\dfrac{166}{360}$	$\dfrac{167}{364}$	$\left(\dfrac{17}{366} + \dfrac{150}{365}\right)$
1 June 2001	$\dfrac{168}{360}$	$\dfrac{168}{365}$	$\dfrac{166}{360}$	$\dfrac{166}{360}$	$\dfrac{168}{364}$	$\left(\dfrac{17}{366} + \dfrac{151}{365}\right)$

EXAMPLE 2

If the interest rate quoted on a deposit from 15 December 2000 to 1 June 2001 is 10% on an ACT/365 basis, the equivalent rate to be quoted on a 30(E)/360 basis would be:

$$10.00\% \times \frac{168}{365} \times \frac{360}{166} = 9.98\%$$

YIELD TO MATURITY (YTM)

Definition

The **yield to maturity** of a bond or other investment is the **internal rate of return** arising from the cashflows of the investment. This is the same as the yield necessary to discount all the investment's cashflows to a net present value (NPV) equal to its current dirty price. For a given set of cashflows, the yield to maturity can vary slightly according to which **bond-basis** convention is used.

HOW IS IT USED?

Suppose that I place £100 on deposit for 1 year and receive back £110 at the end of a year. It is fairly clear that I have earned a return (or 'yield') of 10% on this investment. If, however, I place £100 on deposit for 3 years, and receive back £10 after 1 year, £12 after 2 years and £114 after 3 years – and am also able to reinvest the £10 and £12 when I receive them until the end of the 3 years – it is much less clear what my overall return is. In fact, since I do not know what the reinvestment rates will be, there is an infinite range of possible final results. The yield to maturity – which in this example is 11.85% – provides an answer. It is an internally consistent answer, as it means that if the intermediate cashflows of £10 and £12 can in fact themselves be reinvested at 11.85% also, the overall return will be 11.85% *compounded*. Although the reinvestment rates may well turn out to be different, the figure of 11.85% nevertheless gives the investor an unambiguous summary measure of what he is earning, based on the price he is paying.

Related terminology

Yield to maturity is also known as *YTM, gross redemption yield* or simply *yield*.

Simple yield to maturity and **current yield** are alternative measures of yield which do not take account of time value of money.

The *Moosmüller yield* and other formulas assume slightly different conventions in the calculation.

⟹ *See also* **net present value (NPV)**, **internal rate of return (IRR)**, **dirty price** and **bond basis**.

FORMULAS

It is not possible to write a formula for yield to maturity in a straightforward way such as 'yield to maturity = …'. Instead, the yield can only be incorporated in a formula the other way round, such as:

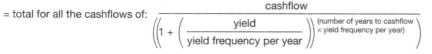

total price paid for investment

= total for all the cashflows of:

For a bond, the conventional yield to maturity is given by:

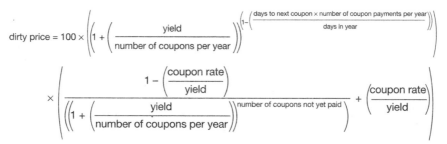

In order to calculate the yield, it is necessary to solve this equation by iteration. That is, by first estimating a value for the yield, then calculating the price to be paid on the basis of this yield, then comparing with the actual price paid, re-estimating the yield, recalculating and comparing, etc.

This formula gives a yield with the same compounding frequency as the coupon. For example, with a bond paying a quarterly coupon, it gives a yield which similarly implies quarterly compounded interest.

EXAMPLE 1

What is the yield to maturity of the investment described above, where the price paid is £100, and the cashflows returned to the investor are £10 after 1 year, £12 after 2 years and £114 after 3 years?

The answer is the yield which solves the following:

$$100 = \left(\frac{10}{(1 + \text{yield})}\right) + \left(\frac{12}{((1 + \text{yield})^2)}\right) + \left(\frac{114}{((1 + \text{yield})^3)}\right)$$

The value for the yield to solve this is 0.1185. That is, 11.85%.

EXAMPLE 2

What is the conventional yield to maturity of a bond paying semi-annual coupons of 9% (that is, 4.5% each 6 months) if the total dirty price paid (including accrued interest) for the bond is 99.25 for each 100 face value of the bond redeemed at maturity, and there are $5\frac{1}{4}$ years remaining until redemption?

The answer is the yield which solves the following:

$$99.25 = 100 \times \left(\left(1 + \left(\frac{\text{yield}}{2}\right)\right)^{(1 - 0.5)}\right) \times \left(\frac{1 - \left(\frac{0.09}{\text{yield}}\right)}{\left(\left(1 + \left(\frac{\text{yield}}{2}\right)\right)\right)^{11}} + \left(\frac{0.09}{\text{yield}}\right)\right)$$

The value for the yield to solve this is 0.0974. That is, 9.74%.

CURRENT YIELD AND SIMPLE YIELD TO MATURITY

Definition

The **current yield** of a bond is the coupon rate of the bond as a proportion of its **clean price** per 100. This is the same as the simple rate of return arising from the coupons of a bond. Current yield does not take into account either principal gain or loss, or time value of money.

The **simple yield to maturity** is the coupon rate plus the principal gain or loss amortized over the time to maturity, as a proportion of the clean price per 100. The simple yield to maturity can vary slightly according to which bond basis convention is used.

HOW ARE THEY USED?

Current yield is useful as a measure of current income – hence the name. For example, a private investor who buys a long-term bond may be much less interested in whether the redemption proceeds will eventually be greater or less than the initial cost, than in the income received each year. To make this income a meaningful number, it is measured as a proportion of the amount invested. This gives a rate of return which, ignoring the capital gain or loss, can be compared, say, to a straightforward cash deposit. In considering the amount invested, the clean price is used rather than the dirty price; the accrued interest included in the dirty price paid up-front can be considered as given back to the investor when he receives his first coupon payment.

The simple yield to maturity does take into account the principal gain or loss but not the *time value of money*. Simple yield to maturity is useful as an alternative to yield to maturity only because it is much easier to calculate. This measure is used in the Japanese markets. As it does not take into account the time value of money, however, it can be misleading. Alternative investments with the same yield to maturity can have significantly different simple yields to maturity (see the two examples below).

Related terminology

Current yield is also known as *running yield*.

⇨ *See also* **yield to maturity**, which does take into account the time value of money.

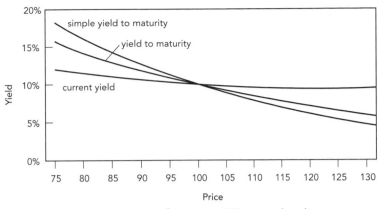

FIGURE 9 Comparison of yield measures for a 7-year 10% coupon bond

FORMULAS

Unlike for yield to maturity, it is possible to give straightforward formulas for both current yield and simple yield to maturity, which require no iteration.

$$\text{current yield} = \frac{\text{coupon rate}}{\left(\dfrac{\text{clean price}}{100}\right)}$$

$$\text{simple yield to maturity} = \frac{\text{coupon rate} + \left(\dfrac{\text{capital gain or loss per 100 face value}}{\text{years to maturity}}\right)}{\left(\dfrac{\text{clean price}}{100}\right)}$$

These formulas give a yield with the same compounding frequency as the coupon. For example, with a bond paying a semi-annual coupon, they give a yield which similarly implies semi-annual compounded interest.

EXAMPLE 1

What are the current yield and simple yield to maturity of a bond paying semi-annual coupons of 9% (that is, 4.5% each 6 months), with a dirty price (including accrued interest) of 99.25 for each 100 face value of the bond redeemed at maturity, a clean price of 97.00, and $5\frac{1}{4}$ years remaining until redemption? This is the same bond as described in example 2 of **yield to maturity**.

$$\text{current yield} = \frac{9\%}{0.9700} = 9.28\%$$

$$\text{simple yield to maturity} = \frac{9 + \left(\dfrac{100.00 - 97.00}{5.25}\right)}{0.9700}\% = 9.87\%$$

EXAMPLE 2

What are the current yield and simple yield to maturity of a bond with semi-annual coupons of 12%, a total dirty price paid (including accrued interest) of 112.10 for each 100 face value of the bond redeemed at maturity, a clean price of 109.10, and $5\frac{1}{4}$ years remaining until redemption?

$$\text{current yield} = \frac{12\%}{1.0910} = 11.00\%$$

$$\text{simple yield to maturity} = \frac{12 + \left(\dfrac{100.00 - 107.78}{5.25}\right)}{1.0910}\% = 9.64\%$$

These yields are different from the results in example 1. The yield to maturity however is 9.74% in each case.

BOND FUTURES, CONVERSION FACTOR AND CHEAPEST-TO-DELIVER (CTD)

Definition

A **bond futures** contract is an agreement on a recognized futures exchange to buy or sell a standard face-value amount of a bond, at an agreed price, for settlement on a standard future delivery date. In some cases, the contract is non-deliverable. In most cases, the contract is based on a notional bond.

The **conversion factor**, for any particular bond deliverable into a futures contract, is a number by which the bond futures delivery settlement price is multiplied, to arrive at the delivery price for that bond.

The **cheapest-to-deliver (CTD)** bond is the one which it is most cost-effective for the futures seller to deliver to the buyer if required to do so.

HOW ARE THEY USED?

Bond futures

In principle, bond futures are transactions where the bond purchased is delivered on some forward date. Indeed, in the case of most bond futures contracts, a buyer can insist on delivery of a bond at maturity of the contract. In some, however, the contract must be closed out before maturity and a profit or loss taken through *variation margin*. In practice, most bond futures are closed out before maturity in this way, regardless of whether they are deliverable.

A futures contract can be used for *hedging, speculation* or *arbitrage*, depending on whether it is taken to offset an existing underlying position, or taken as a new position.

Hedging

A futures contract is an *off-balance-sheet* instrument which can achieve a similar economic effect to buying or selling an actual bond. For example, a fund manager who wishes to protect his portfolio of bonds against the risk of a general price fall could sell those bonds. Alternatively, he could sell bond futures; any subsequent fall in the value of the bonds will then be offset by a gain on the short futures position. Because the futures is usually based on a standardized notional bond (see below), rather than exactly matching his portfolio, the hedge will not be a precise one – there will be *basis risk*. However, the futures market is likely to be liquid, the hedge is quick and easy to put in place and subsequently reverse if necessary, and transaction costs will be low because the *bid/offer* spread is small. Similarly, an **interest rate swap (IRS)** trader or a bond **option** trader might wish to hedge his IRS or option portfolio by buying or selling bonds. Again, a futures contract, although less precise, provides a convenient substitute.

Speculation

The basic trading strategy is to buy bond futures if the trader expects bond prices to rise and to sell futures if he expects prices to fall. The trader does not need to wait until delivery to capture the effect, as he can reverse his position at any time up to then.

Another strategy is a **spread**, to buy one futures contract and sell another, speculating that there will be a relative change in prices, without having an absolute view on whether prices generally are likely to rise or fall. For example, a trader might buy a German Bobl futures contract (based on 3.5- to 5-year bonds) and sell a Bund futures contract (based on 8.5- to 10.5-year bonds) if he expects the medium-term prices to rise relative to longer-term prices.

Arbitrage

If the current price of the futures contract is out of line with the current price of the cheapest-to-deliver bond, it is possible to lock in a profit, either by buying the futures contract and selling the bond, or vice versa. See **cash-and-carry arbitrage**.

Contract specifications

Bond futures contracts are standardized, according to specifications laid down by the relevant exchange. Each contract is based on a standard notional amount, which varies between contracts. For example, US Treasury bond futures and German Bund futures are based on $100,000 and €100,000 face value of bond respectively.

The delivery date is also standardized and the available delivery months are typically only March, June, September and December. In the case of US Treasury bond futures for example, the seller is entitled to deliver on any business day in the delivery month. He will deliver later if the coupon he is accruing is higher than the cost of funding the position and earlier if the coupon is lower. German Bund futures are delivered on the 10th day of the month.

All contracts are completely *fungible*. That is, once a purchase of a certain quantity of a particular contract is added to an existing holding of the same contract, there is no distinction between the two purchases; they simply become a single, larger holding of the contract. When a *long* or *short* position is offset by a subsequent sale or purchase, this closes the position, rather than leaving two offsetting positions.

Margin

Following confirmation of a transaction on the exchange, the *clearing house* substitutes itself for each counterparty, becoming the seller to every buyer and the buyer to every seller.

Members of the exchange who have traded are debited or credited each day with variation margin which reflects the day's loss or profit on contracts held. This valuation (*marking to market*) measures the difference between the closing price each day and the closing price the previous day, multiplied by the notional face value of the contract. By the time the contract is closed, there is therefore no further profit and loss settlement to be made, other than the final day's variation margin.

In order to protect the clearing house for the short period until a position can be revalued and variation margin called for if necessary, clearing members are also required to place collateral with it before each deal is transacted. This collateral is called *initial margin*. As variation margin is paid each day, the initial margin is relatively small in relation to the potential price movements over a longer period. Depending on the size of initial margin, and the exchange's current rules, variation margin may not be called for below a certain level.

Customers, in turn, are required to pay initial margin and variation margin to the member through whom they have cleared their deal.

Conversion factor

A bond futures contract is based on a particular bond. However, any existing bond will change its specification over time, because its remaining maturity will shorten each day. Bond futures prices are therefore usually based on an unchanging, *notional* bond rather than on any one particular existing bond. However, if the contract is deliverable, any one of a range of existing bonds – which can change over time – can usually be delivered at maturity of the contract. In the case of US Treasury bond futures, for example, the contract is based on a notional 6% coupon bond and any bond of at least 15 years' maturity may be delivered, provided that the bond is not callable before 15 years. In the case of Bund futures, the contract is also based on a notional 6% coupon bond and any bond of between 8.5 and 10.5 years' maturity may be delivered.

Because the different deliverable bonds have different coupons, maturities and yields, they need to be put on a common basis with each other and with the notional bond, so that the bond delivered is in a sense 'equivalent' to the notional bond being traded. The mechanism used for this is a different conversion factor for each deliverable bond and each delivery month, published by the futures exchange. In the case of a US Treasury bond futures, for example, this factor is the **clean price** per $1 face value of the deliverable bond at which it has a **yield to maturity** of 6% on the first day of the delivery month (i.e. it has the same yield as the coupon of the notional bond underlying the contract).

At delivery, the seller delivers the bond nominated and receives from the buyer the relevant *invoicing amount*, based on the *Exchange Delivery Settlement Price* (EDSP) – the futures price at the close of trading – multiplied by the conversion factor for that bond.

Cheapest-to-deliver

The seller is able to choose which of the deliverable bonds he will deliver. Because he will always choose to deliver whichever bond is the cheapest for him to do so, this gives rise to the concept of the cheapest-to-deliver (CTD) bond.

The CTD bond will change according to coupon and yield. As yields fall, bonds with lower **duration** are likely to become cheaper to deliver (because the price of a bond with a low duration rises less, as yields fall, than the price of a bond with a high duration) and vice versa.

> ### Related terminology
>
> A conversion factor is also known as a *price factor*.
>
> ⇨ *See also* **accrued interest, cash-and-carry** and **implied repo rate**.

FORMULAS

$$\text{invoicing amount} = \text{face value} \times \left(\frac{\text{EDSP}}{100} \times \text{conversion factor} + \text{accrued coupon rate} \right)$$

theoretical bond futures price

$$= \frac{\left((\text{CTD bond price} + \text{accrued coupon}) \times \left(1 + \left(\text{funding rate} \times \frac{\text{days to delivery}}{\text{days in year}} \right) \right) \right.}{\left. - \text{accrued coupon on CTD at delivery} - \text{intervening coupon on CTD plus reinvestment income} \right)}{\text{conversion factor for CTD bond}}$$

Note that 'days in year' can mean 365 (for example with sterling) or 360 (for example with US dollars) – see **money market basis**.

This theoretical price does not take account of the fact that the seller of a bond futures contract has a choice of which bond to deliver. This optionality implies a slightly lower theoretical futures price than the formula above suggests.

Cheapest-to-deliver

The cheapest-to-deliver bond is the one for which the following has the greatest (or least negative) value:

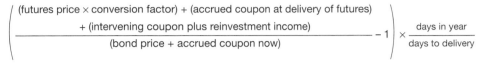

$$\left(\frac{\begin{array}{c}\text{(futures price} \times \text{conversion factor)} + \text{(accrued coupon at delivery of futures)} \\ + \text{(intervening coupon plus reinvestment income)}\end{array}}{\text{(bond price} + \text{accrued coupon now)}} - 1 \right) \times \frac{\text{days in year}}{\text{days to delivery}}$$

$$- \text{ short-term funding rate}$$

Conversion factor

Typically, the conversion factor for a particular deliverable bond

$$= \left(1 + \left(\frac{\text{notional coupon}}{\text{number of coupons per year}} \right) \right)^{\left(1 - \left(\frac{\text{days to next coupon} \times \text{number of coupon payments per year}}{\text{days in year}} \right) \right)}$$

$$\times \left(\frac{1 - \left(\frac{\text{coupon rate}}{\text{notional coupon}} \right)}{\left(\left(1 + \left(\frac{\text{notional coupon}}{\text{number of coupons per year}} \right) \right)^{\text{number of coupons not yet paid}} \right)} + \left(\frac{\text{coupon rate}}{\text{notional coupon}} \right) \right)$$

$$- \left(\text{coupon rate} \times \frac{\text{days since last coupon}}{\text{days in year}} \right)$$

The exact calculation varies from contract to contract. For a US Treasury bond futures, for example, the actual maturity of a deliverable bond is first rounded down to the nearest quarter of a year.

EXAMPLE

What is the theoretical September T-bond futures price on 18 June if the cheapest-to-deliver bond is the Treasury $12\frac{3}{4}\%$ 2020, trading at 142-09 (i.e. $142\frac{9}{32}$)? The conversion factor for this bond is 1.4565. Coupon dates are 15 May and 15 November. Short-term funds can be borrowed at 6.45%.

Payment for the bond purchased by the futures seller to hedge himself is made on 19 June. Coupon on the purchase of the bond is accrued for 35 days (on an ACT/ACT basis – see **bond basis**). The current coupon period is 184 days. Therefore:

$$\text{accrued coupon at start per 100 face value} = 12.75 \times \frac{35}{368} = 1.212636$$

On the basis that delivery of the bond to the futures buyer requires payment to the futures seller on 30 September, the futures seller must fund his position from 19 June to 30 September (103 actual days) and coupon on the sale of the bond will then be accrued for 138 days.

Therefore:

$$\text{accrued coupon at delivery per 100 face value} = 12.75 \times \frac{138}{368} = 4.781250$$

$$\text{theoretical futures price} = \frac{(142.281250 + 1.212636) \times \left(1 + \left(0.0645 \times \frac{103}{360}\right)\right) - 4.781250}{1.4565}$$

$$= 97.0551 = \text{97-02 (i.e. } 97\tfrac{2}{32})$$

CASH-AND-CARRY ARBITRAGE AND IMPLIED REPO RATE

Definition

A **cash-and-carry arbitrage** is the sale of a bond futures contract together with the purchase of a *deliverable bond*, to lock in a profit.

The **implied repo rate** for any deliverable bond is the break-even interest rate at which a purchase of that bond must be funded until delivery of the futures contract so that, when combined with a sale of the futures contract, there is no cash-and-carry arbitrage.

HOW ARE THEY USED?

If the seller of a **bond futures** contract wishes to hedge his position, he can do so by buying the **cheapest-to-deliver (CTD)** bond. He might also do these two trans-actions at the same time deliberately to lock in an arbitrage profit. The opportunity to do this will arise if the current futures price, the bond price and the funding cost of buying the bond and holding it until delivery are not all in line. Such a round trip is called cash-and-carry arbitrage. In calculating the potential arbitrage, account must be taken of any coupon to be paid on the CTD between the trade and delivery, plus re-investment of this coupon. In practice, the two sides of the arbi-trage are likely to be closed out, and the net profit realized, before maturity of the futures contract, rather than taken to delivery.

In order to complete the arbitrage precisely, the face value of the CTD bond pur-chased should not be the same as the notional face value of the futures contract. Rather, it should be this amount divided by the conversion factor for the CTD bond. If the buyer requires delivery of the bond, the seller will then need to buy or sell a small amount of the cash bond at maturity – the difference between the notional futures amount, which must be delivered, and the amount already bought as the hedge. This will be done at the price of the cash bond at maturity, which should converge to (*EDSP* × conversion factor). The difference arises because of the *variation margin* payments during the life of the futures, which are based on the notional bond, not the CTD. The cashflows from the arbitrage are then as follows:

Initially

- pay the purchase cost of the CTD bond
- borrow this amount.

During the life of the contract

- pay or receive variation margin payments
- receive any intervening coupon on the CTD, plus reinvestment income on this amount.

At delivery

- repay the cash borrowed to purchase the CTD bond, plus interest
- pay or receive the cost of the difference between the amount of CTD bond originally purchased, and the amount of the bond to be delivered to the buyer
- receive the settlement from the buyer at delivery.

If the prices are out of line the other way round, it is possible to effect a reverse cash-and-carry arbitrage. That is, borrow a bond (for example through a **reverse repo**), sell the bond, buy the futures contract and take delivery of a bond at maturity of the futures contract. A problem arises however that the buyer of the futures contract has no control over which bond will be delivered. If the CTD bond at maturity is not the same as the bond originally borrowed, the arbitrage will not be complete. The trader must then sell the bond which has been delivered and buy the bond borrowed. In addition to the difference in value of the two bonds, this will involve extra transaction costs. Where the seller may choose the exact delivery date within the month (as in US Treasury bond and UK gilt futures), there is a further uncertainty for the futures buyer.

Implied repo rate

The same strategy as above can be considered in reverse: for any deliverable bond, assuming that we already know the current bond price and the current futures price, what is the interest rate at which it is necessary to fund the bond purchase to ensure that there is no arbitrage profit – that is, a zero result?

This particular interest rate is called the implied repo rate for that bond and is the break-even rate at which the futures sale can be hedged. The reason for the name 'implied repo rate' is that the most effective way to borrow the cash to buy the bond is generally by repoing the bond out. It is thus the 'repo borrowing rate implied by the current futures price'. A cash-and-carry arbitrage is therefore possible if the actual repo rate is lower than the implied repo rate.

The **cheapest-to-deliver** bond will generally be the one with the highest implied repo rate (because any other deliverable bond will require a lower repo rate in order to break even).

Related terminology

The net *cost of carry* in holding any position is the difference between the financing cost of holding it and the interest (or coupon) income from the position.

Basis is the difference between the price of a deliverable bond, and the futures price multiplied by that bond's conversion factor. Buying a bond and selling a futures contract is known as buying the basis. Selling a bond and buying a futures contract is selling the basis.

FORMULAS

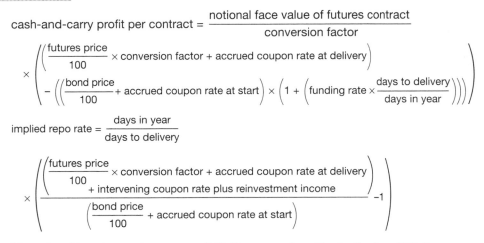

$$\text{cash-and-carry profit per contract} = \frac{\text{notional face value of futures contract}}{\text{conversion factor}}$$

$$\times \left(\left(\left(\frac{\text{futures price}}{100} \times \text{conversion factor} + \text{accrued coupon rate at delivery} \right) \right. \right.$$
$$\left. \left. - \left(\left(\frac{\text{bond price}}{100} + \text{accrued coupon rate at start} \right) \times \left(1 + \left(\text{funding rate} \times \frac{\text{days to delivery}}{\text{days in year}} \right) \right) \right) \right) \right)$$

$$\text{implied repo rate} = \frac{\text{days in year}}{\text{days to delivery}}$$

$$\times \left(\frac{\frac{\text{futures price}}{100} \times \text{conversion factor} + \text{accrued coupon rate at delivery}}{\left(\frac{\text{bond price}}{100} + \text{accrued coupon rate at start} \right)} - 1 \right)$$

Note that 'days in year' can mean 365 (for example with sterling) or 360 (for example with US dollars) – see **money market basis**.

EXAMPLE

CTD Bund 8 7/8% 22/02/2005 price:	105.24
Accrued coupon:	1.9229
Bund futures price:	93.75
Conversion factor for CTD:	1.1181
Repo rate:	3.29%
Days to futures delivery date:	31
Futures contract amount:	€100,000
Accrued coupon on CTD at futures delivery date:	2.6625

Depending on whether the implied repo rate is higher or lower than the actual current repo rate, the cash-and-carry arbitrage is:

either (A)

> buy the cash CTD bond now
> fund this purchase by repoing the bond
> sell the bond futures contract
> deliver the bond at maturity of the futures contract;

or (B) the opposite:

> sell the cash CTD bond now
> borrow this bond (to deliver it now) through a reverse repo, using the cash raised by the bond sale
> buy the futures contract
> take delivery of the futures contract at maturity and use the bond to deliver on the second leg of the reverse repo.

Assume for the moment that the profitable arbitrage is (A). If in fact the result is negative, the profitable arbitrage is (B) instead:

Sell the bond futures contract (notional €100,000)

Buy the cash CTD bond with nominal amount $\dfrac{€100,000}{1.1181} = €89,437.44$

Cost of buying the bond is nominal × (clean price + accrued coupon)

$$= €89,437.44 \times \frac{(105.24 + 1.9229)}{100} = €95,843.75$$

Total borrowing (principal + interest) to be repaid at the end

$$= €95,843.75 \times \left(1 + \left(0.0329 \times \frac{31}{360}\right)\right) = €96,115.29$$

Anticipated receipt from delivering bond

$$= \text{face value of bond} \times \frac{(\text{futures price} \times \text{conversion factor} + \text{accrued coupon})}{100}$$

$$= €89{,}437.44 \times \frac{(93.75 \times 1.1181 + 2.6625)}{100} = €96{,}131.27$$

The futures contract requires that €100,000 nominal of the bond be delivered by the seller, rather than the €89,437.44 which has been purchased as the hedge. The balance of €10,562.56 would need to be purchased at the time of delivery for onward delivery to the counterparty. Apart from transaction costs, this should involve no significant profit or loss, as the futures exchange delivery settlement price should converge by delivery to approximately (CTD cash price × conversion factor).

Profit per futures contract = €96,131.27 – €96,115.29 = €15.98

In practice, the profit in the example above cannot be calculated precisely for several reasons:

● The CTD bond may not be the same at maturity of the futures contract as it is when the arbitrage is established. This provides an advantage to the futures seller, who can profit by switching his hedge from the original CTD bond to a new one during the life of the arbitrage.

● The futures price and the CTD bond cash price may not converge exactly by maturity of the futures contract (that is, the basis may not move exactly to zero).

● The profit or loss on the futures contract is realized through variation margin payments; because the timing of these payments is unknown in advance, it is impossible to calculate their exact value.

ZERO-COUPON SECURITY AND STRIP

Definition

A **zero-coupon security** is a bond that makes no interest payments, paying the investor only the face value at redemption.

A bond **strip** is a zero-coupon bond created by separating each coupon payment and principal payment due from a coupon-bearing bond and allowing each cashflow to be traded as a separate zero-coupon bond.

HOW ARE THEY USED?

Zero-coupon security

Many projects require up-front funding, but are unlikely to give rise to an income stream to service interest costs for some period of time, such as a major building project, in which substantial cash outlays would be needed for construction, whilst income from either rentals or the sale of the building would be received much later. Zero-coupon bonds can be a useful source of funding for such projects because they help to match cash flows.

The only cashflows on a zero-coupon bond are the price paid and the principal amount received at maturity, so that the investor's return is represented by the relationship between these two amounts. With a 'normal' coupon-bearing bond, the investor is vulnerable to the risk that, by the time he receives the coupons, interest rates have fallen so that he can only reinvest the coupons received at a lower rate. Whether the reinvestment rate falls or rises, the final outcome for the investor is not known exactly at the beginning. With a zero-coupon bond however, the outcome is known exactly because there are no coupons to reinvest. Because of this certainty, investors may accept a slightly lower overall yield for a zero-coupon bond. Differences in tax treatment between capital gains/losses and coupon income may also affect the attractiveness of a zero-coupon bond compared with a coupon-bearing bond.

Strip

In order to increase the availability of zero-coupon bonds, various governments (including the US, UK, German and French, for example) facilitate the trading of their securities as strips. Once the cashflows have been separated, they remain obligations of the government as before, but are re-registered as zero-coupon bonds.

Before government securities were officially strippable however, strips were created by investment banks. The bank sets up a special-purpose vehicle to purchase the government security, holds it in custody, and issues a new stripped security in its own name on the back of this collateral. The investor then purchases a bond which is not a government bond, but is fully collateralized by one.

Pricing

Pricing a zero-coupon bond, or a single component of a stripped bond, is similar in concept to pricing a coupon-bearing bond, except that the fraction of an interest period used for discounting – generally taken as the time to the next scheduled coupon date for a coupon-bearing bond – must be determined. For a zero-coupon bond, it is appropriate to use the date which would be the next coupon date if it existed, known as a *quasi-coupon* date. There remains then the same choice as with coupon-bearing bonds of which **bond basis** convention to use. As there is no coupon, the clean price and dirty price are the same. Since there is only one cashflow to be valued in a zero-coupon bond, the price is always at a significant discount to par.

Because the quasi-coupon dates are used as reference points for discounting to a present value but do not reflect actual cashflows, it is possible for two identical zero-coupon bonds stripped from different coupon-bearing bonds to appear to have inconsistent yields, for example, because one was stripped from a bond with annual coupons but the other was stripped from a bond with semi-annual coupons.

Related terminology

'Strip' is an acronym for 'separately traded and registered interest and principal'.

⇨ *See also* **dirty price** and **zero-coupon yield**.

FORMULA

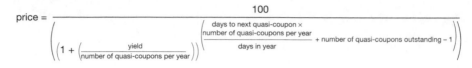

$$price = \frac{100}{\left(\left(1 + \left(\frac{yield}{\text{number of quasi-coupons per year}}\right)\right)^{\left(\frac{\text{days to next quasi-coupon} \times \text{number of quasi-coupons per year}}{\text{days in year}} + \text{number of quasi-coupons outstanding} - 1\right)}\right)}$$

The number of days until the next quasi-coupon date and the number of days in a year are calculated according to conventions which differ between different bond markets – see **bond basis**.

EXAMPLE

What is the price of the following zero-coupon bond?

Maturity date:	24 September 2008
Settlement date:	11 January 2001
Yield:	8.52%
Price/yield calculation basis:	ACT/ACT (semi-annual)

As the quasi-coupon periods are semi-annual, the next quasi-coupon date is 24 March 2001 and the previous one was 24 September 2000 (despite the fact that these are Saturday and Sunday respectively). There are 72 days from 11 January 2001 to 24 March 2001 and 181 days from 24 September 2000 to 24 March 2001. The price is therefore:

$$\frac{100}{\left(\left(1 + \left(\frac{0.0852}{2}\right)\right)^{\left(\frac{72 \times 2}{362} - 15\right)}\right)} = 52.605$$

DURATION, MODIFIED DURATION, PRICE VALUE OF A BASIS POINT (PVB) AND CONVEXITY

Definition

The **duration** of a bond or other series of cashflows is the weighted average life of the cashflows, using the present value of each cashflow as its weighting.

The **modified duration** of a bond or other series of cashflows is the proportional change in its price, relative to a change in yield.

The **price value of a basis point (PVB)** is the price change in an investment arising from a 1-basis-point change in yield.

The **convexity** of an investment is a measure of the curvature of its price/yield relationship – an indication of the extent to which its value does not change in direct proportion to yield.

HOW ARE THEY USED?

Duration

The maturity of a bond is not generally a good indication of the timing of the cash-flows arising from the bond, because a significant proportion of the cashflows may occur before maturity in the form of coupon payments, and also possibly partial redemption payments.

One could calculate an average of the times to each cashflow, weighted by the size of the cashflows. Duration is very similar to such an average. Instead of taking each cashflow as a weighting, however, duration takes the present value of each cash-flow. For a zero-coupon bond, there is only one cashflow, at maturity. The duration of a zero-coupon bond is therefore the same as its maturity.

Consider a 7-year 10% (annual) coupon bond, with a yield of 11.063%. The size and timing of the cashflows of the bond can be shown as follows:

Replacing each cashflow by its present value (discounted at the yield of 11.063%), duration can be considered as their 'balancing point.' (5.3 years):

Duration is useful partly because of its relationship with the price sensitivity of a bond (see modified duration below) and partly because of the concept of investment *immunization*. If I invest in a bond and there is a fall in yields (both short-term and long-term), there are two effects on my investment. First, I will not be able to earn as much as I had expected on reinvesting the coupons I receive. As a result, if I hold the bond to maturity, my total return will be less than anticipated. Second, the price of the bond will rise immediately (yield down, price up). If I hold the bond for only a very short time, therefore, my total return will be more than anticipated because I will not have time to be affected by lower reinvestment rates.

There is some moment between now and the bond's maturity when these two effects – the capital gain from the higher bond price and the loss on reinvestment – are in balance and the total return is the same yield as originally anticipated. The same would be true if yields rise: there is some point at which the capital loss due to the higher bond price would be balanced by the reinvestment gains. It can be shown that this point is the duration of the bond.

If, therefore, an investor wishes to be sure of the total return on his portfolio between now and a particular time in the future, regardless of interest rate movements, he should arrange the portfolio to have a duration equal to that period (rather than have a maturity equal to it). He will then not be vulnerable to yield movements up or down during that period – his portfolio will be immunized.

There are practical problems with this concept. First, the idea assumes that short-term reinvestment rates and long-term bond yields move up or down together. Second, the portfolio's duration itself will change as its yield changes, because the calculation of duration depends on the yield. In order to keep the portfolio's duration equal to the time remaining up to his particular investment horizon, and so remain immunized, the investor therefore needs to adjust his portfolio continually by changing the investments.

Modified duration

It is useful to know the sensitivity to yield of a bond price or of a portfolio's value changes – that is, if yields rise by a certain amount, how much will the bond's price fall? The answer can be seen as depending on how steeply the price/yield curve slopes (as shown in Figure 10).

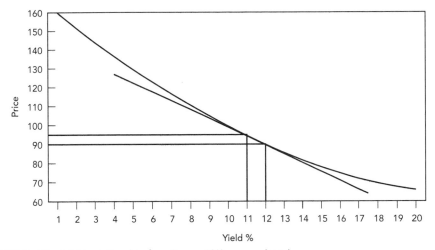

FIGURE 10 Price/yield relationship for a 7-year 10% coupon bond

If the curve is very steeply sloped, then a given move up in the yield will cause a sharp fall in the price. If the curve is not steeply sloped, the price fall will be small. Approximately:

change in price ≈ – (change in yield × slope of curve)

An investor is probably more interested in how much the value of his investment changes relative to the size of the investment (rather than as an absolute amount) – that is, $\frac{\text{change in price}}{\text{dirty price}}$ or $\frac{\text{change in value}}{\text{current value}}$. Mathematically, this proportion is very similar to duration and it is therefore known as modified duration, so that approximately:

$$\frac{\text{change in price}}{\text{dirty price}} \approx (-\text{ change in yield} \times \text{modified duration})$$

Price value of a basis point

The price value of a basis point (PVB) is very closely related to modified duration. It is the change in price due to a 1-basis-point change in yield – usually expressed as a positive number, even though as the yield rises, the price falls. Approximately:

PVB ≈ dirty price × 0.0001 × modified duration

Convexity

For small yield changes, the approximations above are fairly accurate. For larger changes, they become less accurate. This is because the slope of the curve itself changes as you move along the curve. The approximations in fact calculate the change along the straight line shown in Figure 10, rather than along the curve.

As a result, using modified duration to calculate the change in price due to a particular change in yield will generally underestimate the price (because the line is below the curve). When the yield rises, the price does not actually fall as far as the straight line suggests; when the yield falls, the price rises more than the straight line suggests. The difference between the actual price change and the approximation depends on how curved the curve is. The amount of curvature is known as convexity – the more curved it is, the higher the convexity.

Using convexity, it is possible to make a better approximation of the change in price due to a change in yield.

In Figure 10, convexity is a positive number. This is always true for a straightforward bond – that is, the shape of the price/yield curve is roughly as shown in the diagram. It is possible however for convexity to become negative at some point along the curve. Suppose, for example, that the bond issuer has the choice of redeeming the bond early if market yields fall below a certain level. In that case, the price rise will slow as yields fall below a certain point. The result is a reversal of the curvature at low yields. Mortgage-backed securities, where the home-owners are more likely to repay mortgages and re-finance as yields fall, can provide a similar situation.

In general, high positive convexity is good from an investor's point of view. If two very similar bonds have equal price and yield but different convexities, the bond with higher convexity will perform better if the yield changes. In practice therefore, the two bonds should not be priced the same. In the same way, when hedging a portfolio, an investor should try to ensure higher convexity in his long positions and lower convexity in his short positions.

Portfolio duration

The concept of duration – and also modified duration and convexity – can be applied to any series of cashflows, and hence to a whole portfolio of investments rather than to a single bond.

Related terminology

Duration is also known as *Macaulay duration*.

Modified duration is also known as *volatility*.

The price value of a basis point is also known as the *dollar value of a basis point* or the *dollar value of an 01* (DV01).

FORMULAS

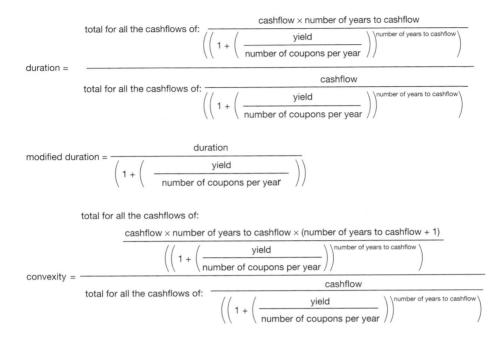

$$\text{duration} = \frac{\text{total for all the cashflows of: } \dfrac{\text{cashflow} \times \text{number of years to cashflow}}{\left(\left(1 + \left(\dfrac{\text{yield}}{\text{number of coupons per year}}\right)\right)^{\text{number of years to cashflow}}\right)}}{\text{total for all the cashflows of: } \dfrac{\text{cashflow}}{\left(\left(1 + \left(\dfrac{\text{yield}}{\text{number of coupons per year}}\right)\right)^{\text{number of years to cashflow}}\right)}}$$

$$\text{modified duration} = \frac{\text{duration}}{\left(1 + \left(\dfrac{\text{yield}}{\text{number of coupons per year}}\right)\right)}$$

$$\text{convexity} = \frac{\text{total for all the cashflows of: } \dfrac{\text{cashflow} \times \text{number of years to cashflow} \times (\text{number of years to cashflow} + 1)}{\left(\left(1 + \left(\dfrac{\text{yield}}{\text{number of coupons per year}}\right)\right)^{\text{number of years to cashflow}}\right)}}{\text{total for all the cashflows of: } \dfrac{\text{cashflow}}{\left(\left(1 + \left(\dfrac{\text{yield}}{\text{number of coupons per year}}\right)\right)^{\text{number of years to cashflow}}\right)}}$$

Approximation

$$\frac{\text{change in price}}{\text{dirty price}} \approx (-\text{ change in yield} \times \text{modified duration})$$

change in price ≈ dirty price × (– change in yield × modified duration)

Better approximation

$$\frac{\text{change in price}}{\text{dirty price}} \approx (-\text{ change in yield} \times \text{modified duration}) + ((\text{change in yield})^2 \times \text{convexity} \times 0.5)$$

change in price ≈ dirty price × ((– change in yield × modified duration)

+ ((change in yield)² × convexity × 0.5))

EXAMPLE

Consider a 7-year 10% (annual) coupon bond, with a price of 95.00 and a yield of 11.063%.

$$\text{duration} = \frac{\begin{pmatrix} \left(\frac{10}{(1.11063^3)} \times 1\right) + \left(\frac{10}{(1.11063^4)} \times 2\right) + \left(\frac{10}{(1.11063^5)} \times 3\right) + \left(\frac{10}{(1.11063^6)} \times 4\right) \\ + \left(\frac{10}{(1.11063^7)} \times 5\right) + \left(\frac{10}{(1.11063^8)} \times 6\right) + \left(\frac{110}{(1.11063^9)} \times 7\right) \end{pmatrix}}{\begin{pmatrix} \left(\frac{10}{(1.11063^3)}\right) + \left(\frac{10}{(1.11063^4)}\right) + \left(\frac{10}{(1.11063^5)}\right) + \left(\frac{10}{(1.11063^6)}\right) \\ + \left(\frac{10}{(1.11063^7)}\right) + \left(\frac{10}{(1.11063^8)}\right) + \left(\frac{110}{(1.11063^9)}\right) \end{pmatrix}} \text{ years}$$

$$= \frac{504.37}{95.00} \text{ years} = 5.31 \text{ years}$$

$$\text{modified duration} = \frac{5.31}{(1 + 0.11063)} = 4.78$$

$$\text{convexity} = \frac{\begin{pmatrix} \left(\frac{10}{(1.11063^3)} \times 1 \times 2\right) + \left(\frac{10}{(1.11063^4)} \times 2 \times 3\right) + \left(\frac{10}{(1.11063^5)} \times 3 \times 4\right) + \left(\frac{10}{(1.11063^6)} \times 4 \times 5\right) \\ + \left(\frac{10}{(1.11063^7)} \times 5 \times 6\right) + \left(\frac{10}{(1.11063^8)} \times 6 \times 7\right) + \left(\frac{110}{(1.11063^9)} \times 7 \times 8\right) \end{pmatrix}}{\begin{pmatrix} \left(\frac{10}{(1.11063^3)}\right) + \left(\frac{10}{(1.11063^4)}\right) + \left(\frac{10}{(1.11063^5)}\right) + \left(\frac{10}{(1.11063^6)}\right) \\ + \left(\frac{10}{(1.11063^7)}\right) + \left(\frac{10}{(1.11063^8)}\right) + \left(\frac{110}{(1.11063^9)}\right) \end{pmatrix}}$$

$$= 31.08$$

Suppose that the yield increases to 12.063%. This causes the price to fall to 90.60 (this can be verified using the price formula given in the **dirty price** section). That is, a price change of –4.40. This compares with the following approximations:

Using only modified duration:

change in price $\approx 95.00 \times (-0.01) \times 4.78 = -4.54$

Using modified duration and convexity:

change in price $\approx 95.00 \times ((-0.01 \times 4.78) + ((0.01)^2 \times 31.08 \times 0.5)) = -4.39$

HEDGE RATIO

Definition

A **hedge ratio** is the face value of one instrument which must be used to hedge another instrument or a portfolio, as a proportion of the face value of the latter.

HOW IS IT USED?

A dealer or fund manager with a position in a bond or a portfolio of bonds may wish to protect against the risk of falling prices. It may not be practical or price-efficient to sell the existing bond or portfolio. For example, if the portfolio contains many bonds, it could take a long time to sell all the portfolio. Also, the dealer might need the protection for only a short time: he might be satisfied in principle with his portfolio but need protection during the announcement of some economic data, or while he is out of the office. He would not want to incur the transaction costs (including significant *bid/offer* spreads) of selling the entire portfolio, only to re-establish it all again subsequently.

One possibility which is administratively easier is to sell an appropriate amount of one single bond so that, if bond prices do fall, the loss on the original portfolio is exactly matched by a gain on the new short position established. The appropriate amount of the hedge depends on the **modified durations** of the original portfolio and the bond being used as a hedge. The hedge ratio tells the dealer how much hedge he needs to put in place, as a proportion of his existing portfolio.

Such modified duration hedging assumes that the yield curve shifts in the same way for all bonds – that is, that the yields on the original portfolio and on the bond used as a hedge move up or down to the same extent. In practice this is unlikely – there is a **basis risk**. It might be that even for a yield curve shift which is parallel in general, the particular bond used as a hedge is expected to respond more sluggishly or less sluggishly than the portfolio. Any such expectation would need to be taken into account in the size of the hedge.

A more cost-effective alternative can be to use bond futures to hedge the portfolio. The number of futures contracts used would depend on the modified duration of the **CTD** bond. Again, there is a basis risk involved in hedging a bond position by an offsetting futures position because the two positions may not move exactly in line.

Related terminology

↪ *See also* modified duration, bond futures and cheapest-to-deliver (CTD).

FORMULAS

If bond B is used to hedge a position in bond A, then:

$$\text{hedge ratio} = \frac{\text{dirty price of bond A}}{\text{dirty price of bond B}} \times \frac{\text{modified duration of bond A}}{\text{modified duration of bond B}}$$

If a bond futures contract is used to hedge a position in bond A, then:

$$\text{hedge ratio} = \frac{\text{dirty price of bond A}}{\text{dirty price of CTD bond}} \times \frac{\text{modified duration of bond A}}{\text{modified duration of CTD bond}}$$

$$\times \frac{\text{conversion factor for CTD bond}}{\left(1 + \left(\text{short-term funding rate} \times \dfrac{\text{days to futures delivery}}{\text{days in year}}\right)\right)}$$

Note that 'days in year' uses the convention appropriate for the funding rate, which is on a **money market basis** and can mean 365 (for example with sterling) or 360 (for example with US dollars).

EXAMPLE 1

A dealer wishes to hedge his bond portfolio, which has a total face value of $350 million, a market value of $370 million and a portfolio modified duration of 4.3. For the hedge, he will sell a bond which currently has a dirty price of 95.37 and a modified duration of 13.7. How much of this bond should he sell?

average price of the portfolio is $\dfrac{370}{350} \times 100 = 105.71$

$$\text{hedge ratio} = \frac{105.71}{95.37} \times \frac{4.3}{13.7} = 0.35$$

Therefore the dealer should sell face value:

$0.35 \times \$350$ million $= \$122.5$ million of the bond

EXAMPLE 2

If the bond described in example 1 is currently the CTD bond for the US Treasury bond futures contract and has a conversion factor of 1.1482, how many futures contracts could he sell as a hedge instead? Assume that the cost of short-term funding is 5.2% and there are 78 days to delivery of the futures contract.

$$\text{hedge ratio} = \frac{105.71}{95.37} \times \frac{4.3}{13.7} \times \frac{1.1482}{\left(1 + \left(0.052 \times \dfrac{78}{360}\right)\right)} = 0.40$$

The dealer should therefore buy 0.40 × $350 million = $140 million nominal of futures. As the nominal size of each futures contract is $100,000, this involves buying $\dfrac{140,000,000}{100,000}$ = 1,400 futures contracts.

REPO AND REVERSE REPO

Definition

A **repo** is a single agreement to sell a bond or other asset and buy it back again from the same counterparty for settlement on a later date at an agreed price.

A **reverse repo** is the same transaction viewed from the counterparty's point of view – a single agreement to buy a bond or other asset and sell it back again to the same counterparty for settlement on a later date at an agreed price.

Where the transaction is between a repo dealer and a customer, the deal is often considered from the repo dealer's point of view: if the dealer is selling first and then buying back, the deal is a repo; if the dealer is buying first and then selling back, the deal is a reverse repo.

HOW ARE THEY USED?

As it is understood from the outset that the first settlement in a repo will be reversed later, it is clear that both parties intend the transfer of the asset in one direction and the transfer of cash in the other to be temporary rather than permanent. The transaction is therefore exactly equivalent to a loan of assets in one direction and a loan of cash in the other. These are the driving forces behind the transaction: repos are driven by either the need to lend or borrow cash, which is collateralized by assets, or the need to borrow a specific asset. The prices for both the original sale and subsequent repurchase are agreed at the outset. The difference between the two prices is calculated to be equivalent to the cost of borrowing secured money (see Figure 11). The asset involved is therefore referred to as the *collateral*.

Legal title to the collateral passes to the buyer for the period of the repo. The effect of this is that if the seller defaults on the cash repayment, the buyer should not (depending on the legal jurisdiction) need to establish his right to the collateral. The legal rights relating to the collateral also pass to the buyer so that, for example, the buyer receives any coupons or partial redemptions due. The repo is structured, however, so that the economic benefit of owning the asset – income and capital gains/losses – should remain with its original owner. The buyer is therefore obliged to make an immediate compensating payment (a *manufactured payment*) to the seller whenever any coupon or other income is paid by the issuer of the security to the buyer, as its new owner.

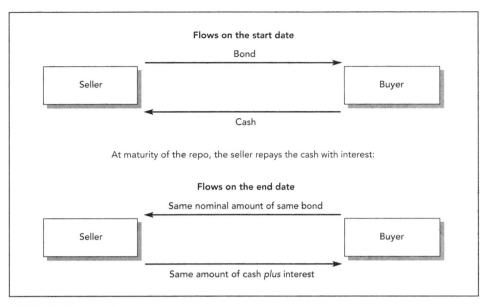

FIGURE 11 Flows on start and end date in a repo

For the lender of cash, a repo has the advantage of double security. If the counterparty defaults, he can rely on the collateral. He can therefore look to the creditworthiness of both the counterparty and the issuer of the collateral. For the borrower of cash, the advantage is that he can make use of an investment in his portfolio to borrow funds either more cheaply, or which he might not otherwise be able to borrow at all.

In addition to providing a means of structuring secured cash borrowing, repos occur in a variety of situations.

Funding a long bond position

Assuming that he is starting from a square position, with no surplus funds, a bond dealer needs to borrow cash, in order to fund any long bond position he takes. In order to borrow the cash easily and cheaply, he repos out the security he is buying (or another which he already has) as collateral against the cash.

Covering a short bond position

Conversely, a bond dealer may acquire a short position in a particular security. In order to be able to deliver on the sale, he must borrow the security. One possibility is via **securities borrowing**. Another is a reverse repo, against the cash which has been generated by the security sale. When the security is in demand by borrowers, the lender of the security can require that the interest rate he is paying on the cash he is borrowing is lower than the normal interest rate. In this case, the security is known as a *special*. Collateral not in particular demand, for example in a repo motivated by the need to borrow cash rather than securities, is known as *general collateral* (GC).

Matched book dealing – taking a view on interest rates

A *matched book dealer* is a repo dealer who does not take speculative positions on the bond market. He does however make a market in repos and might take a position on repo interest rates. If, for example, he expects short-term interest rates to rise, he can borrow cash through a longer-term repo and lend it through a shorter-term reverse. If he is correct, he can then lend out the cash again through a new reverse repo at a higher rate when the first one matures.

Matched book dealing – taking a view on specials

A dealer may reverse in a bond which he believes will become special in due course, repoing it out on the other side for only a short period. If he is correct, he will be able to roll over the repo at a lower rate later.

Fund managers – yield enhancement

If a fund manager does not need funds, but owns a security in demand, he can use this special to repo in cheap cash which he can then reverse out again against general collateral. Because the general collateral can be of the same creditworthiness as the special, he is using his existing portfolio to make an extra yield without sacrificing anything with regard to credit risk. The profit made is simply the difference between the two repo rates, for the period of the repo.

Fund managers – leverage

The manager of a fund can *leverage* his portfolio through repo, by using his existing holdings as collateral to repo in more cash, which he then invests in new securities. The process can be repeated to leverage as far as prudence and **margin** requirements allow. Similarly, he can short securities in a leveraged way by reversing them in against cash, selling them and then repeating the cycle.

Cash-and-carry arbitrage

If the current futures price, bond price and repo rate are not all in line, there will be an arbitrage opportunity available, by selling the futures contract, buying the bond and financing the purchase through a repo (see **cash-and-carry arbitrage**) – or vice versa.

Hedging derivatives positions

When an **interest rate swap (IRS)** dealer establishes a position, he is immediately vulnerable to a change in long-term interest rates. One way of reducing this risk is to buy or sell a bond with similar **modified duration** to the swap. Similarly, when a bond option dealer buys or sells bond options, for example, he is exposed to the risk that the price of the underlying bond will change. He can **delta** hedge by buying or selling an appropriate amount of the bond. In either case, in order to finance the bond purchase or cover the short bond position, the dealer can then repo or reverse the bond.

Central banks

The development of a healthy domestic repo market is important to a central bank, partly because it reduces risk in the banking system (secured lending is safer than unsecured lending), partly because it facilitates derivatives hedging, as mentioned above, and partly as a mechanism for the central bank's intervention in the money market. When there is a shortage of liquidity in the market due to temporary cashflow fluctuations, a central bank can add cash to the banking system by reversing securities in from the banks, and when it wishes to drain liquidity from the banking system it can repo them out. Many central banks also use repos as the mechanism through which changes in interest rate levels are signalled to the market.

Related terminology

Repo is short for *sale and repurchase agreement*. It is also known simply as a *repurchase agreement* or *RP*. It is also called as a *classic repo* or *US-style repo*, to distinguish it from a **sell/buy-back**.

The seller in a repo (the party selling securities at the outset and repurchasing them later) is also known as the lender. The buyer is also known as the borrower or investor. The terminology is taken from the viewpoint of the bond market, not the money market: the lender of cash is usually known as the borrower in a repo.

A *central bank repo* is a repo between the central bank of a country and its banking system; in this case, the terminology is generally viewed from the banking system's side, so that it is the banking system that is doing the repo and the central bank that is doing a reverse repo. In the US, this is also known as a *system repo*, to distinguish it from a *customer repo*, whereby the Federal Reserve does a transaction to lend cash on behalf of one of its own customers (for example another central bank). A central bank reverse repo is similarly a transaction whereby the banking system is doing the reverse repo. A central bank reverse repo in the US is also known as a *matched sale/purchase*.

A repo in which the cash and collateral are denominated in different currencies is known as a *cross-currency repo*.

⇨ *See also* **sell/buy-back** and **securities lending**.

CALCULATION METHOD

A deal can be based on a particular amount of cash to be borrowed, or a particular face-value amount of security to be used as collateral.

The first leg of the repo is usually transacted at the current market price for the security, plus accrued coupon, taking into account any **haircut** if agreed. However, a different price may be agreed, or the amount of collateral rounded up, for example, without affecting the economics of the deal, because the same collateral is returned at the end.

Whatever the cash amount lent on the first leg, the cash amount on the second leg is only the same amount plus the repo interest rate calculated on the appropriate **money market basis**; accrued coupon due on the security at that time is not relevant.

EXAMPLE

A dealer borrows cash in euros at 4.0%, via a repo from 18 July 2001 to 15 August 2001 (28 days), using his holding of €60,000,000 (face value) bond. The bond details are:

Coupon:	8.5% (annual, ACT/ACT basis)
Coupon date:	27 March
Clean price:	108.95

$$\text{accrued coupon on the bond on 18 July 2001} = \frac{113}{365} \times 8.5 = 2.631507$$

dirty price = 108.95 + 2.631507 = 111.581507

$$\text{purchase price} = €60,000,000 \times \frac{111.581507}{100} = €66,948,904.20$$

Flows on 18 July 2001

€60,000,000 bond

Seller   Buyer

€66,948,904.20 cash

On maturity of the repo, the seller repays the cash with interest calculated at 4.0%:

$$\text{principal plus interest} = €66,948,904.20 \times \left(1 + \left(0.04 \times \frac{28}{360}\right)\right) = €67,157,189.68$$

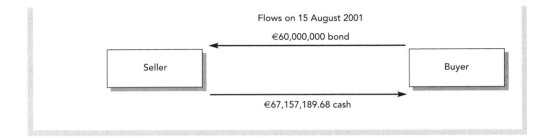

Flows on 15 August 2001

HAIRCUT AND MARGIN

Definition

A **haircut** is additional *collateral* required by the holder of collateral in a **repo, buy/sell-back** or **securities lending** transaction, to protect against the possibility of a fall in the collateral's price.

Margin transfers are payments of cash or transfers of securities to maintain the value of collateral held by the buyer in a transaction equal to the value of the cash held by the seller, adjusted for any haircut requirement.

HOW ARE THEY USED?

In order for the collateral in a repo or similar transaction to be of adequate value, it is important for the buyer to recalculate its value continually and ensure that it is at least equal to the cash lent. This *marking to market* is customarily done at least daily and, if the transactions are to qualify for favourable treatment under **capital adequacy** guidelines, this generally must be done. If the value of the collateral falls, the buyer may make a *margin call*, requiring the seller to transfer more collateral. This can be either in cash or in more securities acceptable to the buyer, to make up the correct value. If cash collateral is used, the buyer would normally pay the seller interest on it at call money rate, or some other agreed rate. Such cash collateral does not affect the cash loan underlying the repo transaction.

If the value of the collateral rises rather than falls, the seller can similarly make a margin call, requiring the buyer to return some of the collateral. If the seller has previously transferred cash to the buyer as collateral, then in any subsequent margin transfer from the buyer, the seller is entitled to ask for cash back first, rather than securities.

When revaluing the collateral, it is the dirty price including accrued coupon which is considered, because this is the amount of money which could be realized by the buyer from selling the collateral, if necessary. Similarly, interest accrued on the cash lent, at the repo interest rate originally transacted, is added to the cash principal amount when valuing the cash loan.

As collateral prices are constantly changing, there would be small transfers of collateral every day if the collateral value were always maintained precisely equal to the cash value. To avoid the administrative costs and burden of this, the two parties agree a threshold, below which changes in the collateral's value do not trigger a margin call.

Under standard repo documentation (the *GMRA*), it is usual to calculate margin calls based on a net current valuation of all the repos and reverses outstanding between the two parties – rather than make margin calls on a deal-by-deal basis.

Because of the risk that the value of the collateral might fall significantly before there is time to ensure that the seller has increased it in response to a margin call, the buyer sometimes requires that the collateral value is always slightly higher than the cash loan. This extra collateral is called a haircut or *initial margin*. Whether a haircut is applied depends on the relative creditworthiness of the two parties. If the seller is of a greater creditworthiness than the buyer, he may insist on having no haircut, or even the opposite, that the cash loan is a few per cent greater than the collateral.

Related terminology

The term *variation margin* is generally used to mean margin transfer. In the UK gilt repo market however, variation margin is used instead to mean the threshold below which a margin call is not made.

The *margin ratio* is the ratio agreed to be maintained for:

$$\frac{\text{market value of collateral}}{\text{amount of cash loan plus accrued interest}}$$

CALCULATION METHOD

Haircut

At the beginning of the repo, and throughout the transaction, the margin ratio should be maintained:

current market value of all collateral held by buyer
= cash lent to seller plus interest accrued so far × (1 + haircut)

Or:

cash lent to seller plus interest accrued so far

$$= \frac{\text{current market value of all collateral held by buyer}}{(1 + \text{haircut})}$$

Margin transfers

Calculate the value of collateral required by buyer:

● add the accrued interest to the amount of the cash loan;

● add any haircut required to this total, as above.

Calculate the current value of the collateral held by the buyer:

- value each security held as collateral in the usual way, including accrued coupon as appropriate;
- add any cash held as collateral;
- subtract the value of any collateral held by the seller arising from previous margin calls.

Calculate the margin call:

- the difference between the two amounts above is the value of transfer required;
- either transfer this amount of cash, or securities which have the same market value.

EXAMPLE 1

A dealer borrows cash in euros at 4.0%, via a repo from 18 July 2001 to 15 August 2001 (28 days), using his holding of €60,000,000 (face value) bond. The counterparty requires a haircut of 2%. The bond details are:

Coupon:	8.5% (annual, ACT/ACT basis)
Coupon date:	27 March
Clean price:	108.95

$$\text{accrued coupon on the bond on 18 July 2001} = \frac{113}{365} \times 8.5 = 2.631507$$

$$\text{dirty price} = 108.95 + 2.631507 = 111.581507$$

$$\text{cash amount without haircut} = €60,000,000 \times \frac{111.581507}{100} = €66,948,904.20$$

$$\text{cash amount adjusting for haircut} = \frac{€66,948,904.20}{1.02} = €65,636,180.59$$

Flows on 18 July 2001

€60,000,000 bond

Seller   Buyer

€65,636,180.59 cash

On maturity of the repo, the seller repays the cash with interest calculated at 4.0%:

$$\text{principal plus interest} = €65,636,180.59 \times \left(1 + \left(0.04 \times \frac{28}{360}\right)\right) = €65,840,382.03$$

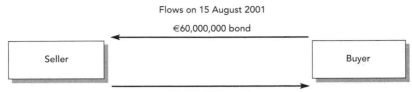

Flows on 15 August 2001

€60,000,000 bond

| Seller | | Buyer |

€65,840,382.03 cash

EXAMPLE 2

Suppose that, in the same transaction as in example 1, the bond price falls to 107.15 on 24 July and a margin call is made.

Collateral required:

cash originally lent plus interest accrued so far at 4.0%

$$= €65,636,180.59 \times \left(1 + \left(0.04 \times \frac{7}{360} \right) \right) = €65,687,230.95$$

allowing for the 2% haircut, the buyer will require that the collateral is now worth:

€65,687,230.95 × 1.02 = €67,000,975.57

Existing collateral:

$$\text{accrued coupon on the bond on 25 July 2001} = \frac{120}{365} \times 8.5 = 2.794521$$

new dirty price = 107.15 + 2.794521 = 109.944521

$$\text{value of existing collateral} = €60,000,000 \times \frac{109.944521}{100} = €65,966,712.60$$

Margin call:

The buyer will therefore call for the shortfall of €67,000,975.57 − €65,966,712.60 = €1,034,262.97 to be made up, either in cash or in securities worth this amount

SELL/BUY-BACK AND BUY/SELL-BACK

Definition

A **sell/buy-back** is a pair of simultaneous transactions: the first is the sale of a bond or other asset and the second is the purchase of the same asset back again from the same counterparty for settlement on a later date. A **buy/sell-back** is the same transaction viewed from the counterparty's point of view.

HOW ARE THEY USED?

A sell/buy-back is essentially the same as a **repo** but the two legs of the deal, although dealt simultaneously, are treated as two separate transactions rather than one. The economics of the deal are the same however and, apart from any effects of **margin** transfers in a repo and adjustments for coupon and other payments on the collateral, the amounts of cash which pass at the beginning and the end are the same as in a repo. As with a repo, a sell/buy-back may incorporate a **haircut** – additional collateral required by the buyer.

The reasons for the transactions are the same as for a repo. Because it is understood from the outset that the first settlement will be reversed later, it is clear that both parties intend the transfer of the asset in one direction and the transfer of cash in the other to be temporary rather than permanent. The transaction is therefore exactly equivalent to a loan of assets in one direction and a loan of cash in the other. These are the driving forces behind the transaction: either the need to lend or borrow cash, which is collateralized by assets – or the need to borrow a specific asset. The difference between the price on the first leg and the price on the second leg is calculated to be equivalent to the cost of borrowing secured money.

The reason for using a sell/buy-back rather than a repo is convenience. Because it is structured as two normal securities transactions, no special documentation (such as the *GMRA* used for repos) is required and there is generally no provision for daily *marking to market* and making margin transfers, although it is possible to have both of these with a sell/buy-back.

In a sell/buy-back, a forward **clean price** must be calculated in order to book the transaction for the second leg of the deal. If there is a coupon payment on the security during the term of the sell/buy-back, it is received by the buyer but not returned to the seller as it would be in a repo. As the economic benefit of the collateral should remain with the seller, the amount of this coupon, together with any investment income the buyer can earn on it until maturity of the sell/buy-back, is therefore deducted from the cash amount repaid by the seller at maturity. A usual assumption for this purpose is that the coupon can be reinvested at the original repo interest rate.

> Related terminology
>
> ⮕ *See also* **repo** and **haircut**.

FORMULAS

Forward clean price

$$= \frac{\text{clean price} + \text{accrued coupon at start}}{(1 + \text{haircut})} \times \left(1 + \left(\text{repo interest rate} \times \frac{\text{days between legs}}{\text{days in year}}\right)\right)$$

$$- \left(\begin{array}{l}\text{intervening coupon amount paid} \\ \text{on 100 face value}\end{array} \times \left(1 + \left(\text{repo interest rate} \times \frac{\text{days from coupon to end}}{\text{days in year}}\right)\right)\right)$$

$$- \text{accrued coupon at end}$$

Note that 'days in year' uses the convention appropriate for the repo rate, which is on a **money market basis** and can mean 365 (for example with sterling) or 360 (for example with US dollars).

EXAMPLE

A dealer borrows cash in euros at 4.0%, via a sell/buy-back from 18 July 2001 to 15 August 2001 (28 days), using his holding of €60,000,000 (face value) bond. The counterparty requires a haircut of 2%. The bond details are:

Coupon:	8.5% (annual, ACT/ACT basis)
Coupon date:	30 July
Clean price:	108.95

accrued coupon on the bond on 18 July 2001 = $\dfrac{353}{365} \times 8.5 = 8.220548$

dirty price = 108.95 + 8.220548 = 117.170548

purchase price without haircut = €60,000,000 × $\dfrac{117.170548}{100}$ = €70,302,328.80

purchase price adjusting for haircut = $\dfrac{€70,302,328.80}{1.02}$ = €68,923,851.76

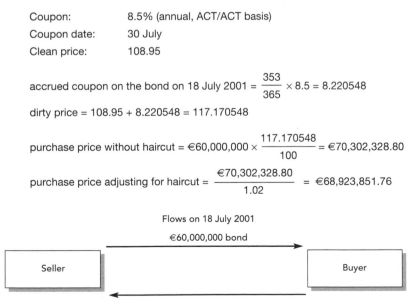

Flows on 18 July 2001

€60,000,000 bond

Seller → Buyer

€68,923,851.76 cash

accrued coupon on the bond on 15 August 2001 $= \dfrac{16}{365} \times 8.5 = 0.372603$

forward clean price $= \dfrac{117.170548}{1.02} \times \left(1 + \left(0.04 \times \dfrac{28}{360}\right)\right)$

$$- \left(8.5 \times \left(1 + \left(0.04 \times \dfrac{16}{360}\right)\right)\right) - 0.372603 = 106.342755$$

amount settled on 15 August =

$$€60,000,000 \times \dfrac{(106.342755 + 0.372603)}{100} = €64,029,214.80$$

Flows on 15 August 2001

€60,000,000 bond

Seller   Buyer

€64,029,214.80 cash

SECURITIES LENDING/BORROWING

Definition

A **securities lending** transaction is a temporary transfer of legal title in a security from one party to another; the transaction is often collateralized by a matching temporary transfer of assets or cash in the opposite direction. **Securities borrowing** is the same transaction viewed from the counterparty's point of view.

HOW IS IT USED?

A dealer may sell a particular security which he does not already own. That is, he deliberately establishes a *short* position because he expects the price to fall so that he can buy the security back later for a profit. He must however deliver on the sale, even though he does not have the bond. If he does not deliver, the deal is not cancelled and he is still liable for delivery eventually. Any delay can be very expensive, as he will not receive the cash until he does deliver, so that the counterparty continues to earn interest on it. On the other side, however, no adjustment will be made to the *accrued coupon* included in the sale price. When the security is finally delivered, the seller has not earned extra coupon on the security but has lost interest on the cash. In addition, dealers in some markets are charged a penalty for non-delivery.

The dealer must therefore borrow the security in order to deliver it. One way of doing this is a **reverse repo**. An alternative is a securities borrowing transaction, whereby the dealer borrows the security, either for an agreed period or until further notice, in return for a fee paid at the end of the loan. The fee is quoted as an interest rate per annum and calculated on the market value (including accrued coupon) of the security borrowed.

The loan may be unsecured, just as a loan of cash may be unsecured. Alternatively, the lender might ask for *collateral* of value equal to, or more than, the value of the security lent. The collateral might be *general collateral* of a similar nature to the security lent. There is however no need for the collateral to be similar, and it can be any collateral acceptable to the lender, such as Treasury bills, CDs, bankers' acceptances or bank letters of credit. A letter of credit has the disadvantage that the bank providing it will charge the borrower for issuing it as a guarantee for him, but the borrower may still be willing to provide this collateral if he has no other available. Cash can also be used as collateral; in this case, the transaction is very similar in all respects to a reverse repo.

When the security borrowed is in particular demand by borrowers, the lender of the security can demand a higher fee – or to borrow cash in return at a significantly lower than normal interest rate. In this case, the security is known as a *special* (see Figure 12).

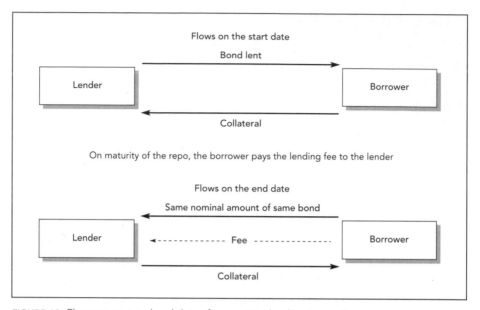

FIGURE 12 Flows on start and end date of a securities lending transaction

In addition to borrowing a security in the market, it is often possible to borrow from the exchange or clearing house through which it is settled (such as Cedel or Euroclear, for example). There are several disadvantages with this: first, the particular security may not be available, although this should often not be a problem as clearing houses have access to large volumes of the security. Second, the cost is usually high. Third, the dealer generally does not know when the security he has borrowed will be demanded back by the lender.

If a coupon, or other payment such as a partial redemption, is payable on the security lent during the transaction, the borrower is obliged to make a compensating payment (a *manufactured payment*) to the lender to compensate him for the loss of the income. Similarly, if there is a payment on the collateral, the lender is generally obliged to make a compensating payment to the borrower. The situation is not the same everywhere however. In some securities lending transactions, the collateral is only pledged, with no transfer of ownership, so that the coupon continues to be paid to the original owner and no compensating payment is required.

Depending on the nature of the security lent, there may also be other rights attached to ownership, such as voting rights, rights to convert the security to a different security (for example from a bond to equity), or rights to purchase more of the security (a rights issue). As far as the issuer of the security is concerned, it is the current registered owner of the security or, in the case of a bearer security, the current holder of the security, who can exercise these rights – that is, the borrower. The treatment of such rights under the securities lending transaction varies according to the documentation used.

Related terminology

Securities lending is also known as *stock lending*.

⤷ *See also* **reverse repo.**

CALCULATION METHOD

- The security borrowed is initially valued at its current market price, including accrued coupon.
- This market value is then increased by any **haircut** agreed.
- The collateral should be equal to this in value – although it can in fact be greater or less, without affecting the economics of the deal.

$$\text{lending fee} = \text{market value of security borrowed} \times \text{fee rate} \times \frac{\text{period of loan in days}}{\text{days in year}}$$

Note that 'days in year' is on a **money market basis** and can mean 365 (for example with sterling) or 360 (for example with US dollars).

EXAMPLE

A dealer borrows €60,000,000 face value of the following bond from 18 July 2001 to 15 August 2001 (28 days):

Coupon:	8.5% (annual, ACT/ACT basis)
Coupon date:	27 March
Clean price:	108.95

The lending fee is 50 basis points per annum and the lender requires a haircut of 2%. The bond used as collateral is as follows:

Coupon:	6.5% (annual, ACT/ACT basis)
Coupon date:	22 September
Clean price:	99.26

The bond borrowed:

$$\text{accrued coupon on 18 July 2001} = \frac{113}{365} \times 8.5 = 2.631507$$

$$\text{dirty price} = 108.95 + 2.631507 = 111.581507$$

$$\text{value of bond} = €60,000,000 \times \frac{111.581507}{100} = €66,948,904.20$$

value of collateral required, including haircut

= €66,948,904.20 × 1.02 = €68,287,882.28

The collateral:

accrued coupon on 18 July 2001 = $\dfrac{299}{365}$ × 6.5 = 5.324658

dirty price = 99.26 + 5.324658 = 104.584658

face value of collateral required = $\dfrac{€68,287,882.28}{\left(\dfrac{104.584658}{100}\right)}$ = €65,294,359.22

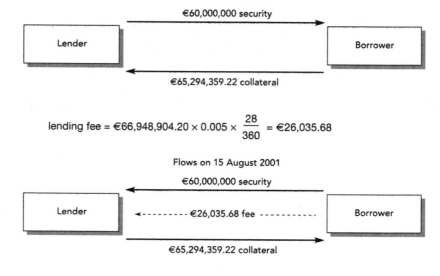

Flows on 19 July 2001

€60,000,000 security

Lender

Borrower

€65,294,359.22 collateral

lending fee = €66,948,904.20 × 0.005 × $\dfrac{28}{360}$ = €26,035.68

Flows on 15 August 2001

€60,000,000 security

Lender

‹- - - - - - - - €26,035.68 fee - - - - - - - - - - -

Borrower

€65,294,359.22 collateral

In practice, the face value of the collateral used is often a rounded amount.

THE SWAPS MARKET

INTEREST RATE SWAP (IRS)

Definition

An **interest rate swap (IRS)** is an exchange of one series of interest payments, at agreed intervals over an agreed period, for another series, each based on an agreed notional principal amount but with no actual exchange of principal. If the timing of the two payments coincides, they are netted.

HOW IS IT USED?

Any swap is the exchange of one set of cashflows for another considered to be of equal value. A straightforward interest rate swap in particular is similar to a **forward rate agreement (FRA)**, but is applied to a series of cashflows over a longer period of time, rather than to a single period.

As with most instruments, an IRS may be used for *hedging, speculation* or *arbitrage*, depending on whether it is used to offset an existing underlying position or taken as a new position.

Hedging

Suppose that a company takes a 5-year borrowing now and will pay LIBOR refixed at 3-monthly intervals throughout the life of the borrowing, plus some lending margin. The cost of the first 3-month period is already fixed at the current LIBOR. The borrower could fix the cost of the second 3-month period of the borrowing with a 3 v 6 FRA. He could also fix the cost of the third 3-month period with a 6 v 9 FRA, and so on. However, if he wishes to hedge the cost of all the 3-month LIBOR settings throughout the 5 years, he could use an IRS, which achieves exactly this (see Figure 13).

An IRS is an *off-balance-sheet* instrument settled as a *contract for differences*. The company pays interest to the lender in the usual way at the end of each 3-month period. Under the IRS, which remains quite separate, he receives or pays the difference between LIBOR and the IRS fixed rate, also at the end of each period. The IRS covers the first period of the borrowing – for which LIBOR is already known – as well as the future periods.

The fixed rate might be paid, for example, 3-monthly, 6-monthly or annually, depending on the terms of the swap. The floating rate might be 1-month LIBOR, 3-month LIBOR or 6-month LIBOR etc. The fixed and floating payments might therefore not have the same frequency. For example the fixed rate might be paid

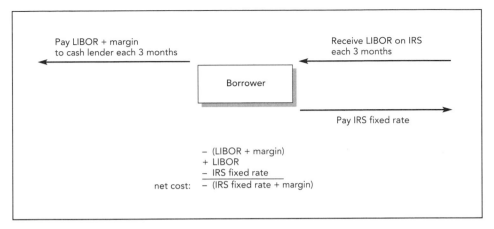

FIGURE 13 Interest flows with an IRS plus underlying borrowing

annually, but the floating rate might be based on 6-month LIBOR and paid semi-annually. A *generic IRS* (i.e. a standard market IRS) is quoted in the market as a fixed interest rate on one side and LIBOR exactly on the other (rather than, say, LIBOR + margin or LIBOR – margin). However, the payments on both sides can be adjusted by the parties if necessary, to match a particular cashflow pattern – see **asset swap** and **liability swap**.

An IRS involves no exchange of principal. Only the interest flows are exchanged and, as long as the timing of the flows in each direction coincides, these are netted rather than transferred gross in both directions.

The motivation for the borrower in the example above might be that he formerly expected interest rates to fall (and therefore took a floating-rate borrowing) but now expects interest rates to rise – that is, he has changed his view. Another motivation might be that, regardless of his view, he has existing floating-rate funding but for commercial purposes needs fixed-rate funding (for example a company funding a long-term project). Another possibility is that a borrower who needs, say, a floating-rate borrowing deliberately takes a fixed-rate borrowing and simultaneously swaps it into a floating-rate borrowing, because this turns out to be a cheaper way of achieving his objective – see **liability swap**.

All these examples are for borrowers. In exactly the same way, an investor can use an IRS to change the fixed- or floating-rate flows on his investment.

Speculation

A dealer deliberately taking a position with a swap is speculating that long-term yields will move up or down. If he expects yields to rise, for example, he will undertake a swap where he is paying the fixed interest rate and receiving LIBOR. If he is

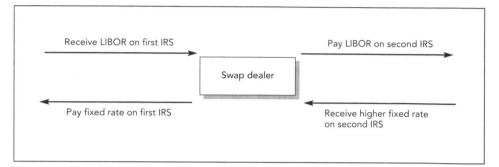

FIGURE 14 Interest flows showing two swaps

correct, he can later offset this with another swap, for the same period, where he is paying LIBOR and receiving the fixed interest rate – which will then be at a higher level, giving him a profit (see Figure 14).

Arbitrage

Interest rate **futures** reflect interest rates for forward-forward periods. By combining a short-term cash borrowing with a series of futures for consecutive periods (a **strip** of futures), it is possible to construct an interest rate for a long period. Because futures are also settled against LIBOR, the result of this should be in line with the fixed interest rate in an IRS. If the two are not in line, it is possible to arbitrage between them.

Related terminology

An IRS involving the payment of a fixed interest rate in one direction and a floating interest rate in the other direction is known as a *coupon swap*.

A swap involving two differently defined floating interest rates – for example the payment of LIBOR and the receipt of a rate based on commercial paper rates – is called a *basis swap* or *index swap*.

A swap where the flows in one or other direction are based on an index (such as a stock index, for example) is also known as an *index swap*.

⇨ *See also* **asset swap**, **liability swap** and **currency swap**.

FORMULA

For a coupon swap when the two payments coincide, the net settlement amount is:

$$\text{notional principal} \times \left(\left(\text{fixed rate} \times \frac{\text{days in current period}}{\text{days in year}} \right) - \left(\text{floating rate} \times \frac{\text{days in current period}}{\text{days in year}} \right) \right)$$

This amount is paid by the fixed rate payer if it is positive or by the fixed rate receiver if it is negative.

'Days in current period' and 'days in year' can be defined according to any of various conventions and might not be the same for the two payments – see **money market basis** and **bond basis**.

EXAMPLE

A company has a $10,000,000 borrowing on which it pays LIBOR + 0.4% each six months. The borrowing has exactly 3 years left until maturity. The company believes that interest rates will rise and wishes to protect itself. It therefore transacts an IRS to pay 6.3% and receive 6-month LIBOR for three years. For each interest period for the remaining 3 years – including the one now just beginning, for which LIBOR has already been fixed – its net cost will therefore be 6.7%:

company pays	LIBOR + 0.4%	to lender
company receives	LIBOR	under IRS
company pays	6.3%	under IRS
net cost	6.7% (IRS fixed rate plus the 0.4% borrowing margin)	

ASSET SWAP AND LIABILITY SWAP

Definition

An **asset swap** is an **interest rate swap** (IRS) or **currency swap** used to change the interest rate exposure and/or the currency exposure of an investment. The term is also used to describe the package of the swap plus the investment itself.

A **liability swap** is an interest rate swap (IRS) or currency swap used to change the interest rate exposure and/or the currency exposure of a borrowing.

HOW ARE THEY USED?

An IRS or a currency swap can be used to change the characteristics of a borrowing – for example, from fixed-rate to floating rate, from floating-rate to fixed-rate, from one floating rate to another (a *basis swap*), and/or from one currency to another. A swap can equally well be used by an investor to change the characteristics of an investment in the same ways.

In the first case, where there is an underlying borrowing, the swap is called a liability swap. In the second case, where there is an underlying investment, the swap is called an asset swap. The swap itself is the same in both cases: the 'asset' or 'liability' tag refers to the package of which it forms a part. The expression asset swap is also often used to describe a whole package – an underlying investment plus a swap.

Asset swap

An investor might for example buy a *floating-rate note* (FRN) and also transact a swap to receive a fixed interest rate and pay LIBOR. The result would be a synthetic fixed-rate investment. Or, in reverse, he might create a synthetic FRN – by buying an underlying fixed-rate investment while receiving fixed and paying floating in the swap.

The advantage of such a structure is that the investor is then able to choose the underlying asset according to such criteria as availability, credit quality, liquidity and competitive pricing. The choice of whether to invest in fixed or floating rate can be separated from the choice of asset. Suppose for example that an investor wishes to buy a 10-year floating-rate note issued by the government (because he wants the highest credit rating possible) but that no such issue exists. He can instead buy a 10-year government fixed-rate bond and swap it. Even if such an FRN does already exist, it might be that the synthetic structure using the swap achieves a slightly better yield, if the two markets are not exactly in line (see Figure 15).

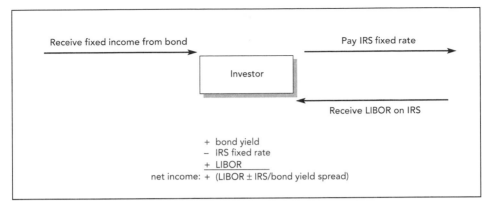

FIGURE 15 Asset swap to create a synthetic FRN

One potential drawback is that the investor is subject to an additional credit risk: the creditworthiness of the swap counterparty. If it is a single-currency IRS, rather than a currency swap, then for a given level of creditworthiness, the size of the credit risk on the IRS is much less than on the underlying asset: the swap is a *contract for differences* and does not involve settlement of the principal amount. Nevertheless, it does add to the risk. A straightforward FRN issued by the government, for example, might be seen as carrying zero credit risk, while a synthetic FRN, created from a government fixed-rate bond and an IRS with a bank, would carry the risk of the bank to some extent.

Liability swap

A liability swap might be used to take advantage of discrepancies in cost between different funding methods.

The long-term borrowing costs of a company with a very strong credit rating are lower than those of a weaker company, regardless of whether we are comparing *fixed-rate* or *floating-rate* borrowing. However, the difference between their costs is generally greater in the fixed-rate market than in the floating-rate market. This is because the strong company would typically issue a bond in order to borrow long-term, which it can do at a good cost. The weaker company however would need to pay a relatively very high yield in order to issue a bond. Floating-rate borrowing however can be achieved through repeated rollovers of a short-term borrowing facility with a bank, for which the weaker company will not have to pay such a high premium relative to the stronger company. This discrepancy means that the weaker company has a relative advantage in borrowing at a floating rate, even though it has an absolute disadvantage compared to the stronger company in both situations.

An IRS provides a mechanism for taking advantage of this discrepancy. Strong companies wishing to borrow floating-rate funds and weaker companies wishing to borrow fixed-rate funds can 'team up': the first can borrow at a fixed rate and the second at a floating rate and the two can then transact an IRS. In practice, the IRS market provides this mechanism on a global rather than an individual scale: each company will deal quite separately with a bank rather than with each other. The bank, whose role is to make a market in swaps, is unlikely to deal with two offsetting counterparties in this way at the same moment for the same period and the same amount.

Typically, the stronger company's bond issue in the structure described above would give rise to various costs – issuing fees, underwriting fees, etc. – which would not arise in a straightforward floating-rate borrowing (see Figure 16). These need to be taken into account in calculating its all-in net floating-rate cost after the swap.

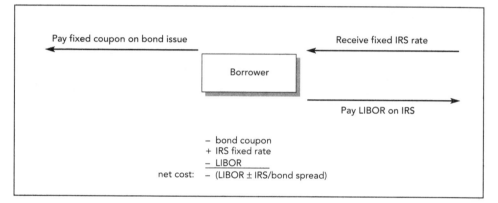

FIGURE 16 Liability swap to create a synthetic floating-rate borrowing

This 'arbitrage' between different borrowing markets can be extended. Suppose that a company arranges to borrow at a floating rate based on something other than LIBOR. For example, the company might be in a position to issue *commercial paper* (CP). If it believes that its cost of borrowing through CP will average less than its cost would be based on a margin over LIBOR over 5 years, it could use a rolling CP borrowing programme instead. Clearly this leaves the company vulnerable to the risk that its CP costs might increase relative to LIBOR because the market's perception of the company's credit rating worsens, or because investors' demand for CP falls. The company might, nevertheless, be prepared to take this risk in return for a possible advantage. As long as the CP rate is below LIBOR, the borrowing cost will be less than the fixed swap rate. If the CP rate rises relative to LIBOR however, so will the all-in cost (see Figure 17).

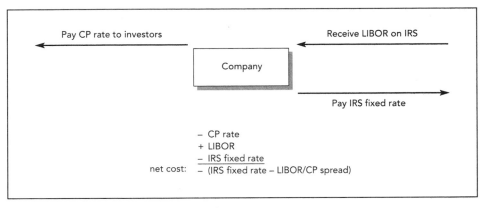

FIGURE 17 Combining a CP programme with a coupon swap

Smoothing the cashflows

Another potential drawback of an asset swap or liability swap is that the resulting cashflows are likely to be more uneven than in a simpler structure. For example the size and timing of cashflows on an underlying asset might not exactly match the size and timing of the offsetting flows on the swap. These can however be smoothed out by the swap counterparty if it is a bank.

Suppose for example that an investor wants an FRN structure. Typically, buying an FRN might mean (for each face value 100 of the FRN):

- investing 100 initially;
- receiving each 6 months a coupon of LIBOR plus a margin;
- receiving the principal of 100 redeemed at maturity.

Investing in a bond and swapping it however might result in the following:

- investing more, or less, than 100 initially, because the bond is unlikely to be priced exactly at par;
- receiving each year a bond coupon;
- paying each year the IRS fixed rate, which is unlikely to be the same as the bond coupon;
- receiving each 6 months exactly LIBOR;
- receiving the principal of 100 redeemed at maturity.

The investor might prefer the bank to 'tidy' the cashflows, so that the second structure looks like the first. In order to do this, the bank can arrange an *off-market* swap – instead of paying the market IRS fixed rate to the investor, the bank will pay a higher or lower fixed rate in order to match the bond coupon exactly. The bank can also introduce a cashflow at the beginning of the swap to match the difference between 100 (the initial amount that the investor would like to spend) and the actual cost of the bond. These adjustments of course have a value – which might be to the customer's advantage or disadvantage. To compensate for them, the bank will therefore also adjust the floating side of the swap, by paying the investor LIBOR plus or minus a spread.

In exactly the same way, a bond issuer using a liability swap to create a synthetic floating-rate borrowing, for example, might prefer the bank to smooth his cash-flows – a mirror image of the process above. After issuing costs, the bond issue would generally generate less cash than par, and the bond coupon payments would not be matched exactly by the fixed receipts from a generic swap. Therefore, as above, the cashflows could be smoothed so that there is a net par inflow at the beginning, a net repayment of par at maturity, and a series of net LIBOR-related outflows over the life of the arrangement.

Related terminology

⇨ *See also* interest rate swap (IRS), currency swap, discount factor and net present value (NPV).

CALCULATION APPROACH

To achieve a swap package with cashflows in a particular pattern:

- Write out a schedule of all the cashflows arising from the underlying asset or liability together with a generic swap.

- Add a further series of cashflows which will adjust the net flows on each date to the pattern required.

- Calculate the NPV of these adjustments, for example using **discount factors** derived from the **zero-coupon** swap yield curve.

- Add another series of regular cashflows which has an equal and opposite NPV to that of the first adjustments, and which maintains the required pattern.

- Each cashflow must be calculated on the appropriate basis (**money market basis** or **bond basis**, annual or semi-annual, etc.).

EXAMPLE 1

Each of the following two companies wishes to borrow for 5 years and each has access to both fixed-rate borrowing and floating-rate borrowing.

Company AAA has access to floating-rate borrowing at LIBOR + 0.1% and also has access to fixed-rate borrowing at 8.0%. Company AAA would prefer floating-rate borrowing.

Company BBB has access to floating-rate borrowing at LIBOR + 0.8% and also has access to fixed-rate borrowing at 9.5%. Company BBB would prefer fixed-rate borrowing.

If AAA borrows at LIBOR + 0.1% and BBB borrows at 9.5%, each company achieves what it requires. There is however a structure which achieves the same result at a lower cost. This is for AAA to take a fixed-rate borrowing at 8.0%, BBB to take a floating-rate borrowing at LIBOR + 0.8% and for AAA and BBB to transact a swap at say 8.3% (which we will assume to be the current market rate for a swap) against LIBOR as follows:

The net cost for AAA is: (8.0% − 8.3% + LIBOR) = LIBOR − 0.3%
The net cost for BBB is: (LIBOR + 0.8% + 8.3% − LIBOR) = 9.1%

In this way, each company achieves what it requires, but at a cost which is 0.4% lower than it would achieve by the 'straightforward' route.

EXAMPLE 2

An investor purchases the following bond and wishes to convert it to a synthetic FRN:

Settlement date:	13 August 2001
Maturity date:	13 August 2004
Coupon:	11.5% (annual)
Price:	102.00
Yield:	10.686%

The 3-year swap rate from 13 August 2001 is quoted at 10.2%/10.3% (annual, 30/360 basis) against LIBOR (semi-annual, ACT/360 basis). The discount factors from 13 August 2001 are given as follows:

13 February 2002:	0.9525
13 August 2002:	0.9080
13 February 2003:	0.8648
13 August 2003:	0.8229
13 February 2004:	0.7835
13 August 2004:	0.7452

Suppose that the principal amount invested is 102, and that the investor transacts a generic 3-year swap based on a notional amount of 100. The bond cashflows and swap cashflows would then be as follows:

Date	Bond	Swap	
13 Aug 2001:	−102		
13 Feb 2002:			$+100 \times \text{LIBOR} \times \frac{184}{360}$
13 Aug 2002:	+11.5	−10.3	$+100 \times \text{LIBOR} \times \frac{181}{360}$
13 Feb 2003:			$+100 \times \text{LIBOR} \times \frac{184}{360}$
13 Aug 2003:	+11.5	−10.3	$+100 \times \text{LIBOR} \times \frac{181}{360}$
13 Feb 2004:			$+100 \times \text{LIBOR} \times \frac{184}{360}$
13 Aug 2004:	+100 +11.5	−10.3	$+100 \times \text{LIBOR} \times \frac{182}{360}$

These cashflows will clearly not provide a 'clean' result in terms of a spread relative to LIBOR based on a principal of 100, for two reasons. First, the difference between the 11.5% coupon on the bond and the 10.3% swap rate is an annual cashflow, but LIBOR is semi-annual. Second, the principal invested is 102 rather than 100. These differences have an NPV of:

$$(11.5 - 10.3) \times 0.9080 + (11.5 - 10.3) \times 0.8229$$

$$+ (11.5 - 10.3) \times 0.7452 + (100 - 102) = 0.9713$$

What interest rate i (semi-annual, ACT/360 basis) is necessary so that a series of cashflows at i based on a principal of 100 would also have an NPV of 0.9713?

$$\left(100 \times i \times \frac{184}{360} \times .9525\right) + \left(100 \times i \times \frac{181}{360} \times .9080\right) + \left(100 \times i \times \frac{184}{360} \times .8648\right)$$

$$+ \left(100 \times i \times \frac{181}{360} \times .8229\right) + \left(100 \times i \times \frac{184}{360} \times .7835\right) + \left(100 \times i \times \frac{182}{360} \times .7452\right) = 0.9713$$

The solution to this is: i = 0.0038 = 0.38%

We can therefore replace the following fixed outflows arising from a generic swap against LIBOR:

annual (30/360 basis) swap outflows of (100 ×10.3%)

by the following cashflows – an off-market swap:

> annual (30/360 basis) swap outflows of (100 × 11.5%)
> plus semi-annual (ACT/360 basis) inflows of (100 × 0.38%)
> plus an initial 'odd' receipt of 2

This 0.38% can be included with the semi-annual swap inflows of (100 × LIBOR) which we already have. We have therefore replaced the generic swap by one with the same NPV, as follows:

> Pay: 11.5% (annual, 30/360 basis)
> Receive: LIBOR + 0.38% (semi-annual, ACT/360 basis)

The net effect is therefore an asset swap giving the investor LIBOR plus 38 basis points, on an investment at par.

CURRENCY SWAP

Definition

A **currency swap** is an exchange of a series of cashflows in one currency for a series of cashflows in another currency, at agreed intervals over an agreed period.

HOW IS IT USED?

Currency swaps usually involve an exchange of cashflows largely analogous to those in an **interest rate swap (IRS)**, but in two different currencies. For example, a company might establish – or have already established – a borrowing in one currency, which it wishes to convert into a borrowing in another currency. One example would be where the existing borrowing, and the effective borrowing arrangement after the swap, are both fixed-rate – a fixed–fixed currency swap. Currency swaps can also be used to convert a fixed borrowing in one currency to a floating borrowing in another, or floating to floating. In the same way, a currency swap can be used to convert the whole stream of flows arising from a fixed- or floating-rate investment in one currency into a series of flows which synthesize a fixed- or floating-rate investment in another currency.

Unlike an IRS, a currency swap which is based on a borrowing or an investment generally involves exchange of the principal amount as well as the interest amounts. In a single-currency IRS, nothing would be achieved by this – each party would simply be required to pay and receive the same principal amount, which would net to zero. In a currency swap however, the value of the principal amount at maturity will vary with the exchange rate at that time. If this is not included in the swap, the all-in result will not be known.

A currency swap can be the conversion of any stream of cashflows in one currency into a stream of cashflows in another currency, not necessarily cashflows arising from a borrowing or an investment. For example, an exporter might wish to hedge the exchange rate risk on foreign currency inflows expected over a number of years from sales of goods. One approach would be to cover each expected inflow using a separate **forward outright**. Another approach however would be to treat all the expected flows as a single package and convert them to a stream of flows in the exporter's domestic currency, using a currency swap.

In order to exchange a series of cashflows in one currency for a series in another currency, the two streams should have the same value at the time of the transaction. An appropriate way to value each series is to calculate its **net present value (NPV)** in its own currency. The spot exchange rate can then be used to equate the two NPVs.

Related terminology

A currency swap is often called a *currency and interest rate swap*, since the swap cashflows usually reflect interest and principal on a borrowing or investment.

⇨ *See also* **interest rate swap (IRS)** and **net present value (NPV)**.

CALCULATION APPROACH

- Calculate the NPV of the series of cashflows in one currency.
- Convert the NPV to the other currency at an agreed spot rate.
- Construct a series of cashflows with the required cashflow profile in the second currency which has this same NPV.

EXAMPLE

You purchase a 5-year USD bond with an annual coupon of 6.7%, at a price of 95.00. Using an asset swap, you convert this investment to a synthetic South African rand (ZAR) investment. The swap rate you achieve is 7.85% for USD against 8.35% for ZAR (both annual bond basis). The current USD/ZAR exchange rate is 6.00. What all-in ZAR yield do you achieve?

The future USD cashflows are as follows for each $100 face value of bond:

Year 1	+ 6.70
Year 2	+ 6.70
Year 3	+ 6.70
Year 4	+ 6.70
Year 5	+106.70

Discounting at a rate of 7.85%, the NPV of these flows is $95.390:

$$\frac{6.70}{1.0785} + \left(\frac{6.70}{(1.0785^2)}\right) + \left(\frac{6.70}{(1.0785^3)}\right) + \left(\frac{6.70}{(1.0785^4)}\right) + \left(\frac{106.70}{(1.0785^5)}\right) = 95.390$$

At an exchange rate of 6.00, $95.390 is equivalent to ZAR 572.341.

For each USD 100 face value of the bond, you invested USD 95.00. This is equivalent to ZAR 570. You therefore wish to receive a series of ZAR cashflows, such that there is a regular ZAR cashflow in years 1 to 5, with an additional cashflow of ZAR 570 in year 5. The NPV of these cashflows, discounting at 8.35%, must be ZAR 572.341. The regular cashflow necessary to give this NPV is ZAR 48.187. There is an infinite number of other possible cashflow patterns which would give this NPV, but this particular pattern provides the par structure at which we are aiming.

The yield on the asset swap is therefore the yield derived from an investment of ZAR 570, a principal amount of ZAR 570 returned at the end of 5 years and an income stream of ZAR 48.187 each year. This can be seen to be a yield of: $\dfrac{48.187}{570} = 0.08454 = 8.454\%$:

Date	Bond USD	Swap USD	ZAR	Net cashflows ZAR
Now	– 95.00			– 570.00
Year 1	+ 6.70	– 6.70	+ 48.187	+ 48.187
Year 2	+ 6.70	– 6.70	+ 48.187	+ 48.187
Year 3	+ 6.70	– 6.70	+ 48.187	+ 48.187
Year 4	+ 6.70	– 6.70	+ 48.187	+ 48.187
Year 5	+ 106.70	– 106.70	+ 618.187	+ 618.187
NPV =		– 95.39	+ 572.341	

FOREIGN EXCHANGE

CROSS-RATE

Definition

Strictly, a **cross-rate** is an exchange rate between any two currencies, neither of which is the US dollar. However, the term is also sometimes used for any exchange rate derived from two other exchange rates.

HOW IS IT USED?

An exchange rate can be quoted between any pair of currencies. In practice however, many pairs are not regularly traded. Rather, banks run trading books in exchange rates against major currencies – in particular, rates against the US dollar but also rates against the euro, sterling etc. Because there is a commercial need for very many currency pairs, as well as a wish to speculate in them, banks need to be able to construct such pairs from the ones which they normally trade.

Suppose, for example, that a bank needs to quote to a counterparty a spot rate between the Swiss franc and the Singapore dollar, but that it does not have a CHF/SGD trading book. The rate can instead be constructed from the prices quoted by the bank's USD/CHF dealer and the bank's USD/SGD dealer.

When dealing in exchange rates involving major currencies, there are conventions in the interbank market for which is the *base currency* and which is the *variable currency*. If, for example, the euro is involved in an exchange rate, it is generally the base currency. Apart from that, if sterling, the Australian dollar, New Zealand dollar or US dollar are involved, they would generally be base currency. In other cases, there is not a universal convention for which way round to quote an exchange rate.

Related terminology

A foreign exchange *spot* price is a price for the purchase of one currency against the sale of another, to be delivered two business days after transaction date.

A **forward outright** price is a price for a similar deal but where delivery takes place on a date after spot.

⇨ *See also* **forward swap.**

An exchange rate is quoted as the number of units of one currency (the *variable currency*) equal to one unit of the other currency (the *base currency*). In this book we always write the base currency on the left and the variable on the right, so that in a 'NOK/SEK' quotation, for example, the NOK is the base currency and the SEK is the variable currency.

The *bid* rate in a spot or forward outright exchange rate is the lower rate, quoted on the left side, at which the bank quoting it (the *market maker*) is prepared to buy one unit of the base currency for a given number of units of the variable currency.

The *offer* rate in a spot or forward outright exchange rate is the higher rate, quoted on the right side, at which the bank quoting it is prepared to sell one unit of the base currency for a given number of units of the variable currency.

The variable currency is also known as the *counter currency* or the *quoted currency*.

CALCULATION METHOD

Spot and forward outright

The following rules apply equally to calculating a spot rate from two spot rates, or a forward outright rate from two forward outright rates.

To calculate an exchange rate from two other rates which share the same base currency or from two other rates which share the same variable currency, divide opposite sides of the exchange rates (i.e. divide the left side of the first rate by the right side of the second rate and divide the right side of the first rate by the left side of the second rate).

To calculate an exchange rate from two rates where the common currency is the base currency in one quotation but the variable currency in the other, multiply the same sides of the exchange rates (i.e. multiply the left side of the first rate by the left side of the second rate and multiply the right side of the first rate by the right side of the second rate).

The construction of one exchange rate from two others in this way can be seen 'algebraically':

Given two exchange rates AAA/BBB and AAA/CCC, the cross-rates are:

> BBB/CCC = AAA/CCC ÷ AAA/BBB
> and CCC/BBB = AAA/BBB ÷ AAA/CCC
> When dividing, use opposite sides.

Given two exchange rates BBB/AAA and AAA/CCC, the cross-rates are:

> BBB/CCC = BBB/AAA × AAA/CCC
> and CCC/BBB = 1 ÷ (BBB/AAA × AAA/CCC)
> When multiplying, use the same sides.

Forward swap

In order to calculate a cross-rate forward swap, it is necessary to:

- first, calculate the cross-rate spot;
- second, calculate the forward outrights for the two underlying rates;
- third, calculate the cross-rate forward outright;
- fourth, subtract the cross-rate spot from the cross-rate forward outright.

EXAMPLE 1

Spot USD/CHF:	1.4874 / 1.4879
Spot USD/SGD:	1.6782 / 1.6792
Spot EUR/USD:	1.2166 / 1.2171
Spot AUD/USD:	0.6834 / 0.6839

(i) To construct spot CHF/SGD:

Consider first the left side of the CHF/SGD price the bank is constructing. This is the price at which the bank will buy CHF (the base currency) and sell SGD. It must therefore ask: at which price does its USD/CHF dealer buy CHF against USD, and at which price does its USD/SGD dealer sell SGD against USD? The answers are 1.4879 and 1.6782 respectively. Since each 1 dollar is worth 1.48 Swiss francs and also 1.67 Singapore dollars, the CHF/SGD exchange rate is the ratio between these two. Effectively, the bank is both selling USD (against CHF) and buying USD (against SGD) simultaneously, with a net zero effect in USD. The right side of the CHF/SGD price the bank is constructing comes from selling CHF against USD at 1.4874 and buying SGD against USD at 1.6792.

$1.6782 \div 1.4879 = 1.1279$ is the rate at which the bank sells SGD and buys CHF
$1.6792 \div 1.4874 = 1.1289$ is the rate at which the bank buys SGD and sells CHF
Therefore the spot CHF/SGD rate is: 1.1279 / 1.1289

(ii) To construct spot SGD/CHF:
$1.4874 \div 1.6792 = 0.8858$ is the rate at which the bank sells CHF and buys SGD
$1.4879 \div 1.6782 = 0.8866$ is the rate at which the bank buys CHF and sells SGD
Therefore the spot SGD/CHF rate is: 0.8858 / 0.8866

(iii) To construct spot EUR/AUD:
$1.2166 \div 0.6839 = 1.7789$ is the rate at which the bank buys EUR and sells AUD
$1.2171 \div 0.6834 = 1.7809$ is the rate at which the bank sells EUR and buys AUD
Therefore the spot EUR/AUD rate is: 1.7789 / 1.7809

(iv) To construct spot EUR/SGD:
$1.2166 \times 1.6782 = 2.0417$ is the rate at which the bank buys EUR and sells SGD
$1.2171 \times 1.6792 = 2.0438$ is the rate at which the bank sells EUR and buys SGD
Therefore the spot EUR/SGD rate is: 2.0417 / 2.0438

EXAMPLE 2

The examples above all construct cross-rates from exchange rates involving the US dollar (which is often the case). The same approach applies when constructing from other rates:

Spot EUR/GBP:	0.7374 / 0.7379
Spot GBP/CHF:	2.1702 / 2.1707
Spot GBP/JPY:	192.70 / 193.00

(i) To construct spot CHF/JPY:

$192.70 \div 2.1707 = 88.77$ is the rate at which the bank buys CHF and sells JPY

$193.00 \div 2.1702 = 88.93$ is the rate at which the bank sells CHF and buys JPY

Therefore the spot CHF/JPY rate is: 88.77 / 88.93

(ii) To construct the spot JPY/CHF:

$2.1702 \div 193.00 = 0.011245$ is the rate at which the bank buys JPY and sells CHF

$2.1707 \div 192.70 = 0.011265$ is the rate at which the bank sells JPY and buys CHF

Therefore the spot JPY/CHF rate is: 0.011245 / 0.011265

(iii) To construct spot EUR/CHF:

$0.7374 \times 2.1702 = 1.6003$ is the rate at which the bank buys EUR and sells CHF

$0.7379 \times 2.1707 = 1.6018$ is the rate at which the bank sells EUR and buys CHF

Therefore the spot EUR/CHF rate is: 1.6003 / 1.6018

(iv) To construct spot CHF/EUR, take the reciprocal of the EUR/CHF:

$1 \div (0.7379 \times 2.1707) = 0.6243$ is the rate at which the bank buys CHF and sells EUR

$1 \div (0.7374 \times 2.1702) = 0.6249$ is the rate at which the bank sells CHF and buys EUR

Therefore the spot CHF/EUR rate is: 0.6243 / 0.6249

EXAMPLE 3

Spot USD/CHF:	1.4874 / 1.4879
3-month USD/CHF swap:	75/80
Spot USD/SGD:	1.6782 / 1.6792
3-month USD/SGD swap:	107/102

Spot CHF/SGD is 1.1279 / 1.1289 (see example 1 above)

3-month forward outright USD/CHF is $(1.4874 + 0.0075)/(1.4879 + 0.0080) = 1.4949 / 1.4959$

3-month forward outright USD/SGD is $(1.6782 - 0.0107)/(1.6792 - 0.0102) = 1.6675 / 1.6690$

3-month forward outright CHF/SGD is therefore $\dfrac{1.6675}{1.4959} / \dfrac{1.6690}{1.4949} = 1.1147/1.1165$

3-month forward swap CHF/SGD is therefore $(1.1147 - 1.1279) / (1.1165 - 1.1289)$

$$= -0.0132 / -0.0124, \text{ quoted as '132/124'}$$

FORWARD OUTRIGHT AND FORWARD SWAP

Definition

A **forward outright** is an outright purchase or sale of one currency in exchange for another currency for delivery on a fixed date in the future other than the spot value date.

A **forward swap** is an exchange of one currency for another currency, to be delivered on one date, together with an exchange in the opposite direction on a given later date.

HOW ARE THEY USED?

Forward outright

Although *spot* in the foreign exchange market is settled two working days in the future, it is not considered as 'future' or 'forward', but as the baseline from which all other dates (earlier or later) are considered. It is possible in theory for settlement to be on any date other than spot, in which case the deal is a forward outright. Forward outright rates are quoted in a similar way to spot rates, with the bank buying the base currency 'low' against the variable currency (on the left side) and selling it 'high' (on the right side).

For example, the spot EUR/USD rate might be 0.9510 / 0.9515, but the forward outright rate for value 1 month after the spot value date might be 0.9550 / 0.9560. The *spread* (the difference between the bank's buying price and the bank's selling price) is wider in the forward quotation than in the spot quotation. Also, in this example, the euro is worth more for forward delivery than for spot delivery: €1 buys $0.9550 for delivery in one month's time as opposed to $0.9510 at present. In a different example, the euro might be worth less for forward delivery than spot delivery.

A company or financial institution uses a forward outright to cover a risk arising from a known or expected transaction which will be settled in the future. For example if a company needs to pay a foreign currency in three months' time to pay for an import, it has a risk because that foreign currency may be more expensive in three months' time. It can remove the risk by buying the required amount of currency at an exchange rate agreed now for delivery in three months' time.

Forward swap

Although forward outrights are important to the end-user, banks do not generally deal between themselves in forward outrights, but rather in forward swaps. A forward swap price is the difference between the spot price and the forward outright price. The forward outright rate can therefore be seen as a combination of the current spot price and the forward swap price (which may be positive or negative) added together.

When a bank sells EUR outright to a counterparty against USD, it can be seen as doing the following:

Bank's spot dealer sells EUR spot	spot deal
Bank's forward dealer buys EUR spot	forward swap deal
Bank's forward dealer sells EUR forward	
Bank sells EUR forward outright	net effect

A forward foreign exchange swap is a temporary purchase or sale of one currency against another. An equivalent effect could be achieved by borrowing one currency for a given period, while lending the other currency for the same period. Therefore the swap price formula (see below) reflects the interest rate differential (generally based on *Eurocurrency* interest rates rather than domestic interest rates) between the two currencies, converted into foreign exchange terms.

If a forward dealer undertakes a similar deal to the one above as a speculative position (rather than in order to construct a forward outright for a customer) – that is, he buys and sells EUR against USD (in that order) – what interest rate view has he taken? He is effectively borrowing euros and lending dollars for the period. He may for example expect EUR interest rates to rise (so that he can re-lend them at a higher rate) and/or USD rates to fall (so that he can re-borrow them at a lower rate). In fact the important point is that the interest differential should move in the EUR's favour. For example, even if EUR interest rates fall rather than rise, the dealer will generally still make a profit as long as USD rates fall even further. In general, a forward dealer expecting the interest rate differential to move in favour of the base currency (for example, base currency interest rates to rise or variable currency interest rates to fall) will 'buy and sell' the base currency, and vice versa.

Consider how the following swap and outright rates change as the spot rate and interest rates move:

Spot rate	EUR interest rate	USD interest rate	31-day forward outright	31-day forward swap
0.9550	3.0%	5.0%	0.9566	+ 0.0016
0.9650	3.0%	5.0%	0.9667	+ 0.0017
0.9650	3.0%	4.5%	0.9662	+ 0.0012

A movement of 100 points in the exchange rate from 0.9550 to 0.9650 has affected the forward swap price only slightly. A change in the interest rate differential from 2.0% to 1.5% however has changed it significantly. Essentially, a forward swap is an interest rate instrument rather than a currency instrument. If bank dealers traded outrights, they would be combining two related but different markets in one deal, which is less satisfactory.

The forward outright rate is therefore effectively the spot rate, adjusted to take account of the interest rates in the two currencies. However, it must simultaneously be a reflection of the market's assessment of where the spot rate will be in the future – because if it were not, then market supply and demand would push the spot rate and/or the interest rates to levels where this was the case.

Swap prices are generally quoted as *points* so that the last digit of the price co-incides with the same decimal place as the last digit of the spot price. For example, if the spot price is quoted to four decimal places (0.9556) and the swap price is '20 points', this means '0.0020'.

When a bank quotes a swap rate, it buys the base currency forward on the left side, and sells the base currency forward on the right side. That is, the bank 'sells and buys' the base currency (in that order) on the left side and 'buys and sells' the base currency on the right side. Therefore on a EUR/USD 1-month forward swap quote of 20 / 22, the bank quoting the price does the following:

20	/	22
sells EUR spot		buys EUR spot
buys EUR forward		sells EUR forward

Although only one single price is dealt, a forward swap transaction has two separate settlements:

- a settlement on the spot value date;
- a settlement on the forward value date.

There is no net outright position taken, and the spot dealer's spread will therefore not be involved, but some benchmark spot rate will nevertheless be needed in order to arrive at the settlement rates. As the swap is a representation of the interest rate differential between the two currencies quoted, as long as the 'near' and 'far' sides of the swap quotation preserve this differential, it does not generally make a significant difference which exact spot rate is used as a base for adding or subtracting the swap points. The rate must however generally be a current rate.

Corporate use of swaps

Suppose that in June a euro-based company sells €10 million for value 15 August against USD, at a forward outright rate of 0.9700, to cover the cost the company expects to pay for some US imports. On 13 August, the company realizes that it will not need to pay the dollars until a month later than it previously expected. It can therefore roll over the foreign exchange cover by using a forward swap – selling the USD spot (value 15 August) and buying them back again one month forward.

Covered interest arbitrage

The link between interest rates and forward swaps allows banks and others to take advantage of different opportunities in different markets. This can be seen in either of two ways. First, suppose that a bank needs to fund itself in one currency but can borrow relatively more cheaply in another; it can choose deliberately to borrow in the second currency and use a forward swap to convert the borrowing to the first currency. The reason for doing this would be that the resulting all-in cost of borrowing is slightly less than the cost of borrowing the first currency directly.

Second, even if it does not need to borrow, a bank can still borrow in the second currency, use a forward swap to convert the borrowing to the first currency and then make a deposit directly in the first currency; the reason for doing this would be that a profit can be locked in because the interest rates available to the bank are out of line with the swap price.

These strategies are known as 'covered interest arbitrage'.

Discounts and premiums

When the base currency interest rate is lower than the variable currency rate, the forward outright exchange rate is always greater than the spot rate. That is, the base currency is worth more units of the variable currency forward than it is spot. This can be seen as compensating for the lower interest rate: if I deposit money in the base currency rather than the variable currency, I will receive less interest. Therefore if I sell forward the maturing deposit amount, the forward exchange rate is correspondingly better. In this case, the base currency is said to be at a *premium* to the variable currency, and the forward swap price must be positive.

The reverse also follows: the currency with the higher interest rate is worth fewer units of the other currency forward than spot and is said to be at a forward *discount* to the other currency. When the base currency is at a discount to the variable currency, the forward swap points are negative.

When the swap points are positive, and the forward dealer applies a *bid/offer spread* to make a two-way swap price, the left price is smaller than the right price as usual. When the swap points are negative, he must similarly quote a more negative number on the left and a more positive number on the right in order to make a profit. However, the minus sign ' – ' is generally not shown. The result is that the larger number appears to be on the left. As a result, whenever the swap price *appears* larger on the left than the right, it is in fact negative, and must be subtracted from the swap rate rather than added.

If a forward swap price includes the word *par* it means that the spot rate and the forward outright rate are the same: 'par' in this case represents zero. 'A/P' is 'around par', meaning that the left-hand side of the swap must be subtracted from spot and the right side added. This happens when the two interest rates are the same or very similar. This is often written '–6 / +4', which means the same as '6 / 4 A/P' but indicates more clearly how the outrights are calculated.

Related terminology

A clear terminology is to say 'the EUR is at a premium to the USD' or 'the USD is at a discount to the EUR'; there is then no ambiguity. In London however, if a dealer does not specify to which of the two currencies he is referring, he is generally referring to the variable currency: 'the EUR/USD is at a discount' would mean that the variable currency, USD, is at a discount and that the swap points are to be added to the spot. Similarly 'the GBP/JPY is at a premium' would mean that the variable currency, JPY, is at a premium and that the points are to be subtracted from the spot. Elsewhere in the world, this loose terminology would generally be taken to mean the opposite.

⇨ *See also* non-deliverable forward.

FORMULAS

theoretical forward swap

$$= \text{spot} \times \frac{\left(\left(\text{variable currency interest rate} \times \frac{\text{days in period}}{\text{days in year}}\right) - \left(\text{base currency interest rate} \times \frac{\text{days in period}}{\text{days in year}}\right)\right)}{\left(1 + \left(\text{base currency interest rate} \times \frac{\text{days in period}}{\text{days in year}}\right)\right)}$$

theoretical forward outright

$$= \text{spot} \times \frac{\left(1 + \left(\text{variable currency interest rate} \times \frac{\text{days in period}}{\text{days in year}}\right)\right)}{\left(1 + \left(\text{base currency interest rate} \times \frac{\text{days in period}}{\text{days in year}}\right)\right)}$$

Note that 'days in year' can mean 365 (for example with sterling) or 360 (for example with US dollars) – see **money market basis**.

actual forward outright quoted = spot + forward swap

Approximation

If 'days in year' is the same for the two currencies, the number of days is sufficiently small, and the base currency interest rate is not too great, the following approximation holds:

theoretical forward swap $\approx$ spot $\times$ interest rate differential $\times \dfrac{\text{days in period}}{\text{days in year}}$

In reverse, an approximate interest rate differential can be calculated from the swap rate as follows:

$$\text{interest rate differential} \approx \frac{\text{forward swap}}{\text{spot}} \times \frac{\text{days in year}}{\text{days in period}}$$

Covered interest arbitrage

variable currency interest rate synthetically created from base currency interest rate

$$= \left(\left(1 + \left(\text{base currency interest rate} \times \frac{\text{days in period}}{\text{days in base year}} \right) \right) \times \frac{\text{rate for far date}}{\text{rate for near date}} - 1 \right) \times \frac{\text{days in variable year}}{\text{days in period}}$$

base currency interest rate synthetically created from variable currency interest rate

$$= \left(\left(1 + \left(\text{variable currency interest rate} \times \frac{\text{days in period}}{\text{days in variable year}} \right) \right) \times \frac{\text{rate for near date}}{\text{rate for far date}} - 1 \right) \times \frac{\text{days in base year}}{\text{days in period}}$$

Note that 'rate for near date' and 'rate for far date' normally mean 'spot' and 'forward outright' respectively. For a *tom/next* arbitrage however, they would mean 'outright value tomorrow' and 'spot' respectively.

EXAMPLE 1

Spot GBP/USD rate:	1.5168
183-day GBP interest rate:	7% / 6.9%
183-day USD interest rate:	5.1% / 5%

$$\text{theoretical forward outright (left side)} = 1.5168 \times \frac{\left(1 + 0.05 \times \frac{183}{360}\right)}{\left(1 + 0.07 \times \frac{183}{365}\right)} = 1.5026$$

$$\text{theoretical forward outright (right side)} = 1.5168 \times \frac{\left(1 + 0.051 \times \frac{183}{360}\right)}{\left(1 + 0.069 \times \frac{183}{365}\right)} = 1.5041$$

theoretical outright price is therefore 1.5026 / 1.5041

$$\text{theoretical forward swap (left side)} = 1.5168 \times \frac{\left(\left(0.05 \times \frac{183}{360}\right) - \left(0.07 \times \frac{183}{365}\right)\right)}{\left(1 + \left(0.07 \times \frac{183}{365}\right)\right)} = -0.0142$$

$$\text{theoretical forward swap (right side)} = 1.5168 \times \frac{\left(\left(0.051 \times \frac{183}{360}\right) - \left(0.069 \times \frac{183}{365}\right)\right)}{\left(1 + \left(0.069 \times \frac{183}{365}\right)\right)} = -0.0127$$

theoretical swap price is therefore –0.0142 / –0.0127, quoted as '142 / 127'

GBP is at a discount to USD

USD is at a premium to GBP

EXAMPLE 2

Spot EUR/USD: 0.9566 / 0.9571

Forward swap: 145 / 150

forward outright = (0.9566 + 0.0145) / (0.9571 + 0.0150) = 0.9711 / 0.9721

EXAMPLE 3

Spot EUR/USD: 0.9566 / 0.9571

Forward swap: 150 / 145

forward outright = (0.9566 − 0.0150) / (0.9571 − 0.0145) = 0.9416 / 0.9426

EXAMPLE 4

Spot EUR/USD: 0.9566 / 0.9571

Forward swap: 6 / 4 A/P

forward outright = (0.9566 − 0.0006) / (0.9571 + 0.0004) = 0.9560 / 0.9575

EXAMPLE 5

Spot EUR/USD: 1.2166 / 1.2171

31-day USD interest rate: 5.0%

31-day EUR interest rate: 3.0%

31-day forward swap: 20 / 22

Our bank's dealer expects EUR interest rates to rise. He therefore asks another bank for its price, which is quoted as 20 / 22. Our dealer buys and sells €10 million at a swap price of 20 (that is, + 0.0020). The spot rate is set at 1.2168 and the forward rate at 1.2188. The cashflows are therefore:

spot	*31 days forward*
buy €10,000,000	sell €10,000,000
sell $12,168,000	buy $12,188,000

Immediately after dealing, EUR rates in fact fall rather than rise, but USD rates also fall, as follows:

Spot EUR/USD: 1.2166 / 1.2171

31-day USD interest rate: 4.5%

31-day EUR interest rate: 2.75%

31-day forward swap: 17 / 19

Our dealer now asks another counterparty for a price, is quoted 17 / 19, and deals to close out his position. Thus he now sells and buys EUR at a swap price of 19 (that is, + 0.0019). The spot rate is set at 1.2168 again and the forward rate at 1.2187. The new cashflows are:

spot	31 days forward
sell €10,000,000	buy €10,000,000
buy $ 12,168,000	sell $ 12,187,000

The net result is a profit of $1,000, 31 days forward. The dealer has made a profit because the interest differential between EUR and USD has narrowed from 2.0% to 1.75%, even though it did not narrow in the way he expected.

EXAMPLE 6

USD/CHF spot:	1.4810 / 1.4815
3-month swap:	116 / 111
USD 3-month interest rates:	7.43% / 7.56%
CHF 3-month interest rates:	4.50% / 4.62%

The 3-month period is 92 days and the bank needs to borrow CHF 10 million. It deals on rates quoted to it as above by another bank.

Bank borrows $ 6,749,915.63 for 92 days from spot at 7.56%.

At the end of 92 days, the bank repays principal plus interest of $ 6,880,324.00 calculated as:

principal $ 6,749,915.63

plus interest $ 6,749,915.63 $\times$ 0.0756 $\times \frac{92}{360}$ = $130,408.37

The bank 'sells and buys' $ against CHF at a swap price of 111, based on a spot of 1.4815:

The bank sells $ 6,749,915.63 / buys CHF 10,000,000.00 spot at 1.4815

Bank buys $ 6,880,324.00 / sells CHF 10,116,828.41 3 months forward at 1.4704

The net $ flows balance to zero.

The effective cost of borrowing is therefore interest of CHF 116,828.41 on a principal sum of CHF 10,000,000 for 92 days:

$$\frac{116,828.41}{10,000,000} \times \frac{360}{92} = 0.0457 = 4.57\%$$

The net effect is thus a CHF 10 million borrowing at 4.57%. This is 5 basis points cheaper than the 4.62% at which the bank could borrow directly.

This rate can be calculated as follows:

CHF interest rate synthetically created from $ interest rate

$$= \left[\left(1 + \left(0.0756 \times \frac{92}{360} \right) \right) \times \frac{1.4704}{1.4815} - 1 \right] \times \frac{360}{92} = 0.0457 = 4.57\%$$

If the bank is in fact not looking for funds, but is able to deposit CHF at higher than 4.57%, it can instead 'round trip', locking in a profit.

SHORT DATES

Definition

A **short date** is a foreign exchange **forward swap** or **forward outright** transaction for value less than 1 month after *spot*.

HOW ARE THEY USED?

Value dates earlier than 1 month are referred to as 'short dates'. There are certain regular dates usually quoted, and the terminology used is the same as in the deposit market, as follows:

'Overnight'   –   a deposit or foreign exchange swap from today until 'tomorrow'
'Tom/next'   –   a deposit or foreign exchange swap from 'tomorrow' to the 'next' day (spot)
'Spot/next'   –   a deposit or foreign exchange swap from spot until the 'next' day
'Spot-a-week' –   a deposit or foreign exchange swap from spot until a week later

'Tomorrow' means 'the next working day after today' and 'next' means 'the next working day following'.

When referring to outright deals rather than swaps, one refers to 'value today', 'value tomorrow', 'value spot/next', 'value a week over spot'.

Overnight prices are the only regular swap prices not involving the spot value date. To calculate an outright value today price, it is therefore necessary to combine the spot price with both an overnight price and a tom/next price.

Deals cannot always be done for value today. For example, when London and European markets are open, Japanese banks have already closed their books for today, so deals in yen can only be done for value tomorrow. Similarly in London, most European currencies can only be dealt early in the morning for value today, because of the time difference and the mechanical difficulties of ensuring good value. Even the market for value tomorrow generally closes during the morning.

In considering swaps and outrights for short dates later than the spot date, exactly the same rules apply as in calculating longer dates. However, confusion can arise in considering outright prices for dates earlier than spot – that is, outright value today and outright value tomorrow. The bank quoting the price still 'sells and buys' (in that order) the base currency on the left and 'buys and sells' the base currency on the right – regardless of whether it is before or after spot. The confusion can arise because the spot value date – effectively the baseline date for calculation of the outright rate – is the 'near' date when calculating most forward prices. For value today and tomorrow however, the spot date becomes the 'far' date and the outright date is the near date.

Note that, because short dates refer to short swap periods, the prices can be very small and are therefore sometimes quoted as fractions or decimals of a *point*. A swap price of say '1¾' or 1.75' therefore means 1.75 points. If the spot is quoted to four decimal places, this would be a swap price of 0.000175.

> ### Related terminology
>
> Overnight, tom/next, spot/next and spot-a-week are often abbreviated as *O/N*, *T/N*, *S/N* and *S/W* respectively.

CALCULATION METHOD

To calculate forward outrights for value earlier than spot, i.e. value outright tomorrow and value outright today:

- first, change the sign of the swap points;
- second, add the right side of the swap points to the left side of the spot and add the left side of the swap points to the right side of the spot rate.

A trick to remember for this is 'reverse the swap points and proceed exactly as for a forward later than spot'. **However, it is important always to remember to make this reversal only in your head! Never quote the price in reverse!**

> ### EXAMPLE
>
> | Spot EUR/USD: | 0.9505 / 10 |
> |---|---|
> | O/N swap: | 0.75 / 1 |
> | T/N swap: | 0.25 / 0.5 |
> | S/N swap: | 5 / 7 |
>
> Outright value the day after spot is (0.9505 + 0.0005) / (0.9510 + 0.0007) = 0.9510 / 0.9517. Note that this calculation is similar to the calculation for any forward outright after spot, regardless of whether it is a short date.
>
> Outright value tomorrow is (0.9505 − 0.00005) / (0.9510 − 0.000025) = 0.95045 / 0.950975.
>
> Outright value today is (0.9505 − 0.00005 − 0.0001) / (0.9510 − 0.000025 − 0.000075) = 0.95035 / 0.9509.

FORWARD-FORWARD EXCHANGE RATE

Definition

A **forward-forward** exchange rate is the price for a **forward swap** transaction from one forward date to another forward date.

HOW IS IT USED?

A forward-forward swap is a swap deal between two forward dates rather than from spot to a forward date – for example, to sell US dollars 1 month forward and buy them back in 3 months' time. In this case, the swap is for the 2-month period between the 1-month date and the 3-month date. A company might undertake such a swap because it has previously bought dollars forward but wishes now to defer the transaction by a further two months, as it will not need the dollars as soon as it thought.

From the bank's point of view, a forward-forward swap can be constructed from two separate swaps, each based on spot.

Related terminology

⇨ *See also* forward swap.

FORMULAS

Forward-forward price after spot

left side of forward-forward swap price

= (left side of far-date swap) – (right side of near-date swap)

right side of forward-forward swap price

= (right side of far-date swap) – (left side of near-date swap)

Note that the bid-offer spread of the resulting price is the sum of the two separate bid-offer spreads.

Forward-forward price from before spot to after spot

left side of forward-forward swap price

= (left side of near-date swap) + (left side of far-date swap)

right side of forward-forward swap price

= (right side of near-date swap) + (right side of far-date swap)

Forward swaps are always quoted as how the quoting bank 'sells and buys' the base currency (that is, it sells the base currency on the 'near' date and buys it back on the 'far' date) on the left, and 'buys and sells' the base currency (that is, it buys the base currency on the 'near' date and sells it back on the 'far' date) on the right.

As with a swap from spot to a forward date, the two settlement prices in a forward-forward must be based on a current market rate. Thus the settlement rate for the 'near' date is set as a current market rate for that date and the settlement rate for the far date is set as the same rate, adjusted by the forward-forward swap points transacted.

EXAMPLE

USD/CHF spot rate:	1.5325 / 1.5335
T/N swap:	4 / 6
1-month swap:	65 / 69
3-month swap:	160 / 165

1 v 3 forward-forward price is (160 − 69) / (165 − 65) = 91 / 100

forward-forward price for tomorrow against 1 month after spot is (4 + 65) / (6 + 69) = 69 / 75

NON-DELIVERABLE FORWARD (NDF)

Definition

A **non-deliverable forward** is a foreign exchange **forward outright** where, instead of each party delivering the full amount of currency at settlement, there is a single net cash payment to reflect the change in value between the forward rate transacted and the spot rate two working days before settlement.

HOW IS IT USED?

Suppose that someone wishes to transact a forward outright where one of the currencies is non-convertible, so that it is not possible for that currency to be delivered to or by a non-resident of that country. This outright might be because he has a need to hedge a commercial transaction or because he wishes to speculate in that currency.

A normal forward outright is not permitted in the case of non-convertibility. If the purpose of the deal is speculative, the NDF itself is sufficient – the cash settlement of the NDF provides the same economic effect as if a normal forward outright had been dealt and then closed out 2 days before maturity by an offsetting spot deal. If the purpose of the deal is to hedge a commercial transaction, the same economic effect as a normal outright can be achieved by first transacting and settling the NDF, and then buying or selling the non-convertible currency for spot value at the same time as the NDF is settled.

An NDF also has the effect of reducing counterparty credit risk, as the risk is limited to the settlement amount and does not involve the usual *settlement risk* of the whole nominal amount of the deal. The rationale for NDFs is therefore not limited to non-convertible currencies.

Related terminology

A *contract for differences* is any transaction which is cash settled against a reference rate, rather than delivered in full. That is, where a net cash payment is made from one party to the other to reflect the difference between a price or rate fixed at the time of transaction and a reference price or rate determined later, or between two such reference prices or rates.

➩ *See also* **forward outright**.

FORMULAS

If settlement is in the variable currency:

settlement amount = notional amount of base currency × (NDF rate transacted – reference spot rate)

If settlement is in the base currency:

$$\text{settlement amount} = \frac{\text{notional amount of base currency} \times (\text{NDF rate transacted} - \text{reference spot rate})}{\text{reference spot rate}}$$

EXAMPLE 1

On 27 March, a company buys HUF against USD (amount $2 million) at a USD/HUF rate of 254.10 for value 29 September, using an NDF.

On 27 September, the spot USD/HUF rate is 251.30.

Settlement is for the difference between 254.10 and 251.30, on an amount of $2 million:

the company's profit is 2,000,000 × HUF(254.10 – 251.30) = HUF5,600,000

Assuming that settlement is made in dollars, the settlement amount on 29 September is:

$$\$ \frac{5,600,000}{251.30} = \$22,284.12$$

EXAMPLE 2

Suppose that in the example above, the company needs the HUF for commercial purposes. On 27 September, it can sell both the $2,000,000 and the settlement amount, for spot value against HUF at 251.30. The net effect is then as if it had originally purchased the HUF for normal forward delivery at 254.10:

receive:	$22,284.12	in settlement of NDF	
sell:	$2,022,284.12	at 251.30 against:	HUF508,200,000
net sale of:	$2,000,000.00	and purchase of:	HUF508,200,000

$$\text{effective exchange rate} = \frac{508,200,000}{2,000,000} = 254.10$$

OPTIONS

CALLS AND PUTS

Definition

A **call** option is a deal giving one party the right, without the obligation, to buy an agreed amount of a particular instrument or commodity, at an agreed rate, on or before an agreed future date. The other party has the obligation to sell if so requested by the first party.

A **put** option is a deal giving one party the right, without the obligation, to sell an agreed amount of a particular instrument or commodity, at an agreed rate, on or before an agreed future date. The other party has the obligation to buy if so requested by the first party.

HOW ARE THEY USED?

An option is one-sided. For one of the two parties, it is similar to a forward deal but with the difference that he can always choose whether or not to fulfil the deal. For the second party, it is similar to a forward deal but with the difference that he does not know whether or not he will be required to fulfil it. Clearly, the first party will choose to insist on the deal only if it turns out to be profitable for him compared to the current market price at the time of choosing. These circumstances will equally imply a loss at that time for the second party. In return for this flexibility, the first party must give something to the second party, to compensate him for his risk. This something is an up-front cash payment, known as a *premium*. The party paying the premium is the buyer of the option and the other party is the seller of the option.

Hedging

For someone using an option as a *hedge* rather than as a trading instrument, it can be considered as a form of insurance. An insurance policy is not called upon if circumstances are satisfactory. The insured person is however willing to pay an insurance premium in order to be able to claim on the insurance policy if circumstances are not satisfactory. An option is similar. If an option enables a hedger to buy something at a certain rate but it turns out to be cheaper in the market than that rate, the hedger does not need the option. If however it turns out to be more expensive than the option rate, he can 'claim' on the option. He thus has 'insurance protection' at the option rate, for which he pays a premium.

For the trader selling the option, the situation is similar to that of the insurer – he is exposed to the risk that he will be obliged to deliver at the agreed rate but be able to cover his position in the market only at a worse rate.

For example, a company with a short yen position which it wishes to hedge against euros has three basic choices. It can do nothing and remain unhedged, it can buy the yen forward, or it can buy a yen call option. In general, the option will never provide the best outcome because of the premium cost: if the yen rises, the company would be better buying forward; if the yen falls, the company would be better remaining unhedged. On the other hand, the option provides the safest overall result because it protects against a yen rise while preserving opportunity gain if the yen falls. Essentially, if the company firmly believes the yen will rise, it should buy forward; if the company firmly believes the yen will fall, it should do nothing; if the company believes the yen will fall but cannot afford to be wrong, it should buy a yen call option. The outcomes of the three possibilities are as follows. Figure 18 shows the effective net outcome (in terms of the EUR/JPY exchange rate achieved net of the option premium cost) for a hedger with an underlying position.

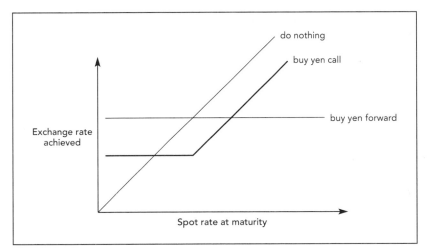

FIGURE 18 Hedging a short yen exposure against euros

A parallel situation arises in interest rate hedging. A company with a short-term borrowing rollover in the future also has three basic choices. It can remain unhedged, buy a forward rate agreement (or sell futures), or buy a call option on a forward rate agreement (or a put option on futures).

Speculation

An option can be bought or sold speculatively. For example, someone who expects an instrument's price to fall might buy a put option on that instrument. His maximum loss is then the premium he has paid (because if the price rises instead, he will simply not exercise the option). His profit however is limited only by how far the price can fall (see Figure 19).

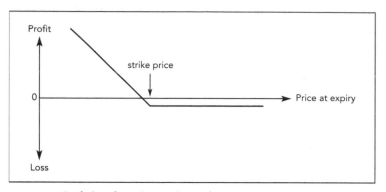

FIGURE 19 Profit/loss from the purchase of a put

Alternatively, the same speculator might sell a call option on that instrument. This is a riskier strategy. His maximum profit is the premium he has received (because if the price does fall, the other party will not exercise the option). His loss however is limited only by how far the price can rise if he is wrong (see Figure 20).

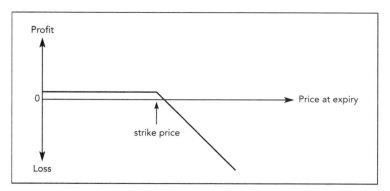

FIGURE 20 Profit/loss from the sale of a call

Options are available in a wide range of underlying instruments, including currencies, interest rates, bonds, equities and commodities.

Related terminology

The instrument or commodity which is being bought or sold in an option is referred to as the *underlying*. Thus in a bond option, the underlying is the bond. In a EUR/USD option, the underlying is the value of a euro measured in dollars; in a short-term interest rate option, the underlying is an FRA or an interest rate futures contract.

The purchaser of the option is known as the *holder*. The seller is known as the *writer*.

To *exercise* an option is to use it. The final day on which the option can be exercised is known as the *expiry date*.

With a *European* option, the holder can exercise the option only at expiry. With an *American* option, he can choose to exercise at any time between the purchase of the option and expiry. European and American options are both available everywhere; the terms are technical, not geographical.

The price agreed in the transaction – the *strike price* or *strike rate* or *exercise price* – is not necessarily the same as the current market rate for the same value date, but is chosen to suit the option buyer (with a corresponding increase or decrease in how much premium the buyer must pay for the option). If it is more advantageous to the option buyer than the current market rate, the option is referred to as *in-the-money*. If it is less advantageous to the option buyer than the current market rate, it is *out-of-the-money*. If the strike is the same as the current market rate, the option is *at-the-money (ATM)*. As the market moves after the option has been written, the option will move in- and out-of-the-money.

If an option is in-the-money, the difference between the strike price and the current market price is known as the *intrinsic value* of the option. The intrinsic value of an out-of-the-money option is zero rather than negative. The remaining part of the premium paid for the option, above this intrinsic value, is known as the *time value*.

A *naked option* is an option bought or sold for speculation, with no offsetting natural position behind it. A *covered option* is an option bought or sold against an underlying position.

An *interest rate guarantee (IRG)* is effectively an option on a forward rate agreement. An IRG can be either a *borrower's option* (i.e. a call on an FRA) or a *lender's option* (i.e. a put on an FRA).

EXAMPLE 1

Suppose that a US company will need to pay €1,000,000 for some imports, in 6 months' time. The current spot rate for EUR/USD is 0.9650 and the current 6-month forward outright rate is 0.9700. The company believes that the euro will be cheaper in 3 months' time and therefore does not wish to buy euros forward. However, it cannot afford to be wrong by a large margin. The company therefore buys a European euro call/dollar put at a strike of 0.9800 and a premium cost of 1.2% of the euro amount.

The premium cost can be seen as 0.0116 in exchange rate terms paid now (1.2% × 0.9650 = 0.0116). If the euro strengthens by 6 months' time to above 0.9800, the company will exercise the option and buy euros at a net exchange rate of 0.9916 (= 0.9800 + 0.0116). This is therefore the company's worst-case rate, whereas if the exchange rate falls, the company remains in a position to buy euros more cheaply.

EXAMPLE 2

A trader believes that the price of a particular instrument will rise. He buys a call option on it at a strike of 125.3, at a premium cost of 1.9. At expiry, the instrument's price is 129.4. The trader exercises the option to buy the instrument at 125.3 and simultaneously sells it in the market at 129.4. He makes a net profit of 2.2 (= 129.4 − 125.3 − 1.9). If the price had fallen, the trader would not have exercised the option and would have made a loss of the premium of 1.9.

Neither of these analyses takes account of the small cost of funding the option premium payment from the start until expiry.

THE BLACK AND SCHOLES PRICING MODEL

Definition

The **Black and Scholes** model is a formula for calculating *option* prices, named after Fischer Black and Myron Scholes, who developed it.

HOW IS IT USED?

The pricing of an option depends on probability. In principle, ignoring *bid/offer spreads*, the *premium* paid by the buyer should represent his expected profit on *exercising* the option. The profit arises from the fact that he is always entitled to exercise an option which expires *in-the-money* and simultaneously cover himself in the market at a better price. The buyer will never be obliged to exercise the option at a loss to himself. As with insurance premiums, assuming that the option writer can accurately assess the probability of each possible outcome, his total payments out on *expiry* of a portfolio of options should approximate to the premiums received. Option pricing theory therefore depends on assessing these probabilities and deriving from them an expected outcome, and hence a fair value for the premium.

The factors on which these probabilities depend are as follows:

- *Probability distribution*: different assumptions about the probability distribution for price movements – effectively what is the probability of any particular price movement – affect the value placed on an option.
- *Strike*: the more advantageous the strike price is to the buyer at the time of pricing, the greater the probability of the option being exercised, at a loss to the writer, and hence the greater the option premium.
- *Volatility*: this is a measure of how much the price fluctuates. The more volatile the price, the greater the probability that the option will become of value to the buyer at some time.
- *Maturity*: the longer the maturity of the option, the greater the probability that it will become of value to the buyer at some time, because the price has a longer time in which to fluctuate.
- *Interest rates*: the premium is payable up-front. The value of an option is therefore affected by the **present value** of the strike, and hence by the interest rate. The *rate of discount* therefore affects the premium to some extent. The *forward price* – and hence the relationship between the strike and the forward – is also

affected by interest rate movements. In the case of an option on a bond or other interest-rate instrument, the interest rate itself also directly affects the underlying price.

Fischer Black and Myron Scholes developed a model which is widely used for pricing options on financial instruments. This model depends on the following assumptions:

- The probability distribution of relative price changes is *lognormal*. The assumption of a lognormal distribution implies a smaller probability of significant deviations from the mean than is generally the case in practice. This is reflected in how fat or thin the 'tails' of the bell-shaped probability curve are and affects the pricing of deep in-the-money and deep out-of-the-money options.

- Future relative price changes are independent both of past changes and of the current price.

- Volatility and interest rates both remain constant throughout the life of the option. In practice, volatility and interest rates are not constant throughout the option's life. In the case of a bond option for example, this causes significant problems. First, volatility tends towards zero as the bond approaches maturity, because its price must tend to *par*. Secondly, the price of the bond itself is crucially dependent on interest rates, in a way that say an exchange rate is not.

- There are no transaction costs.

> **Related terminology**
>
> ⇨ *See also* **binomial pricing model**, an alternative approach to pricing options.

FORMULAS

Based on the Black and Scholes model, and assuming an *underlying* asset which does not pay dividends:

call premium = (spot price $\times$ N(d$_1$)) – (strike price $\times$ N(d$_2$) $\times$ e^{-rt})

put premium = – (spot price $\times$ N(– d$_1$)) + (strike price $\times$ N(– d$_2$) $\times$ e^{-rt})
            = call premium + (strike price $\times$ e^{-rt}) – spot price

where:

$$d_1 = \frac{LN\left(\frac{\text{spot price} \times e^{rt}}{\text{strike price}}\right) + \frac{\sigma^2 t}{2}}{\sigma \sqrt{t}}$$

$$d_2 = \frac{LN\left(\frac{\text{spot price} \times e^{rt}}{\text{strike price}}\right) - \frac{\sigma^2 t}{2}}{\sigma\sqrt{t}}$$

t = the time to expiry of the option expressed as a proportion of a year (365 days).

σ = the annualized volatility.

r = the **continuously compounded** interest rate.

N( ) = the standardized normal cumulative probability distribution.

LN( ) = the natural logarithm (i.e. the logarithm to base e).

The normal distribution function N( ) cannot be expressed precisely as a formula. Tables giving values of the function are widely available. Alternatively, it can be approximated. One such approximation is:

$$N(d) = 1 - \frac{\frac{0.4361836}{1+0.33267d} - \frac{0.1201676}{(1+0.33267d)^2} + \frac{0.937298}{(1+0.33267d)^3}}{\sqrt{2\pi}\, e^{\frac{d^2}{2}}} \quad \text{when } d \geq 0$$

and: $N(d) = 1 - N(-d)$ when $d < 0$

In the case of a currency option, the Black and Scholes formula can be re-written slightly as:

call premium $= ((\text{forward outright price} \times N(d_1)) - (\text{strike price} \times N(d_2))) \times e^{-rt}$

put premium $= (-(\text{forward outright price} \times N(-d_1)) + (\text{strike price} \times N(-d_2))) \times e^{-rt}$

$\qquad\qquad\quad = \text{call premium} + ((\text{strike price} - \text{forward price}) \times e^{-rt})$

where: the option is a call on one unit of the *base currency* and the premium is expressed in units of the *variable currency*.

$$d_1 = \frac{LN\left(\frac{\text{forward outright}}{\text{strike rate}}\right) + \frac{\sigma^2 t}{2}}{\sigma\sqrt{t}}$$

$$d_2 = \frac{LN\left(\frac{\text{forward outright}}{\text{strike rate}}\right) - \frac{\sigma^2 t}{2}}{\sigma\sqrt{t}}$$

r = the continuously compounded interest rate for the variable currency.

The expressions e^{rt} and e^{-rt} in the formulas above can be replaced respectively by:

$$\left(1 + \left(\text{simple interest rate} \times \frac{\text{days in period}}{\text{days in year}}\right)\right) \quad \text{and} \quad \frac{1}{\left(1 + \left(\text{simple interest rate} \times \frac{\text{days in period}}{\text{days in year}}\right)\right)}$$

EXAMPLE

Using the Black and Scholes formula, what is the cost (expressed as a percentage of the EUR amount) of a 91-day EUR put against USD at a strike of 0.9500? The spot rate is 0.9600, the forward outright is 0.9650, volatility is 9.0%, and the USD 3-month interest rate is 6.5%.

With the same notation as above:

$$r = \frac{365}{91} \times LN\left(1 + \left(0.065 \times \frac{91}{360}\right)\right) = 0.0654$$

$$d_1 = \frac{LN\left(\frac{0.9650}{0.9500}\right) + \frac{0.09^2 \times \frac{91}{365}}{2}}{0.09\sqrt{\frac{91}{365}}} = 0.3711$$

$$d_2 = \frac{LN\left(\frac{0.9650}{0.9500}\right) - \frac{0.09^2 \times \frac{91}{365}}{2}}{0.09\sqrt{\frac{91}{365}}} = 0.3261$$

$$\begin{aligned}
\text{put premium} \quad &= ((-0.9650 \times N(-0.3711)) + (0.9500 \times N(-0.3261))) \times e^{-0.0654 \times \frac{91}{365}} \\
&= ((-0.9650 \times 0.3553) + (0.9500 \times 0.3722)) \times 0.9838 = 0.0106
\end{aligned}$$

The cost is therefore 0.0128 USD for each one euro underlying the option. As a percentage of the euro amount, this is:

$$\frac{0.0106}{0.9600} = 0.011 = 1.1\%$$

HISTORIC VOLATILITY AND IMPLIED VOLATILITY

Definition

Volatility is the standard deviation, generally annualized, of the continuously compounded rate of return on an instrument.

Historic volatility is the actual volatility observed using historic data over a particular period.

Implied volatility is the current measure of volatility being used by a particular dealer or by the market in general to calculate premiums, i.e. it is the volatility implied by an option premium.

HOW ARE THEY USED?

Volatility is used as a measure of how much the price of something fluctuates. This is significant in valuing *options*, because the more volatile the price, the greater the probable profit that will be available at some time to the buyer of an option.

It is possible to measure precisely the volatility of actual historic prices recorded over any particular past period. This forms a basis for estimating what volatility might be in the future but the future will not necessarily be the same. When a dealer calculates an option price, he will therefore not in practice use a historic volatility exactly. Instead, he will blend recent actual experience of volatility, his own forecast for volatility, the current general market estimate of volatility and the requirements of his current trading position.

The volatility which is then used to calculate an option premium – either the price quoted by a particular dealer or the current general market price – is known as the implied volatility. This is because, given a particular pricing model, the price, and all the other factors, it is possible to work backwards to calculate what volatility is implied in that calculation. Implied volatility therefore means current volatility as used by the market in its pricing.

Related terminology

Implied volatility is sometimes known simply as the *implied*.

⇨ *See also* standard deviation and variance.

CALCULATION METHOD

Historic volatility

(i)   From a series of historic prices for an instrument, divide each price by the previous price to give a relative price.

(ii)   Calculate the natural logarithms of these relative prices, to give the continuously compounded rates of return on the instrument in each period.

(iii)   Total these rates of return and divide by the number of them, to give their *mean*.

(iv)   Calculate the differences between each rate of return and the mean.

(v)   Square each difference.

(vi)   Total these squares and divide by one less than the number of squares, to give the estimated **variance** of the rates of return.

(vii)   Take the square root of the variance to give the standard deviation of the rates of return.

(viii)   Multiply by the square root of the frequency of the original data per year to give the annualized standard deviation, i.e. the volatility.

Implied volatility

As implied volatility is one of the variables on which the value of an option depends, it is part of the 'raw material' of the market, from which other prices are derived, rather than something which can itself be derived by a formula.

However, given a particular option premium quoted by a trader, the volatility implied by that price can be calculated in reverse, using any chosen pricing model, such as the **Black and Scholes** model, for example. It is not possible to invert the Black and Scholes formula. Rather, *iteration* must be used to solve for the volatility, given the price.

EXAMPLE

Given five daily price data for an exchange rate, the historic volatility is calculated as follows:

Day	Exchange rate	LN $\left(\frac{1.8345}{1.8220}\right)$ etc.	Difference from mean	(Difference)^2
1	1.8220			
2	1.8345	0.00684	0.00622	0.000039
3	1.8313	– 0.00175	– 0.00237	0.000006
4	1.8350	0.00202	0.00140	0.000002
5	1.8265	– 0.00464	– 0.00526	0.000028
		Mean = 0.00062		Total = 0.000074

$$\text{estimated variance} = \frac{0.000074}{3} = 0.000025$$

$$\text{standard deviation} = \sqrt{0.000025} = 0.00497$$

$$\text{volatility} = 0.00497 \times \sqrt{252} = 0.079 = 7.9\%$$

This calculation assumes that the frequency of the original data is 252 per year, i.e. that weekends and bank holidays are ignored for daily data, leaving 252 working days in the year. If data for these days are included, then the frequency per year is 365. If the data are weekly, the annualized volatility would be:

$$0.00497 \times \sqrt{52} = 0.036 = 3.6\%$$

BINOMIAL PRICING MODEL

Definition

A **binomial pricing model** is a method of valuing an option based on building a lattice of all the possible paths up and down that the *underlying* price might take from start until *expiry*, assuming that, at each price change, the price either rises by a given amount (or proportion), or falls by a given amount (or proportion).

HOW IS IT USED?

One way of building a model for option pricing is to simplify the assumptions to the possibility that the price of something may move up by a certain amount or down by a certain amount in a particular time period. Suppose for example that the price of a particular asset is now 1 and that, each month, the price may rise by a multiplicative factor of 1.010000 or fall by a factor of $\frac{1.0000}{1.0100} = 0.990099$. After two months, the price may have moved along any of the following four routes, with three possible outcomes:

>   from 1 to 1.010000 and then to (1.010000 × 1.010000) = 1.020100
>   from 1 to 1.010000 and then to (1.010000 × 0.990099) = 1.000000
>   from 1 to 0.990099 and then to (0.990099 × 1.010000) = 1.000000
>   from 1 to 0.990099 and then to (0.990099 × 0.990099) = 0.980296

Suppose also that the probability each time of a move up in the price is 0.75 and that the probability of a move down is therefore 0.25. The possible paths that the price can take can therefore be shown as follows:

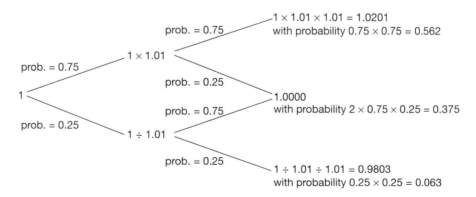

After 3 months, there are eight possible routes (up, up, up, or up, up, down, or up, down, up etc.) and four possible outcomes. A lattice of possible paths for the price, known as a *binomial tree*, can be built up in this way. Depending on the relative probabilities of an up movement or a down movement, we can calculate the probability of each possible outcome at the end, and hence a probability-weighted expected outcome at the end. From this, we can assess the expected outcome of exercising an option at any given strike price at the end. The price paid for this option at the beginning should be the present value of this expected profit.

In order for the model to be useful, the period of each change must be small – for example, looking at daily changes rather than monthly changes as above.

Such a model can be particularly useful for pricing an option whose value depends not only on the price of the underlying at expiry, but also on its price at every time during the life of the option – known as *path-dependent* options. An American option's value for example depends partly on the possibility of exercising the option during its life. *Asian options*, **barrier options** and *lookback options* also depend on the value of the underlying during the option's life.

> Related terminology
>
> ⟼ *See also* **Black and Scholes**, an alternative option pricing model.

CALCULATION METHOD

In order to use the binomial model, it is necessary to calculate what are the appropriate movements up and down at each step, and the probabilities of a move up or a move down. The size of the movements up and down depends on the volatility of the underlying price. The probabilities used depend on the extent to which the underlying price is expected to show a rising trend over time – which is related to the *risk-free rate of return* which would be earned by investing initially in a risk-free cash investment, rather than in an option.

There are various approaches to this. One approach, for example, uses the following. In this approach, increasing the number of steps (i.e. shortening the time period of each step) indefinitely, results in an option valuation consistent with the Black and Scholes model:

$$u = e^{\sigma\sqrt{\frac{t}{n}}}$$

$$d = \frac{1}{u}$$

$$p = \frac{(1 + i \times t)^{\frac{1}{n}} - d}{u - d}$$

where: u = multiplicative up movement.

d = multiplicative down movement.

p = probability.

σ = volatility.

t = time to expiry expressed in years.

n = number of periods in the binomial tree.

i = interest rate per annum to expiry.

EXAMPLE

What is the cost of a 2-month European call at a strike of 1.0040, based on the following?

Current price: 100

Volatility: 3.4%

Interest rate: 6%

$$u = e^{\left(0.034 \times \sqrt{\left(\frac{\left(\frac{2}{12}\right)}{2}\right)}\right)} = 1.01$$

$$d = \frac{1}{1.01} = 0.99$$

$$p = \frac{\left(1 + \left(0.06 \times \frac{2}{12}\right)\right)^{\left(\frac{1}{2}\right)} - 0.99}{1.01 - 0.99} = 0.75$$

The parameters are thus the same as in the example described earlier:

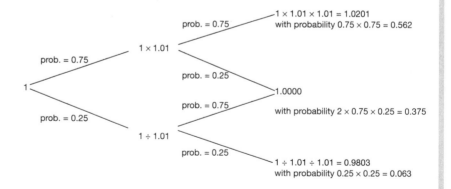

There is a probability of 0.562 that the underlying price is 1.0201 after 2 months, in which case the option can be exercised at a profit of 0.0161 (= 1.0201 – 1.0040). There is a probability of 0.375 that the underlying price is 1 and a probability of 0.063 that it is 0.9803 – in either case, the option will not be exercised.

The expected profit is therefore 0.562 × 0.0161 = 0.009. The option premium paid up-front should therefore be the present value of this amount:

$$\frac{0.0090}{\left(1 + 0.06 \times \dfrac{2}{12}\right)} = 0.0089 = 0.89\%$$

The price of this 2-month call option is therefore 0.89%.

THE PUT/CALL PARITY

Definition

The **put/call parity** is the theoretical relationship between the value of a **put** option and the value of a **call** option at the same *strike* price.

HOW IS IT USED?

There must be a relationship between the premium cost of a call option and the premium cost of a put option at the same strike rate, because otherwise there would be an arbitrage opportunity between the two – it would be possible to buy one, sell the other and lock in a profit. This can be seen as follows.

Suppose that I buy a European call option and sell a European put option on the same instrument, at the same strike, for the same expiry date. At the same time, I also sell the instrument for forward delivery on the same date.

At expiry, if the instrument's market price is higher than the strike, I will exercise the call, thereby buying the instrument at the strike price. However, if the instrument's price is lower than the strike, my counterparty will exercise the put against me, forcing me again to buy the instrument at the same strike price. Whatever happens, therefore, I end up buying the instrument at the strike price. Because I have also sold it forward at the original market forward price, I must end up with a guaranteed profit or loss – the difference between the strike price and the forward price.

On the basis that guaranteed profits and losses are not available (because supply and demand theoretically eliminate them in a free market), this difference must be offset by the difference between the call premium I have paid and the put premium I have received.

Given this relationship, if a call or a put is mis-priced in the market, it is possible to establish a call more cheaply via a put, or vice versa. Suppose, for example, that a trader wishes to buy a call but that the call is relatively expensive. It is possible instead for him to establish exactly the same economic position by buying a put at the same strike and simultaneously buying forward for the same date. Similarly, for example, a short put position can be created synthetically by selling a call at the same strike and buying forward.

Related terminology

A *synthetic forward* is the combination of a purchase (or sale) of a call option on an instrument and a sale (or purchase) of a put option at the same strike. This combination, theoretically, has the same economic effect as a forward purchase (or sale) of that instrument.

FORMULAS

For European call and put options at the same strike:

value of call option – value of put option
= **present value** of (current forward price – strike price)

For currency options, 'value of option' should be interpreted as the value of an option to buy or sell one unit of the base currency, expressed in units of the variable currency. Similarly, the forward and strike prices are the prices of one unit of the base currency, expressed in units of the variable currency.

For American call and put options at the same strike:

value of call option – value of put option = current spot price – strike price

---

EXAMPLE 1

A 182-day USD put option against NOK at a strike of 6.9500 costs 1.5% of the USD amount. What should a USD call at the same strike rate cost, also expressed as a percentage of the USD amount, based on the following?

USD/NOK spot:	7.0000
USD/NOK 6-month forward outright:	7.0690
NOK 6-month LIBOR:	7%

premium for put on USD 1, expressed in NOK = 1.5% × NOK 7.0000 = NOK 0.10500

Therefore:

$$\text{USD call premium} - \text{NOK } 0.10500 = \text{NOK } \frac{7.0690 - 6.9500}{\left(1 + \left(0.07 \times \frac{182}{360}\right)\right)} = \text{NOK } 0.11493$$

Therefore:

USD call premium = NOK 0.10500 + NOK 0.11493 = NOK 0.21993

$$\text{NOK } 0.21993 = \text{USD } \frac{0.21993}{7.0000} = \text{USD } 0.0314$$

Therefore the cost of a USD call is 3.14% of the USD amount.

EXAMPLE 2

Suppose that the price of a put option, at a strike of 95.00, on the euro interest rate June futures contract, is 1.47 and the price of a call option at the same strike is 0.13. Theoretically, what should the current futures price be?

$$0.13 - 1.47 = \text{futures price} - 95.00$$

Therefore:

$$\text{futures price} = 0.13 - 1.47 + 95.00 = 93.66$$

CAP, FLOOR, COLLAR AND ZERO-COST OPTION

Definition

A **cap** is a package of interest rate options whereby, at each of a series of future *fixing* dates, if an agreed reference rate such as *LIBOR* is higher than the strike rate, the option buyer receives the difference between them, calculated on an agreed notional principal amount for the period until the next fixing date.

A **floor** is a package of interest rate options whereby, at each of a series of future fixing dates, if an agreed reference rate such as LIBOR is lower than the strike rate, the option buyer receives the difference between them, calculated on an agreed notional principal amount for the period until the next fixing date.

A **collar** is the purchase of a cap combined with the sale of a floor.

A **zero-cost option** is a combination of options bought and sold, such that the premiums paid and received net to zero.

HOW ARE THEY USED?

Cap

Suppose that a borrower has a 5-year loan which he rolls over each 3 months based on the 3-month LIBOR then current. He can buy a 5-year cap with 3-monthly fixings which will put a maximum cost on each of the rollovers. At each fixing date, the cap strike rate is compared with LIBOR at that time. Whenever the rollover LIBOR rate exceeds the cap strike rate, he receives the difference. Whenever the rollover LIBOR rate is below the cap strike rate, nothing is paid or received. Therefore the borrower has a maximum borrowing cost of LIBOR at each rollover date, but will still borrow more cheaply whenever LIBOR is lower than the strike rate at rollover. This ignores any margin above LIBOR which the borrower pays on his underlying borrowing, which will apply whether the cap is exercised or not on any particular fixing date (see Figure 21). It is possible to have different strikes for different future periods of a cap, floor or collar. Any difference paid under the cap is paid at the end of the rollover period to which it applies.

Floor

A floor similarly protects an investor against the risk that the interest rate will fall. If the investor purchases an *FRN* with 6-monthly fixings based on LIBOR for

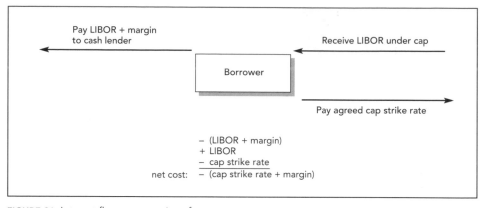

FIGURE 21 Interest flows on exercise of a cap

example, he will be at risk at each of the fixings to LIBOR falling. Alternatively, the investor may be protecting a deposit which he rolls over indefinitely, say each 3 or 6 months, and on which he expects to receive, say, *LIBID* prevailing at that time. In either case, whenever LIBOR at the time of rollover is less than the floor strike rate, he receives the difference. Whenever the rollover LIBOR rate is above the floor strike rate, nothing is paid or received. If the floor reference rate is LIBOR but the investor is rolling over his deposit at LIBID, his net income on any rollover when he exercises the cap will not be the strike rate. Rather, it will be the strike rate less the LIBID/LIBOR spread at that time.

Collar

A collar provides similar protection to a cap or a floor for a borrower or an investor. The protection is however more limited, in return for a lower initial cost. Suppose for example that a borrower is considering buying a 3-year cap at a 9% strike. A comparable collar would involve buying this same cap at 9% but also, at the same time, selling a floor to the bank at, say, 7%. The net initial cost would be lower because the borrower would receive back from the bank a premium for the floor it has purchased from him. If LIBOR is fixed at any time above 9%, the borrower will receive the difference from the bank. However, if LIBOR is fixed at any time below 7%, the borrower must pay the difference to the bank, because the bank is the buyer of the option. He will thus have (ignoring any margin above LIBOR which he pays on his underlying borrowing) a maximum cost of 9% but a minimum cost of 7% over the life of the collar. He might be prepared to accept this minimum on the cost because he is keen to reduce the initial premium of the arrangement, and/or because he does not expect LIBOR to fall that low over the period anyway. Furthermore, even if LIBOR does fall below 7%, he may then be borrowing at a cost which, from a commercial point of view, he finds acceptable (see Figure 22).

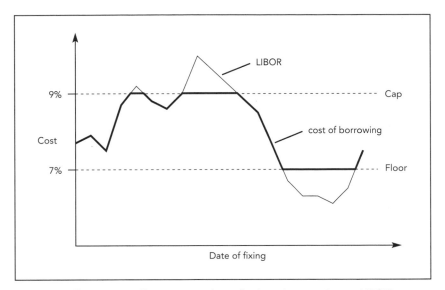

FIGURE 22 Effective cost of borrowing with a collar (ignoring margin over LIBOR)

Zero-cost option

A zero-cost option is a strategy made up of more than one option – for example a collar as described above – where the customer is effectively buying one or more options and also selling one or more options at the same time. If the premiums paid for the options bought are equal in total to the premiums received for the options sold, the net premium is zero. A zero-cost collar for example is therefore a collar, exactly as above, with net zero premiums. In this case, the strike of the cap and the strike of the floor would need to be set either side of a long-term fixed interest rate for the period (i.e. an **interest rate swap (IRS)** rate) to achieve this zero cost. If the borrower chooses a particular cap strike rate for example, the bank then calculates what floor strike rate is necessary to achieve the net zero cost.

> **Related terminology**
>
> A cap is also known as a *ceiling*.
>
> The term *collar* is also used to refer to the purchase of a put and the sale of a call (or the purchase of a call and the sale of a put), both *out-of-the-money*, for a single maturity date, in other instruments such as foreign exchange. See **range forward**, which is effectively the same instrument as a zero-cost collar.
>
> A collar can also be known as a *cylinder, tunnel, fence* or *corridor*.
>
> ⇨ *See also* **forward rate agreement (FRA)**, which is the instrument effectively exercisable at each date in a cap or floor.

FORMULA

settlement amount paid to buyer under cap (if LIBOR is greater than the strike rate)

$$= \text{notional principal} \times (\text{LIBOR} - \text{strike}) \times \frac{\text{days in rollover period}}{\text{days in year}}$$

settlement amount paid to buyer under floor (if LIBOR is less than the strike rate)

$$= \text{notional principal} \times (\text{strike} - \text{LIBOR}) \times \frac{\text{days in rollover period}}{\text{days in year}}$$

In either case, the settlement is paid at the end of the rollover period.

'LIBOR' is the LIBOR reference rate at the beginning of each rollover period – or in the case of a *Eurocurrency*, LIBOR two working days before the beginning of the period.

Note that 'days in year' can mean 365 (for example with sterling interest rates) or 360 (for example with US dollar interest rates) – see **money market basis**.

EXAMPLE

A company has a deposit of $2,000,000 which it rolls over each 6 months at LIBID. To protect against interest rates falling, it buys a floor at a strike of 6.00%. At the time of one particular 6-month rollover (for a period of 183 days), the 6-month cash market rate is 5.70% / 5.80%. The company earns LIBID on the rollover (5.70%) but receives 0.20% (= 6.00% – 5.80%) from the floor.

The settlement under the floor will be as follows:

$$\$2,000,000 \times (0.06 - 0.058) \times \frac{183}{360} = \$2,033.33$$

The result is as follows:

company receives	5.70% (LIBID)	from deposit
company receives	6.00%	under floor
company pays	5.80% (LIBOR)	under floor
net income	5.90% (floor strike rate less the LIBOR–LIBID spread)	

The company will have paid a premium for the floor. The cost of this must therefore also be taken into account. Although the premium would have all been paid up-front when the floor was first put in place, it could be considered as amortized over the life of the floor, taking account of the funding cost of the premium up-front.

BREAK FORWARD, RANGE FORWARD AND PARTICIPATION FORWARD

Definition

A **break forward** is a *forward* deal where the customer is allowed to reverse the deal at an agreed break rate.

A **range forward** is a forward deal with two forward rates, where settlement takes place at the higher forward rate if the *spot* rate at maturity is higher than that, at the lower forward rate if the spot rate at maturity is lower than that, or at the spot rate at maturity otherwise.

A **participation forward** is a forward deal where, if the spot rate at maturity turns out to be more advantageous than the forward rate, the customer receives a share of the better result that he would have had if he had not dealt forward.

HOW ARE THEY USED?

Various *OTC option*-based products are offered by banks to their customers, some of which can be constructed from straightforward options. These three are some of the products available. They are designed partly for companies who prefer not to trade in products which are described as 'options', even though in fact they are option products. In each of these three cases, although the products are described as 'forwards' – and, like a forward, they do involve a commitment by both parties to settlement at maturity regardless of the outcome – the 'forward' rate transacted is not as good for the customer as the 'true' **forward outright** rate for the same maturity. This is effectively to absorb the cost of the optionality built into the product. Throughout this section, we have used examples based on exchange rates but the same principle applies to examples based on any instrument.

Break forward

A break forward is a forward deal at a fixed rate (the worst-case level) with another 'break' level at which the customer may reverse the forward deal if he chooses. For example, a break forward to sell USD against CHF at 1.52 in 3 months' time with a break at 1.55 obliges the customer to sell USD at 1.52 but allows him to buy USD back at 1.55 if he chooses. The result is:

Either, if the spot rate at maturity is less than 1.55, the customer simply sells USD at 1.52. This is equivalent to selling USD at 1.55 but also paying a cost of CHF 0.03 at the same time.

Or, if the spot rate at maturity is greater than 1.55, the customer sells USD at 1.52 and buys them back at 1.55, giving him a net cost of CHF 0.03. The customer is then able to sell USD at the market spot rate.

This outcome is exactly the same as a USD put against CHF at a strike of 1.55 and a premium which has a future value at maturity of CHF 0.03. It is therefore effectively a straightforward USD put option with deferred payment of the premium.

The 'forward' rate chosen by the customer in the break forward can be any rate that is not as good as the forward outright. The bank can then calculate (see below) what the break rate should be, which is the strike rate of an exactly equivalent option (see Figure 23).

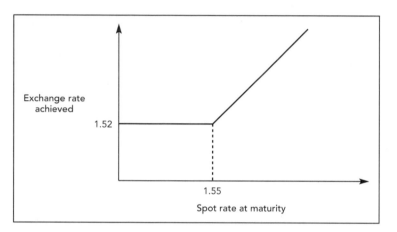

FIGURE 23 Break forward to sell USD against CHF at 1.52, with a break rate at 1.55

Range forward

A straightforward option provides a fixed worst-case level at which the customer can deal, but allows him to deal at the market rate if this turns out better. A range forward allows the customer to deal at a better market rate, but only up to a certain level. Beyond that level, the customer must deal at another fixed best-case level.

Such an arrangement can be constructed by the bank, by buying one option and selling another. The premium earned from the second option offsets the premium paid on the first option. The obligation to deal at the strike rate of the second option determines the best-case level. As the net premium is zero, setting either of the two strike rates determines the other one.

There is generally a technical difference between a range forward and a zero-cost **collar**. With a range forward, the customer is usually obliged to deal with the bank providing the range forward, regardless of the outcome. If neither of the range limits is reached (i.e. neither option is exercised) at maturity, the customer must deal at the spot rate with the bank. With a collar however, the customer is not obliged to deal with any particular bank if neither option is exercised. Also, the term 'range forward' usually applies to a deal with a single future maturity date, but in general a collar can be applied to any underlying instrument (see Figure 24). It is often used for example to describe the simultaneous purchase of a **cap** and sale of a **floor**.

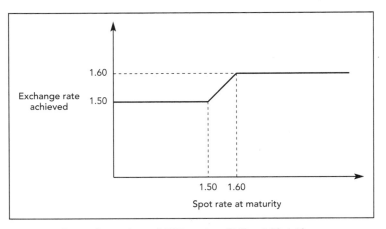

FIGURE 24 Range forward to sell USD against CHF at 1.50–1.60

Participation forward

A participation forward provides a worst-case level (the 'forward' rate) in the same way as an option. However, if the customer would have been better off not locking himself in at this level because the market level at maturity is better, he can take advantage of this better level, but must share the benefit with the bank. For example, a participation forward to sell USD against CHF at 1.50 with a participation rate of 70% provides a worst-case level of 1.50. If the market rate is 1.60, the customer receives 70% of the difference between 1.50 and 1.60, i.e. 0.07, and sells USD at 1.57. There is no premium to pay for this participation forward, but there is a 30% loss of potential advantage compared with a straightforward option (see Figure 25).

A participation forward can be constructed by buying an option (in this case a USD put option) and selling a smaller amount of an opposite option (in this case a USD call option) at the same strike rate.

If the customer chooses the participation 'forward' rate, this will determine the participation rate. If the customer chooses the participation rate, this will determine the participation 'forward' rate.

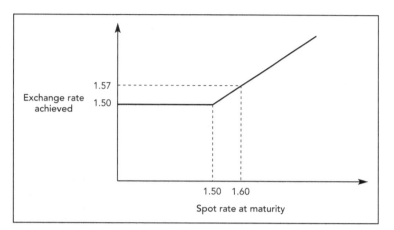

FIGURE 25 Participation forward to sell USD against CHF at 1.50, with a 70% participation rate

> **Related terminology**
>
> A break forward can also be known as a *forward with optional exit.*

FORMULAS

If the following are used for currency options, the cost of a premium should be expressed as units of the variable currency for an option on one unit of the base currency.

Break forward

To calculate the break rate, for any chosen 'forward' rate, use an option pricing model (e.g. **Black and Scholes**) to calculate call and put premiums for a series of strikes. The break rate is then the strike where:

(for a break forward to buy)
strike rate + future value of call premium = 'forward' rate

(for a break forward to sell)
strike rate – future value of put premium = 'forward' rate

'Future value of premium' is the premium plus the cost of funding it from the time of transaction to settlement.

Assuming that the **put/call parity** holds, a convenient method of calculating the correct strike is as follows:

(for a break forward to buy) first calculate the premium for a straightforward put:

put premium = present value of ('forward' rate – 'true' forward outright rate)

Then use an option pricing model in reverse to calculate from this put premium the corresponding strike rate, which is the break rate required.

(for a break forward to sell) first calculate the premium for a straightforward call:

call premium = present value of ('true' forward outright rate – 'forward' rate)

Then use an option pricing model in reverse to calculate from this call premium the corresponding strike rate, which is the break rate required.

Participation forward

To calculate the participation rate for any chosen participation 'forward' rate:

$$\text{participation rate to buy} = 1 - \left(\frac{\text{premium for a call with strike = 'forward'}}{\text{premium for a put with strike = 'forward'}} \right)$$

$$\text{participation rate to sell} = 1 - \left(\frac{\text{premium for a put with strike = 'forward'}}{\text{premium for a call with strike = 'forward'}} \right)$$

To calculate the participation 'forward' rate for any chosen participation rate, use the option pricing model to calculate call premiums and put premiums for a series of strikes. The 'forward' rate is the strike where:

(for a participation forward to buy)

$$\frac{\text{call premium}}{\text{put premium}} = 1 - \text{participation rate}$$

(for a participation forward to sell)

$$\frac{\text{put premium}}{\text{call premium}} = 1 - \text{participation rate}$$

EXAMPLE

A dollar-based company needs to buy euros 3 months forward. Its bank offers the following products:

A forward outright at 0.9500
A break forward at 0.9700 with a break rate of 0.9500
A range forward at 0.9350 and 0.9700
A participation forward at 0.9700 with a participation rate of 70%

What effective rate would the company achieve under each of these products if the spot rate in 3 months' time is 1.0000, 0.9600 or 0.9200?

Spot rate is 1.0000
Forward outright: 0.9500
Break forward: 0.9700 (break rate is better than the spot rate)
Range forward: 0.9700 (spot is above the top of the range)
Participation forward: 0.9700 (participation 'forward' rate is better than the spot rate)

Spot rate is 0.9600
Forward outright: 0.9500
Break forward: 0.9700 (break rate is better than the spot rate)
Range forward: 0.9600 (spot is within the range)
Participation forward: 0.9630 (= 0.9700 less 70% of the difference between 0.9700 and the 0.9600 spot rate)

Spot rate is 0.9200
Forward outright: 0.9500
Break forward: 0.9400 (buy at 0.9700, sell back at the break rate of 0.9500 and then buy at the 0.9200 spot rate)
Range forward: 0.9350 (spot is below the bottom of the range)
Participation forward: 0.9350 (= 0.9700 less 70% of the difference between 0.9700 and the 0.9200 spot rate)

OPTION TRADING STRATEGIES: STRADDLE, STRANGLE, SPREAD, BUTTERFLY, CONDOR, RATIO SPREAD AND RISK REVERSAL

Definition

A **straddle** is the purchase of a call combined with the purchase of a put at the same strike (generally purchased with both at-the-money).

A **strangle** is the purchase of a call combined with the purchase of a put at a lower strike (generally purchased with both out-of-the-money).

A **spread** is the purchase of one call (or put) and the sale of another at a worse strike to the buyer (generally out-of-the-money).

A **butterfly spread** is the purchase of a call (or put) (generally out-of-the-money) combined with the purchase of another call (or put) at a different strike (generally in-the-money) and the sale of two calls (or puts) at a mid-way strike (generally at-the-money).

A **condor** is the purchase of a call (or put) (generally out-of-the-money) combined with the purchase of another call (or put) at a different strike (generally in-the-money) and the sale of two calls (or puts) at two different strikes between the first two (generally one in-the-money and one out-of-the-money).

A **ratio spread** is the purchase of a certain number of calls (or puts) combined with the sale of a different number of calls (or puts).

A **risk-reversal** is the purchase (or sale) of a call combined with the sale (or purchase) of a put at a lower strike (generally transacted with both out-of-the-money, at net zero premium).

HOW ARE THEY USED?

Option traders adopt various strategies to speculate on the value of options. Typically, the positions are taken because the trader expects a move up or down in the price of the *underlying* (a *directional trade*), because he expects an increase or decrease in *volatility* (a *volatility trade*), or both.

Straddle

A straddle is a volatility strategy. To go long of a straddle is to buy both a put and a call at the same strike price. The buyer expects either the underlying price to move sufficiently far up or down (but he does not know which way), or volatility to increase. In return for paying two premiums, the buyer benefits if the underlying moves far enough in either direction (see Figure 26). Or he can reverse the position subsequently at a profit if volatility increases, because the value of each option will increase with volatility. The seller of a straddle assumes unlimited risk in both directions but receives a double premium (see Figure 27). He therefore benefits if volatility is low or falls.

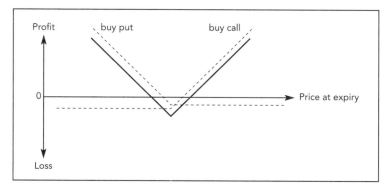

FIGURE 26 Profit/loss from a long straddle

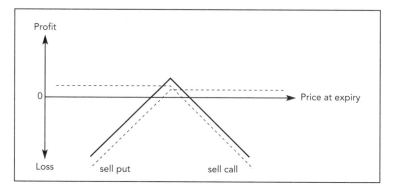

FIGURE 27 Profit/loss from a short straddle

Strangle

A strangle is a volatility strategy similar to a straddle but the premiums are reduced by setting the two strike prices apart – generally each strike will be out-of-the-money. Profits are only generated on a long strangle position if the underlying moves significantly (see Figure 28). The buyer must therefore expect a significant move up or down in the underlying price (see Figure 29).

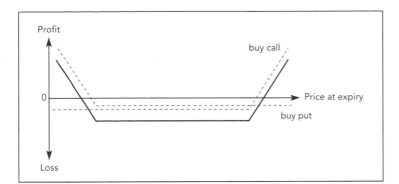

FIGURE 28 Profit/loss from a long strangle

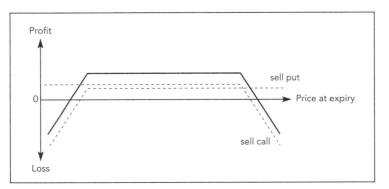

FIGURE 29 Profit/loss from a short strangle

Spread

Spreads involve the simultaneous purchase and sale of two different calls, or of two different puts. A long call spread is the purchase of a call at one strike price, offset by the simultaneous sale of a call at another strike less in-the-money (or more out-of-the-money) than the first. Compared with the simple purchase of a call, this limits the potential gain if the underlying goes up, but is a cheaper strategy because the premium received from selling the second call partly finances the purchase of the first call. A call spread may also be advantageous if the purchaser thinks there is only limited upside in the underlying anyway.

A long put spread is similarly the purchase of a put at one strike price, offset by the simultaneous sale of a put less in-the-money (or more out-of-the-money) than the first – similarly used to reduce the premium cost and/or if the purchaser thinks there is limited downside for the underlying.

A spread is a directional strategy. Each of a call spread and a put spread can be either *bullish* or *bearish*, depending on the strikes chosen. To buy a call spread (for example, buy a call in-the-money and sell one out-of-the-money, at a net premium cost) is bullish because the buyer profits if the underlying price rises but loses if it falls (see Figure 30). Similarly to sell a call spread (the opposite) is bearish (see Figure 32). However, to buy a put spread (for example, buy a put in-the-money and sell one out-of-the-money, at a net premium cost) is bearish because the buyer profits if the underlying price falls but loses if it rises, and to sell a call spread (the opposite) is bearish (see Figures 31 and 33).

A calendar spread is the purchase of a call (or put) and the simultaneous sale of a call (or put) with the same strike price but a different maturity. For example, if one-month volatility is high and one-year volatility low, a trader might buy one-year options and sell one-month options, thereby selling short-term volatility and buying long-term volatility. If short-term volatility falls relative to long-term volatility, the strategy can be reversed at a profit.

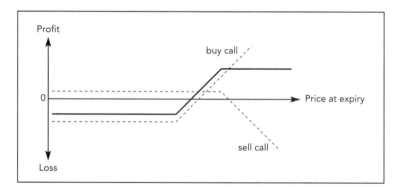

FIGURE 30 Profit/loss from a long (bullish) call spread

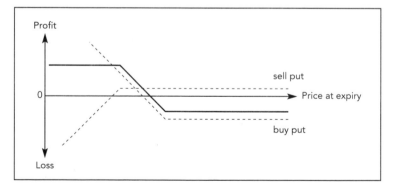

FIGURE 31 Profit/loss from a long (bearish) put spread

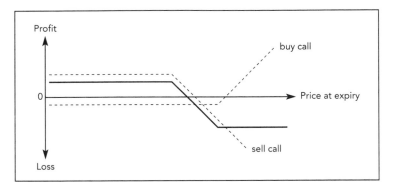

FIGURE 32 Profit/loss from a short (bearish) call spread

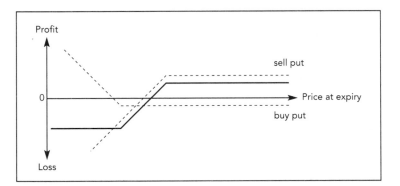

FIGURE 33 Profit/loss from a short (bullish) put spread

Butterfly

A butterfly spread is, for example, to purchase an out-of-the-money put, sell two at-the-money puts and buy an in-the-money put. This strategy profits if the underlying remains stable, and has limited risk in the event of a large move in either direction: it is a volatility strategy and is directionally neutral (see Figure 34). A butterfly spread can alternatively be constructed out of calls (see Figure 35).

Because of the **put/call parity** relationship, it is also possible to construct a butterfly spread as the purchase of a strangle and sale of a straddle. This is also equivalent to the purchase of a put spread and the simultaneous sale of a call spread (buy call out-of-the-money, sell call at-the-money, buy put out-of-the-money, sell put at-the-money).

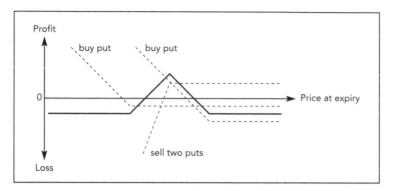

FIGURE 34 Profit/loss from a long butterfly spread

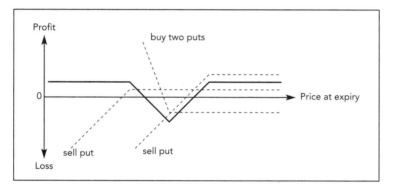

FIGURE 35 Profit/loss from a short butterfly spread

Condor

A condor is, for example, the purchase of one out-of-the-money put, sale of one slightly out-of-the-money put, sale of one slightly in-the-money put and purchase of one more in-the-money put.

A condor is a volatility strategy similar to a butterfly. It bears the same relationship to a butterfly that a strangle does to a straddle. The potential profit is less, but the risk is also less (see Figures 36 and 37).

Ratio spread

A ratio spread is a spread where the number of calls (or puts) purchased is not the same as the number sold. It can be seen as a directional strategy and as a volatility strategy. For example, a long ratio call spread could be the sale of one at-the-money call and the purchase of two out-of-the-money calls, such that the net premium cost is close to zero. The buyer will make a profit as long as the underlying moves up far enough (see Figures 38 and 39). If volatility falls, he is in greater danger of making a loss.

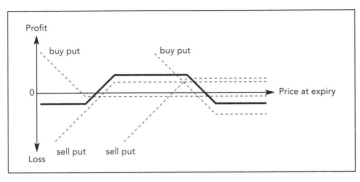

FIGURE 36 Profit/loss from a long condor

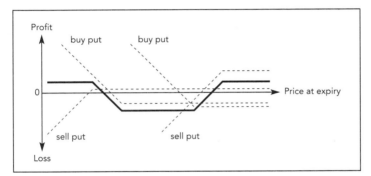

FIGURE 37 Profit/loss from a short condor

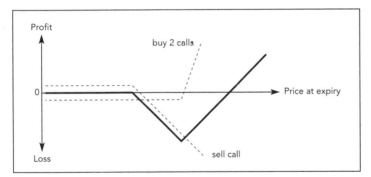

FIGURE 38 Profit/loss from a long ratio call spread

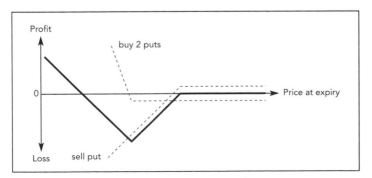

FIGURE 39 Profit/loss from a long ratio put spread

Risk reversal

Risk reversal is the purchase of a call (or put) and sale of a put (or call), both generally out-of-the-money, and generally at a net premium of around zero. This bears a
similarity to a forward purchase (or sale) of the underlying, since, if the two strikes
are in fact brought together to be both at-the-money, the strategy would be a *synthetic forward* purchase. This is therefore a directional strategy. The risk reversal
however has no profit or loss if the underlying only moves a little, so it provides
protection in the event of a small underlying fall (or rise) (see Figure 40).

A risk reversal also provides a means of reversing the risk on an existing position.
For example, if a trader's position is currently bullish (say, long of calls or short of
puts), he can reverse his directional risk by buying puts and selling calls, to re-
establish his position as bearish (see Figure 41).

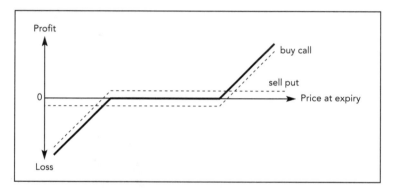

FIGURE 40 Profit/loss from a risk reversal

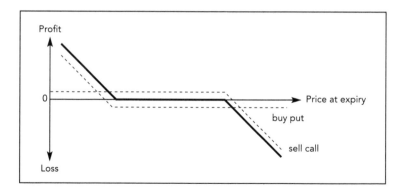

FIGURE 41 Profit/loss from a risk reversal

Related terminology

With combination strategies such as straddles and strangles, a *top combination* is one such as a straddle sale or a strangle sale which has a top limit to its profitability, and a *bottom combination* is the reverse, such as a straddle purchase or a strangle purchase.

Spreads constructed from options with the same maturity but different strikes are sometimes known as *vertical spreads*, while calendar spreads are *horizontal spreads*. A spread constructed from both different strikes and different maturities is a *diagonal spread*.

EXAMPLE

A trader buys a butterfly spread – buying a call at 98, selling two calls at 100 and buying a call at 102, for a net premium of 0.5. What is his profit or loss at maturity, if the underlying is then 96, 98.5, 100, 101 or 104?

Underlying at maturity is 96
Loss is 0.5 (nothing is exercised; premium paid is 0.5)

Underlying at maturity is 98.5
Zero profit/loss (98 call is exercised at a profit of 0.5; premium paid is 0.5)

Underlying at maturity is 100
Profit is 1.5 (98 call is exercised at a profit of 2; premium paid is 0.5)

Underlying at maturity is 101
Profit is 0.5 (98 call is exercised at a profit of 3; both 100 calls are exercised at a total loss of 2; premium paid is 0.5)

Underlying at maturity is 104
Loss is 0.5 (98 call is exercised at a profit of 6; both 100 calls are exercised at a total loss of 8; 102 call is exercised at a profit of 2; premium paid is 0.5).

This analysis does not take account of the cost of funding the premium from the start until maturity.

BARRIER OPTIONS: KNOCK-OUT OPTION AND KNOCK-IN OPTION

Definition

A **barrier option** is a class of options, including knock-out and knock-in options, which are either cancelled or activated if the *underlying* price reaches a predetermined barrier or *trigger level*.

A **knock-out option** is an option which is cancelled if the trigger level is reached.

A **knock-in option** is an option which is activated if the trigger level is reached.

HOW ARE THEY USED?

Barrier options are usually straightforward European options until, or from, the time the underlying reaches the trigger level. With a knock-out option, the option exists in the usual way – and either it is exercised at expiry or it expires worthless, depending on the underlying price at that time – unless the underlying price reaches an agreed trigger level before then. If it does, the option is immediately cancelled.

With a knock-in option, the option cannot be exercised at expiry, regardless of the underlying rate at that time, unless an agreed trigger level has been reached at some time during the life of the option. If this level has been reached, the option becomes a standard European option from that time on.

Because of these cancelling or activating features, barrier options are usually cheaper than ordinary options. This is because there are some circumstances under which a normal option would be exercised, but a knock-in or knock-out cannot be. There is therefore less probability of the seller of the option paying out on the option, and hence a lower value to the option.

They can therefore provide a hedge at a lower cost than a straightforward option, while still providing adequate protection. For example, the trigger level can be set by the buyer so that, if the trigger point is reached, he is then happy not to be protected, because the underlying is better anyway.

Because of the lower premium, barrier options can also provide a more *leveraged* speculative instrument than a straightforward call or put. If the underlying moves as anticipated, the buyer achieves the same profit for less initial cost.

Related terminology

Barrier options are also known as *trigger options*, *exploding options* and *extinguishing options*.

The trigger level in a knock-out option is also known as an *outstrike*. The trigger level in a knock-in option is also known as an *instrike*.

An *up-and-in option* and a *down-and-in option* are knock-in options where the trigger is respectively higher than, or lower than, the underlying rate at the start. An *up-and-out option* and a *down-and-out option* are knock-out options where the trigger is respectively higher than, or lower than, the underlying rate at the start.

A *reverse knock-out option* (or *kick-out option*) and a *reverse knock-in option* (or *kick-in option*) are a particular type of knock-out and knock-in option respectively, where the trigger level is such that, at the point of its being triggered, the option would be in-the-money rather than out-of-the-money.

A *double knock-out option* and a *double knock-in option* are a knock-out option and a knock-in option respectively, with two trigger levels – one above and one below the underlying rate at the start – either of which will trigger the cancellation or activation of the option.

Path-dependent option is a general term for options such as barrier options, *American options* and *average options*, where the decision or ability to exercise them, and hence their value, depends not only on the underlying price at expiry, but also on the path that the price of the underlying has taken during the life of the option.

Exotic option is a general term for any complex option, including barrier options.

EXAMPLE 1

A dollar-based company needs to buy €1,000,000 in 3 months' time. The current spot EUR/USD rate is 0.9500. The company buys a knock-out euro call option with a strike of 0.9700 and a trigger level of 0.9200. If, at any time over the next 3 months, the rate falls to 0.9200, the option will be cancelled and the company will no longer be protected. However, at that level, the company will be happy to have no further option protection, because it would consider 0.9200 to be a very satisfactory level to buy euros forward anyway. If the trigger is reached, the company will therefore be able to make a decision as to whether to buy the euros forward at that point or wait for further developments in the market. There would therefore be no reason to pay for protection that includes the possibility of the rate falling to 0.9200 and then rising again later to 0.9700.

EXAMPLE 2

A dollar-based company needs to buy €1,000,000 in 3 months' time. The current spot EUR/USD rate is 0.9500. The company buys a knock-in euro call option with a strike of 0.9700 and a trigger level of 0.9900. As long as the underlying rate remains below 0.9900, the company is comfortable remaining unprotected. However, if the rate rises above that level, it would want protection. If at any time over the next 3 months, the rate rises to 0.9900, the option will therefore come into existence and the company will be protected, able to buy euros at 0.9700 at expiry if necessary.

THE 'GREEKS': DELTA, GAMMA, VEGA, THETA AND RHO

Definition

The **delta** (Δ) of an *option* is the change in the value of the option as a proportion of the change in the value of the *underlying*.

The **gamma** (Γ) of an option is the change in the value of the option's delta as a proportion of the change in the value of the underlying.

The **vega** of an option is the change in the value of the option as a proportion of the change in volatility.

The **theta** (Θ) of an option is the change in the value of the option as a proportion of the change in time.

The **rho** (ρ) of an option is the change in the value of the option as a proportion of the change in the interest rate.

Each of these sensitivities assumes infinitesimally small changes and also assumes that other factors remain constant.

HOW ARE THEY USED?

In principle, an option *writer* could sell options without *hedging* his position. If the premiums received accurately reflect the average expected payouts at expiry, there is theoretically no profit or loss on average. This is analogous to an insurance company not reinsuring its business. In practice however, the risk that any one option may move sharply *in-the-money* makes this too dangerous. In order to manage a portfolio of options, therefore, the option dealer must know how the value of the options he has sold and bought will vary with changes in the various factors affecting their price, so that he can hedge them. He may also wish to take a position which is deliberately exposed to changes in one particular variable (such as volatility) but not to others, because he wishes to speculate on the change in that variable. The 'Greeks' are measures of the sensitivity of the value of an option to changes in each of these various factors, assuming that each of the other factors remains constant.

Delta

An option's delta measures how the option's value (which is the same as its current *premium*) varies with changes in the price of the underlying. For example, if an option has a delta of 0.7 (i.e 70%), a $100 increase in the value of the underlying will cause a $70 increase in the value of the option.

For a *call* option which is deep *out-of-the-money*, the premium will increase very little as the price of the underlying increases – essentially the option will remain worth almost zero. For an option deep *in-the-money*, however, an increase in the price of the underlying will be reflected completely in the call premium. The delta is therefore close to zero for deep out-of-the-money call options, 0.5 *at-the-money*, and 1 for deep in-the-money call options. For put options, delta is close to zero deep out-of-the-money, –0.5 at-the-money, and –1 deep in-the-money.

Consider, for example, a call option on an asset with a strike price of 99. When the underlying price is also 99, the option will have a certain premium value. If the underlying price rises to 100, the option will have a higher value because it could be exercised for a profit of 1 if the underlying price remains at 100. However, there is still a probability of approximately 50% that the price will fall and the option will expire worthless. The premium increase is therefore only approximately 50% of the underlying increase.

When an option trader wishes to hedge an option he has written, against changes in the underlying price, he has several choices:

● Buy an exactly matching option.

● Buy or sell the underlying. In this case, the trader will buy or sell enough of the underlying so that if the price changes, he will make a profit or loss which exactly offsets the loss or profit on the option position. In the example above, he would buy the underlying asset to the extent of 50% of the option amount. In this way, if the price rises from 99 to say 100, he will make a profit of 1 on half the amount of the option. This would offset a loss on the option position of 0.5 on the whole amount. In general, the amount of the hedge is equal to:

   delta × the notional amount of the option.

This is known as 'delta hedging' and demonstrates the importance of knowing the delta.

● Buy or sell another instrument with the same (but opposite) value for (delta × notional amount), so that again any change in the underlying price gives rise to a change in the hedge value which exactly offsets the change in the option's value. In the example above, such a hedge might be the purchase of another option with a different strike price – say a larger amount of an option on the same asset which is slightly out-of-the-money (and hence has a smaller delta).

If a trader is short of a *call* (as in this example) or long of a *put*, he has a negative delta and needs to buy the underlying in order to hedge. If he is long of a call or short of a put, he has a positive delta and needs to sell the underlying in order to hedge. For more complicated strategies, the direction of the delta may be less obvious. For a long butterfly position for example, the delta becomes positive as the underlying price falls and negative as the underlying price rises.

Gamma

One problem with delta hedging an option or portfolio of options is that the delta itself changes as the underlying price changes, so that although a portfolio may be hedged, or *delta neutral,* at one moment, it may not be so the next moment. An option's gamma (Γ) measures how much the delta changes with changes in the underlying price.

The delta does not change rapidly, when an option is deep out-of-the-money (the delta remains close to zero) or when an option is deep in-the-money (the delta remains close to 1 or –1), so that gamma is very small. When an option is close to the money however, the delta changes rapidly, and the gamma of a call is at its greatest slightly out-of-the-money. Gamma is positive for long option positions, both calls and puts, and negative for short calls and short puts.

Ideally, a trader who wishes to be fully hedged against changes in the underlying price would like to be *gamma neutral* – that is, to have a portfolio of options where the delta does not change at all.

Vega

An option's vega measures how much the option's value changes with changes in the volatility of the underlying. This is important to an option trader who is deliberately taking a position with a directional view, because he may not wish his position to be distorted by changes in volatility, and will therefore wish to be *vega neutral* (i.e. superimpose a hedge to make vega zero overall). It is similarly important to a trader who is taking a volatility strategy, because he will wish to know how much he will profit if his view on volatility is correct.

Vega is at its highest when an option is at-the-money and falls as the market and strike prices diverge. Options closer to expiration have a lower vega than those with more time to run. Positions with positive vega will generally have positive gamma. To be long vega (to have a positive vega) can be achieved by purchasing either call or put options.

Theta

An option's theta (Θ) measures how much the option's value changes with changes over time. This is significant in time to expiry because as an option approaches expiry, time value will inevitably disappear. Theta is defined so that it is negative for a long call or put position and positive for a short call or put position. The more the market and strike prices diverge, the less effect time has on an option's price and hence the smaller the theta. Positive theta is generally associated with negative gamma and vice versa.

Rho

An option's rho (ρ) measures how much the option's value changes with changes in interest rates. Rho tends to increase with maturity; it is generally a less significant sensitivity than the others described here.

> **Related terminology**
>
> Vega is sometimes known as *lambda* (Λ) or *kappa* (K).
>
> The *elasticity* of an option is the proportional change in the value of the option as a proportion of the proportional change in the value of the underlying.

FORMULAS

Calculation of these sensitivities depends on the mathematical model being used to value the options. Based on the Black and Scholes formula, for example, the sensitivities are calculated as follows:

$$\text{delta } (\Delta) = \frac{\text{change in option's value}}{\text{change in underlying's value}} = N(d_1) \text{ for a call or} - N(-d_1) \text{ for a put}$$

$$\text{gamma } (\Gamma) = \frac{\text{change in delta}}{\text{change in price}} = \frac{1}{\left(S\sigma\sqrt{2\pi t}\ e^{\left(\frac{d_1^2}{2}\right)}\right)}$$

$$\text{vega} = \frac{\text{change in option's value}}{\text{change in volatility}} = \frac{S\sqrt{\left(\frac{t}{2\pi}\right)}}{e^{\left(\frac{d_1^2}{2}\right)}}$$

$$\text{theta } (\Theta) = -\frac{\text{change in option's value}}{\text{change in time to maturity}} = \frac{-S\sigma}{\left(2\sqrt{(2\pi t)}e^{\left(\frac{d_1^2}{2}\right)}\right)} - \left(Kre^{(-rt)}N(d_2)\right) \text{ for a call}$$

$$\text{or } \frac{-S\sigma}{\left(2\sqrt{(2\pi t)}e^{\left(\frac{d_1^2}{2}\right)}\right)} + \left(Kre^{(-rt)}N(-d_2)\right) \text{ for a put}$$

$$\text{rho } (\rho) = \frac{\text{change in option's value}}{\text{change in interest rate}} = Kte^{(-rt)}N(d_2) \text{ for a call}$$

$$\text{or} - Kte^{(-rt)}N(-d_2) \text{ for a put}$$

where: $d_1 = \dfrac{LN\left(\dfrac{Se^{rt}}{K}\right) + \dfrac{\sigma^2 t}{2}}{\sigma\sqrt{t}}$

$d_2 = \dfrac{LN\left(\dfrac{Se^{rt}}{K}\right) - \dfrac{\sigma^2 t}{2}}{\sigma\sqrt{t}}$

$N()$	=	standardized normal cumulative probability distribution.
S	=	spot price.
K	=	strike price.
σ	=	annualized volatility.
t	=	time to expiry of the option expressed as a proportion of a year (365 days).
r	=	**continuously compounded** interest rate.
$LN()$	=	natural logarithm (i.e. the logarithm to base e).

EXAMPLE 1

Suppose, for example, that an option portfolio is currently delta-neutral, but has a portfolio gamma (= gamma × portfolio size) of –60. Suppose that a particular option which could be used to hedge this has a delta of 0.5 and a gamma of 0.6. The gamma of the portfolio could be reduced to zero by adding a long position of $\frac{60}{0.6} = 100$ units of this option. However, the delta of the portfolio would now be $100 \times 0.5 = 50$. It is therefore necessary to superimpose on this, for example, a further hedge of a short position of 50 in the underlying – to reduce the delta back to zero. This will not affect the portfolio's gamma, because the underlying has a delta of 1 but a gamma of zero. The portfolio would still need to be hedged dynamically – because the gamma itself, as well as the delta, will change as the underlying moves – but it would be less vulnerable.

EXAMPLE 2

Consider a 90-day call option at a strike of 97. The underlying price is 95, volatility is 9% and the continuously compounded interest rate is 5%. The current value of the call, i.e. its premium, is 1.33 according to the Black and Scholes model. What would be the various sensitivities, according to the same model?

$$d_1 = \frac{LN\left(\dfrac{95 \times e^{\left(0.05 \times \frac{90}{365}\right)}}{97}\right) + \left(0.09^2 \times \dfrac{\frac{90}{365}}{2}\right)}{0.09 \times \sqrt{\left(\dfrac{90}{365}\right)}} = -0.1680$$

$$d_2 = \cfrac{LN\left(\cfrac{95 \times e^{\left(0.05 \times \frac{90}{365}\right)}}{97}\right) - \left(\cfrac{0.09^2 \times \frac{90}{365}}{2}\right)}{0.09 \times \sqrt{\left(\frac{90}{365}\right)}} = -0.2127$$

delta = N(–0.1680) = 0.43 = 43%

Therefore the value of the call will increase by approximately 43% of the increase in the underlying, i.e. it will rise by approximately 0.43 to 1.76, if the underlying rises 1 to 96. (Because the delta is only an approximation, this is not precise; the value of the call according to the Black and Scholes model actually rises to 1.81.)

$$gamma = \cfrac{1}{95 \times 0.09 \times \sqrt{\left(2 \times \pi \times \frac{90}{365}\right)} \times e^{\left(\frac{(-0.1680)^2}{2}\right)}} = 0.09 = 9\%$$

Therefore the value of the delta will increase by approximately 0.09 for an increase of 1 in the underlying, i.e. it will rise by approximately 0.09 to 0.52, if the underlying rises 1 to 96. (Because the gamma is only an approximation, this is not precise; the value of the delta according to the Black and Scholes model actually rises to 0.53%.)

$$vega = \cfrac{95 \times \sqrt{\left(\cfrac{\left(\frac{90}{365}\right)}{(2 \times \pi)}\right)}}{e^{\left(\frac{(-0.1680)^2}{2}\right)}} = 19$$

Therefore the value of the call will increase by approximately 19 for an increase of 1 in the volatility, i.e. it will rise by approximately 0.19 to 1.52, if volatility rises 1% to 10%. (Because the vega is only an approximation, this is not precise; the value of the call according to the Black and Scholes model actually rises to 1.51.)

$$theta = \cfrac{-95 \times 0.09}{2 \times \sqrt{\left(2 \times \pi \times \frac{90}{365}\right)} \times e^{\left(\frac{(-0.1680)^2}{2}\right)}} - \left(97 \times 0.05 \times e^{\left(-0.05 \times \frac{90}{365}\right)} \times N(-0.2127)\right)$$

$$= -5.378$$

Therefore the value of the call will fall by approximately $\frac{5.3781}{365} = 0.015$ to 1.31, after one day.

$$rho = 97 \times \frac{90}{365} \times e^{\left(-0.05 \times \frac{90}{365}\right)} \times N(-0.2127) = 10$$

Therefore the value of the call will increase by approximately 10 for an increase of 1 in the interest rate, i.e. it will rise by approximately 0.10 to 1.43, if the interest rate rises 1% to 6%.

RISK MANAGEMENT

VARIANCE AND STANDARD DEVIATION

Definition

The **variance** of a series of numbers is the mean of all the squares of the differences between each number and the mean of all the numbers.

The **standard deviation** of a series of numbers is the square root of their variance.

HOW ARE THEY USED?

The *arithmetic mean* (or simply *mean*) of a series of numbers is the average of the numbers as we normally understand it. If we have the following five numbers:

52, 53, 57, 58, 60

then their mean is:

$$\frac{(52 + 53 + 57 + 58 + 60)}{5} = 56$$

The mean is useful, because it gives us an idea of how big the numbers are – 'about 56'. However, if we knew only this mean, 56, it would not give us any idea of how 'spread out' all the numbers are around 56; perhaps they are all very close to 56, or perhaps they are very spread out.

The standard deviation of the same numbers is a measure of how spread out the numbers are around this mean. If all the numbers were exactly the same, the standard deviation would be zero. If the numbers were very spread out, the standard deviation would be very high. Effectively, the standard deviation gives an idea of the answer to the question: 'On average, how far are the numbers away from their mean?' The standard deviation is defined as the square root of the variance. The variance in turn is defined as the average of the squared difference between each number and their average.

Consider the two following sets of numbers. They also each have a mean of 56, but the first set is closely packed together and the second set is very spread out. In fact, the first set has a standard deviation of 1.4 (see Figure 42) and the second set has a standard deviation of 4.3 (see Figure 43). If the standard distribution or variance is lower, the histogram is compressed horizontally – it looks taller and thinner – and there is a lower probability that any particular number is a long way from the mean. If the standard distribution or variance is greater, the histogram is more stretched out horizontally – it looks lower and fatter – and more numbers are further from the mean.

Related terminology

Volatility is the standard deviation, generally annualized, of the **continuously compounded** rate of return on an instrument.

52 53 53 54 54 54 54 54

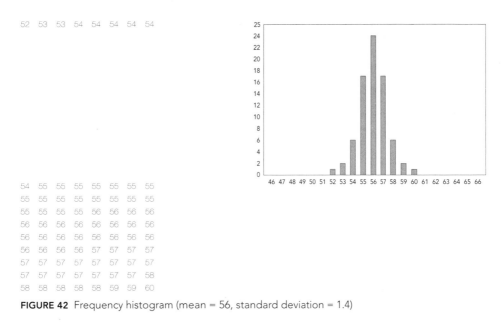

54 55 55 55 55 55 55 55
55 55 55 55 55 55 55 55
55 55 55 55 56 56 56 56
56 56 56 56 56 56 56 56
56 56 56 56 56 56 56 56
56 56 56 56 57 57 57 57
57 57 57 57 57 57 57 57
57 57 57 57 57 57 57 58
58 58 58 58 58 59 59 60

FIGURE 42 Frequency histogram (mean = 56, standard deviation = 1.4)

46 47 48 48 49 49 50 50

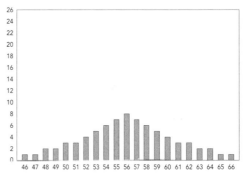

50 51 51 51 52 52 52 52
52 53 53 53 53 53 54 54
54 54 54 54 54 55 55 55
55 55 55 55 56 56 56 56
56 56 56 56 57 57 57 57
57 57 57 58 58 58 58 58
58 58 59 59 59 59 59 60
60 60 60 60 61 61 61 62
62 62 63 63 64 64 65 66

FIGURE 43 Frequency histogram (mean = 56, standard deviation = 4.3)

FORMULAS

$$\text{mean} = \frac{\text{sum of all the values}}{\text{the number of values}}$$

$$\text{variance} = \frac{\text{sum of all the (difference from the mean)}^2}{\text{the number of values}}$$

This gives the variance of a set of numbers, given that all the numbers are known. Very often, however, only a sample of the numbers is used. For example, a representative sample of prices for a particular instrument might be the daily closing prices over a period of only 1 year, rather than over the entire history of that instrument since it began trading. In this case, a better estimate of the variance of all the numbers is:

$$\text{variance} = \frac{\text{sum of all the (difference from the mean)}^2}{\text{(the number of values} - 1)}$$

Whichever formula is used,

$$\text{standard deviation} = \sqrt{\text{variance}}$$

EXAMPLE 1

What are the variance and standard deviation of the following numbers?

52, 53, 57, 58, 60

As above, their mean is:

$$\frac{(52 + 53 + 57 + 58 + 60)}{5} = 56$$

Numbers	Difference between the numbers and 56	(Difference)^2
52	−4	16
53	−3	9
57	+1	1
58	+2	4
60	+4	16
Mean = 56		Total = 46

The variance is therefore $\frac{46}{5}$ = 9.2 and the standard deviation is $\sqrt{9.2}$ = 3.03.

EXAMPLE 2

If the numbers above were only a sample of all the possible numbers, a better estimate of the variance of all the numbers would be found by dividing by 4, rather than by 5. The estimated variance would therefore be $\frac{46}{4}$ = 11.5 and the estimated standard deviation would be $\sqrt{11.5}$ = 3.39.

CORRELATION AND COVARIANCE

Definition

Correlation and **covariance** are measures of the extent to which two things do, or do not, move together. The precise mathematical formulas are given below.

HOW ARE THEY USED?

Consider for example the price of a 10-year government bond and the price of an 11-year government bond (issued by the same government). Generally, the price of one will rise and fall in line with the price of the other. The two prices are therefore closely correlated. On the other hand, when house prices rise, a government bond price might fall (because rising inflation pushes up interest rates) and vice versa. There might therefore be a negative correlation between government bond prices and the value of shares in a building materials producer. There might well be very little relationship at all between government bond prices and the price of rubber, so that the price of one moving up or down suggests no information about whether the other has risen or fallen (no correlation).

A correlation coefficient lies between +1 and –1. If two series of numbers are perfectly correlated (they move exactly in line), their correlation coefficient is +1. If they move exactly in line but in opposite directions, their correlation coefficient is –1. If there is no link at all between the two series, their correlation coefficient is 0.

First series	Second series	Correlation coefficient	First series	Second series	Correlation coefficient	First series	Second series	Correlation coefficient
1	2		1	–2		1	10	
2	4		2	–4		2	2	
3	6	+1	3	–6	–1	3	4	0
4	8		4	–8		4	6	
5	10		5	–10		5	9	

Covariance is a concept linking correlation and **variance**. Whereas variance quantifies how much the value of one particular thing varies, covariance measures how much two things vary, relative to each other.

Related terminology

⇨ *See also* **variance**.

FORMULAS

correlation coefficient

$$= \frac{\text{sum of } (x \times y) - (n \times (\text{average of } x) \times (\text{average of } y))}{\sqrt{((\text{sum of } (x^2) - (n \times (\text{average of } x)^2)) \times (\text{sum of } (y^2) - (n \times (\text{average of } y)^2)))}}$$

covariance

$$= \text{correlation coefficient} \times \sqrt{((\text{variance of } x) \times (\text{variance of } y))}$$

Where 'n' is the number of pairs of data and 'average' is the straightforward arithmetic mean.

EXAMPLE

What are the correlation coefficient and covariance of the following two series of prices?

	First price x	Second price y	$x \times y$	x^2	y^2	$(x - \text{average of } x)^2$	$(y - \text{average of } y)^2$
Day 1:	94	75	7,050	8,836	5,625	1	4
Day 2:	95	74	7,030	9,025	5,476	4	1
Day 3:	93	73	6,789	8,649	5,329	0	0
Day 4:	91	72	6,552	8,281	5,184	4	1
Day 5:	92	71	6,532	8,464	5,041	1	4
Totals:	465	365	33,953	43,255	26,655	10	10

$$\text{average of } x = \frac{465}{5} = 93 \quad \text{average of } y = \frac{365}{5} = 73$$

$$\text{correlation coefficient} = \frac{33,953 - (5 \times 93 \times 73)}{\sqrt{((43,255 - (5 \times (93^2))) \times (26,655 - (5 \times (73^2))))}} = 0.80$$

This is a reasonably high level of correlation, indicating that the price of x and the price of y move to some extent in parallel (see Figure 44).

$$\text{variance of } x = \frac{10}{5} = 2 \quad \text{variance of } y = \frac{10}{5} = 2$$

$$\text{covariance} = 0.80 \times \sqrt{(2 \times 2)} = 1.6$$

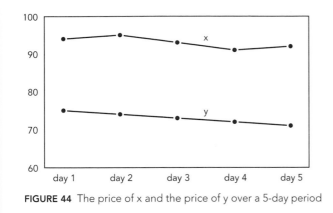

FIGURE 44 The price of x and the price of y over a 5-day period

VALUE AT RISK (VAR)

Definition

Value at risk (VAR) is the maximum potential loss which a bank expects to suffer on its positions over a given time period, estimated with a given confidence level.

HOW IS IT USED?

In order to control market risk, a bank needs to be in a position to measure it. Banks have therefore increasingly developed computer models with a view to deriving an overall measurement of the bank's market risk – value at risk (VAR) or *earnings at risk*. For any given *probability distribution*, it is possible to estimate what is the probability of any particular number being greater than, or less than, a particular level. In financial risk management, this translates into being able to estimate the probability of a profit or loss being greater than or less than a particular amount.

Suppose for example that a bank has a VAR of $10 million with a time horizon of 30 days and a confidence level of 95%. This means that if the bank's positions remain unchanged, there is a 95% probability that the total losses will not exceed $10 million over the next 30 days – or to put it another way, only a 5% probability that the total losses will exceed this amount. This can also be seen as saying that, during 1 month out of every 20 months (i.e. 5% of the time), it expects that its loss

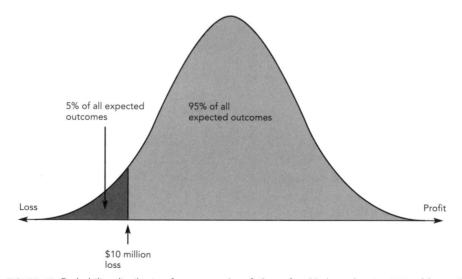

FIGURE 45 Probability distribution for expected profit/loss after 30 days, showing VAR of $10 million with a confidence level of 95%

would exceed this level. Intuitively, the total expected loss would be smaller (greater) if the time horizon were less (more) than a month and smaller (greater) if the confidence level were lower (higher) than 95%.

In arriving at this summary number of $10 million, the bank must make certain assumptions. First, there is an assumption about what is the 'pattern' of price movements for each instrument in which the bank has a position, and whether the price changes up and down are expected to be large or small. Mathematically, this means what is the probability distribution of rates of return on each instrument and what is their **standard deviation**? Banks often use an assumption that returns show a *normal* probability distribution as the basis for risk assessment, and the standard deviation used is often based on historic movements.

Second, the bank will take into account **correlation** between different instruments. Suppose for example that a particular dollar-based bank is long of 1 million euros and short of an equivalent amount of Swiss francs. Because there is a reasonably close (although of course not perfect) correlation between the two currencies, the bank is much less vulnerable to market movements than if it was only long of 1 million euros without any offsetting position. In this particular case, the greater the correlation, the less risky the position. If the two positions are both long (rather than one long and one short), then the riskiness of the total position would increase with higher correlation rather than decrease.

In general, a portfolio is less risky if it is more *diversified*. In other words, it may be safer to invest half in government bonds and half in rubber, rather than wholly in rubber. If the rubber market collapses, there is probably no reason to expect the government bond market to collapse at the same time. All other things being equal, diversification is less risky than non-diversification.

Problems with VAR calculations

One obvious difficulty with a VAR calculation lies in the assumption of a normal probability distribution. In practice, the probability distribution relating to financial returns tends to have fatter *tails* than suggested by the normal curve (the left-hand and right-hand ends of the graph are fatter than shown above). This suggests a greater probability of large profits or losses.

There is also a likelihood of *negative skewness* – a greater probability of a large downward movement in prices than of a large upward movement. This is because a falling market can trigger panic stop-loss sales which accelerate prices downward.

Standard deviation (i.e. volatility) is also not constant. The standard deviation seen in the past is not necessarily a good guide to the future.

A problem with assumptions about correlation is that historic relationships sometimes break down under extreme circumstances. For example, in quiet markets, bond prices and equity prices might be negatively correlated, so that a portfolio spread across both looks relatively safe: if one falls in value, the other might hopefully rise. When the market panics however, the prices of both might fall together. The use of correlation in assessing risk, like volatility, must therefore be partly based on historic data and partly subjective.

In using VAR for risk management, a bank must also make a decision on the holding period and confidence level (30 days and 95% in the example above). These parameters are clearly arbitrary and depend on the bank's willingness to accept risk and the speed with which it believes it can close out a loss-making position.

Variance/covariance, *Monte Carlo* and historic approaches

The approach considered so far for estimating VAR is the *variance/covariance* approach: a probability distribution is assumed, and the **variance** (based on historic standard deviations of financial instruments) and **covariance** (correlation between different financial instruments) are applied to this.

An alternative is to apply use a *Monte Carlo* simulation. This involves generating a very large number of random price changes, applying these to the current portfolio of instruments and measuring the net effect. The VAR is then taken as the worst net result, excluding the worst 5% of cases (for a 95% confidence level for example). Although the computer-generated series of prices is random, it must still fit an assumed probability distribution. For example, if the current price of an asset is 100, a move to 50 is clearly much less likely than a move to 99. This technique is more expensive in terms of computer time than the variance/covariance approach, but can be rather more reliable for *option*-related instruments. In the case of options, the fact that small changes in the *underlying* price can cause a large change in an option's value means that the variance/covariance approach is not always satisfactory.

Another possibility is to apply historic price movements over a long period to the current portfolio of instruments, on the assumption that future price movements will mimic past ones, and look at the net effect as with a Monte Carlo simulation. This is clearly a simpler technique mathematically than the variance/covariance approach, but still suffers from the drawback that the size of future price movements (i.e. standard deviation) and the relationships between price movements of different instruments (i.e. correlations or covariances) may not be the same as those implied by past movements.

BIS recommendations on VAR

The Bank for International Settlements (BIS) recommends that a supervisory authority should allow a bank to use its own internal VAR model for assessing **capital adequacy**. The VAR should be taken as the greater of: the average of the last 60 days'

VAR measurements multiplied by a factor (at least 3) determined by the supervisory authority, or the latest VAR measurement. However, the recommendation is that an internal VAR model can only be used if the following conditions are met:

- There should be a 'qualitative' check on the model's use: the bank should have a risk control unit which is independent of the dealers, and also the model's results should be integrated into the bank's day-to-day controls.

- There should be a 'quantitative' check: a test portfolio should be run through the model to check its measurements.

- The model should be run to calculate VAR at least daily.

- The holding period used should be 10 days and the confidence level should be 99% (i.e. there is only a 1% probability of the loss exceeding the VAR number over a 10-day period).

- The model should be tested against the last year's historic data (*backtesting*) to check that any losses actually incurred by the bank did not exceed the results estimated by the model more often than would have been expected. Four exceptions or less would be acceptable; between five and nine exceptions would require the multiplicative factor to be increased from 3; ten exceptions or more would require the model to be investigated before it could be used.

- VAR should be measured for four separate areas of business or 'portfolios' interest rate instruments, equities, foreign exchange and commodities – and the four figures added. The bank is allowed to take correlation (i.e. diversification) into account to reduce the measured VAR within each portfolio, but not across portfolios. That is, it may not consider any correlation effects arising from positions in two different portfolios.

Related terminology

⇨ *See also* standard deviation and correlation.

THE CAPITAL ADEQUACY RATIO

Definition

The **capital adequacy ratio** is the minimum level which supervisors require a bank to maintain for the size of its *own funds* (available capital and reserves) as a proportion of its *risk-weighted assets* (the amount of money which it has put at risk in the course of its business).

HOW IS IT USED?

When a bank or other financial institution lends money or deals in financial instruments, it is clearly taking risks. Two of the major risk categories are:

- *credit risk* – the risk that the borrower, or the counterparty to the deal, or the issuer of a security, will default on repayment or not deliver its side of the deal;
- *market risk* – the risk that the value of the bank's deal falls; for example the bank buys a security whose price subsequently falls.

In order to prevent banks from taking excessive risks (and hence to protect the banking system as a whole), the European Union (EU) and the *BIS* have established guideline limits to the risks which each bank may take. In turn, each country's financial supervisory authority enforces these limits, or stronger ones if it prefers, on the banks under its control. The details of these guidelines are complex, and the following remarks are necessarily a simplification of them. The concept is that a bank should always have adequate capital so that, if some of the risks are realized, the bank can still remain in business without jeopardizing its depositors, hence the term capital adequacy.

Each bank is therefore required to maintain the following *risk asset ratio* at or above the capital adequacy ratio (which is currently 8%):

$$\frac{\text{own funds (i.e. available capital and reserves)}}{\text{risk-weighted assets (i.e. the amount of money which it has put at risk in the course of its business)}}$$

The various directives from the EU which together set out the risk measurement rules are known as the *Capital Adequacy Directives* (CAD).

Own funds

The risk limits are defined in terms of the size of each bank's own funds, roughly equivalent to the value of its shareholders' equity in the bank plus reserves and certain other funding raised by the bank. There are three tiers within own funds:

Tier 1: equity
   reserves
   retained profit
   minority interests
   less goodwill, other intangibles and current losses

Tier 2: reserves from fixed asset revaluations
   medium-term subordinated debt
   less holdings of other banks' issues

Tier 3: daily trading profits
   short-term subordinated debt

Tier 3 capital can be used only to cover *trading book* risks (see 'risk-weighted assets') and there are various other restrictions on the uses and relative sizes of the three tiers in covering different aspects of risk.

Risk-weighted assets

A bank's business is split into two areas: the trading book and the *banking book* (or *investment book*). Essentially, a transaction is in the banking book if it is a cash loan made by the bank for normal lending purposes rather than trading purposes, or a long-term investment. A transaction is in the trading book if it involves trading in financial instruments for the purpose of making trading profits, or is a hedge against something else in the trading book – largely the type of activity undertaken by a bank's dealing rooms rather than by its lending departments.

The effect of the CAD is to limit the amount, and type, of business which a bank does. If the types of deals undertaken by a particular bank are measured as mostly having a low risk, it can do more of them than if they are measured as having a high risk.

If a bank's overheads are large in comparison with its business, the risk-weighted assets are taken as being 25% of the previous year's fixed overheads. Normally however, this constraint is not relevant and the risk-weighted assets are the total of the following:

- *currency risk* on both trading activities and banking business;
- *large exposure risk* on both trading activities and banking business;
- *counterparty risk* on both trading activities and banking business;
- *settlement risk* on trading activities
- *position risk* on trading activities.

Currency risk

This measures the net exposure to foreign currencies, as the greater of the following:

- the sum of all net long positions in each currency;
- the sum of all net short positions in each currency.

An amount of 2% of own funds is then deducted from this total. Banks are however allowed to net and/or reduce the measured exposures for closely related currencies, provided that the supervisory authorities allow this.

Large exposure risk

A bank is required to allocate more capital to its assets if the total exposure to any one counterparty is a particularly large proportion of the total.

Counterparty and settlement risk

Settlement risk is the risk that the counterparty will not settle a transaction for which the settlement date has now arrived or has already passed. The risk is limited to mark-to-market profit which has already been made, multiplied by a factor which increases toward 100% as the delay increases.

The counterparty risk for any transaction takes account of two aspects: the creditworthiness of the counterparty and the nature of the transaction. For example, a US$1 million **forward rate agreement (FRA)** dealt with a particular counterparty does not expose the bank to the same potential loss as a US$1 million loan made to the same counterparty. With the FRA, if the counterparty defaults, the bank can lose only the difference between two interest rates. With a loan, the bank can lose the entire principal amount as well as the interest on it. Counterparty risk is therefore measured as:

risk-weighting factor for the counterparty × risk-weighting factor for the transaction

Examples of some of the weightings applied for certain counterparty and transaction types are shown in Tables 1 and 2:

TABLE 1 Risk weighting for counterparty type

government in 'Zone A' (mostly OECD countries) or local currency transactions with government in 'Zone B'	0%
bank in 'Zone A'	20%
corporate (for mortgages)	50%
corporate (for derivative transactions)	50%
corporate (other transactions)	100%

TABLE 2 Risk weighting for transaction type

'on-balance-sheet' (e.g. loan or bond purchase)	100% of amount
'off-balance-sheet' but not *derivative* transaction	0% for 'low risk' (e.g. undrawn, uncommitted, short-term credit facility); 20% for 'medium/low risk' (e.g. documentary credits with goods as collateral); 50% for 'medium risk' (e.g. documentary credits and indemnities); 100% for 'full risk' (e.g. bill acceptances and guarantees)
exchange-traded derivatives with daily *margin* requirements	0%
interest rate-related derivative transactions (such as FRA or *IRS*) with maturity up to 1 year	*mark-to-market* profit
interest rate-related derivative transactions with maturity more than 1 year	mark-to-market profit plus 0.5% of amount of deal
FX-related derivative transactions with maturity up to 1 year	mark-to-market profit plus 1.0% of amount of deal
FX-related derivative transactions with maturity more than 1 year	mark-to-market profit plus 5.0% of amount of deal
(Derivative transactions can alternatively be weighted by ignoring the mark-to-market profits but considering the original exposures and using different factors)	
repos, buy/sell-backs and securities lending in the trading book	any amount of under-collateralization (including accrued coupon on the collateral and accrued interest on the cash)

Thus for example:

> The risk for a US$1 million loan to a corporate counterparty is:
>
> US$1 million × 100% × 100% = US$1 million
>
> The risk for a US$1 million FRA 3 v 6 dealt with a Zone A bank is:
>
> 20% × the current mark-to-market profit on the deal

In the case of the FRA, if the deal is currently running at a loss, there is clearly no mark-to-market exposure if the counterparty defaults. The 'add-on' of 0.5%, etc for longer term positions is to allow for the possibility of the deal moving into profit before a mark-to-market calculation is next made.

> For a reverse repo of US$1 million with a Zone A bank, where our bank has taken a margin of 2%, the risk is:
>
> > 20% × zero = zero
>
> For a reverse repo of US$1 million with a Zone A bank, where the other bank has taken a margin of 2%, the risk is:
>
> > 20% × (US$1.02 million – US$1 million) = US$4,000

Position risk

Position risk, which applies only to the trading book, measures exposure to changes in interest rates and security prices. The measurement is of net positions in particular issues and net positions in 'closely matched interest rate positions' (i.e. net positions in each *time bucket*). For FRAs, **futures**, *forward* purchases and **interest rate swaps**, the bank must consider both sides of the position. For example, a long 3 v 4 FRA is considered as a short 3-month position and a long 4-month position.

The risk is measured in two components. The first is 'specific risk', which considers the issuer of a security held by the bank, with the amount of risk-weighted asset being between 0% and 8% of the nominal amount of the risk, depending on the nature of the issuer. The second is 'general risk' for the market position. This can be measured by using the CAD's complex and detailed rules for each type and maturity of position. Alternatively, because of the complexity of assessing such risk, which varies widely from one bank's portfolio to another's, the CAD allows for each bank to use its own internal **VAR** models, provided that this is approved by the supervising authority.

Related terminology

⇨ *See also* value at risk (VAR)

APPENDICES

GLOSSARY

Accrued coupon ▶ *See accrued interest.*

Accrued interest The proportion of a bond's coupon which has been accrued, or 'earned but not yet paid', since the last coupon payment.

American option An **option** where the **holder** can choose to **exercise** at any time between the purchase of the option and **expiry**.
▶ *See European option.*

Amount of discount For those discount instruments traded on the basis of a **discount rate**, such as a US **Treasury bill**, the amount subtracted from the instrument's face value to arrive at the consideration paid for it.

Annuity (Or **annuity certain**.) A regular stream of future cash receipts which can be purchased by an initial cash payment, or a regular stream of cash payments to repay an initial borrowing.

Annuity certain ▶ *See annuity.*

Annuity due An **annuity** where the payments are made at the beginning of each period.

Arbitrage A simultaneous operation in two related markets, to take advantage of a discrepancy between them, which will lock in a profit.
▶ *See covered interest arbitrage.*

Arithmetic mean Average.

Asian option ▶ *See average option.*

Asset An investment, or some other thing owned.

Asset swap An **interest rate swap** or **currency swap** used to change the interest rate exposure and/or the currency exposure of an investment. Also used to describe the package of the swap plus the investment itself.

ATM ▶ *See at-the-money.*

At-the-money An **option** where the **strike** is the same as the current **spot** or **forward** market rate.
▶ *See in-the-money, out-of-the-money.*

Average option (Or **Asian option**.) An **option** whose value depends on the average value of the **underlying** over the option's life.

Backtesting Testing a **VAR** model against historic data to check its validity.

Banking book (Or **investment book**.) Under the **capital adequacy directives**, those of a bank's outstanding transactions which relate to customer lending or long-term strategic investments.
▶ *See trading book.*

Barrier option   (Or **trigger option** or **exploding option** or **extinguishing option**.) An option which is either cancelled or activated if the underlying price reaches a predetermined barrier or trigger level.
> *See knock-out option and knock-in option.*

Base currency   An exchange rate is quoted as the number of units of one currency (the **variable currency**) equal to one unit of the other currency (the base currency).

Basis (Or **simple basis**.) The difference between the actual **STIR futures** price trading in the market and (100 – the current cash interest rate).

The difference between the price of a **deliverable bond** and the futures price, multiplied by that bond's **conversion factor**.

Basis risk   The risk that the price or rate of one instrument or position might not move exactly in line with the price or rate of another instrument or position which is being used to hedge it.

Basis swap   (Or **index swap**.) An **interest rate swap** in which the two legs are based on differently defined floating interest rates.
> *See coupon swap.*

Bearish   Expecting a fall in prices.

Bid   The price at which the dealer quoting a price or rate is prepared to buy or borrow. The bid price of a foreign exchange quotation is the rate at which he will buy the **base currency** and sell the **variable currency**.

In a **repo**, the interest rate at which the dealer will borrow the **collateral** and lend the cash.
> *See offer.*

Binomial pricing model   A method of valuing an **option** based on building a lattice (a 'tree') of all the possible paths up and down that the **underlying** price might take from start until expiry, assuming that, at each price change, the price either rises or falls by a given amount or proportion.

Binomial tree ▶ *See binomial pricing model.*

BIS   Bank for International Settlements.

Black and Scholes model   A formula for calculating **option** prices, developed by Fischer Black and Myron Scholes.

Bond basis   The calculation of interest on the basis of a 'bond' year, approximating to the assumption that there are 365 days in each year.
> *See money market basis.*

Bond futures   An agreement on a recognized **futures** exchange to buy or sell a standard face value amount of a bond, at an agreed price, for settlement on a standard future delivery date. In some cases, the contract is non-deliverable. In most cases, the contract is based on a notional bond.

Bootstrapping   The process of building up a theoretical **spot yield curve** by calculating **zero-coupon yields** for successively longer maturities from those for shorter maturities.

Borrower's option ▶ *See interest rate guarantee.*

Bottom combination An **option** strategy such as a **straddle** purchase, which has a lower limit to its profitability.

Break forward (Or **forward with optional exit**.) A **forward** deal, equivalent to a straightforward **option**, where the customer is allowed to reverse the deal at an agreed break rate.

Broken date (Or **odd date**.) A maturity date other than the standard ones normally quoted.

Bullish Expecting a rise in prices.

Butterfly spread The purchase of a **call** (or **put**) (generally **out-of-the-money**) combined with the purchase of another call (or put) at a different **strike** (generally **in-the-money**) and the sale of two calls (or puts) at a mid-way strike (generally **at-the-money**).

Buy/sell-back The purchase of a bond or other **asset** and the simultaneous sale of the same asset back again to the same counterparty for settlement on a later date.
 ▶ *See sell/buy-back and repo.*

CAD ▶ *See capital adequacy directives.*

Calendar spread The simultaneous purchase (or sale) of a **futures** or **option** contract for one date and the sale (or purchase) of a similar contract for a different date.
 ▶ *See spread.*

Call option A deal giving one party the right, without the obligation, to buy an agreed amount of a particular instrument or commodity, at an agreed rate, on or before an agreed future date. The other party has the obligation to sell if so requested by the first party.
 ▶ *See put option.*

Call spread The purchase of a **call option** coupled with the sale of another call option at a different **strike**, expecting a limited rise or fall in the value of the **underlying**.

Cap (Or **ceiling**.) A package of interest rate **options** whereby, at each of a series of future fixing dates, if an agreed reference rate such as **LIBOR** is higher than the **strike** rate, the option buyer receives the difference between them, calculated on an agreed **notional** principal amount for the period until the next fixing date.

Capital adequacy directives The various directives from the EU which together set out risk measurement rules for banks.

Capital adequacy ratio The minimum level which supervisors require a bank to maintain for the size of its own funds (available capital and reserves) as a proportion of its risk-weighted assets (the amount of money which it has put at risk in the course of its business).

Cash market The market for trading an **underlying** financial instrument, where the whole value of the instrument will potentially be settled on the normal delivery date. As opposed to **contracts for differences** (where the cash amount to be settled is not intended to be the full value of the underlying), **futures**, **options** or **forwards** (where delivery is for a later date than normal).
 ▶ *See derivative.*

Cash-and-carry arbitrage The sale of a **bond futures** contract together with the purchase of a **deliverable bond**, to lock in a profit.

CD ▶ *See certificate of deposit.*

Ceiling ▶ *See cap.*

Central bank repo When a central bank initiates a **repo** or a **reverse repo** with the market, the terminology is viewed from the market's viewpoint and not from the central bank's. Thus a central bank repo is when the central bank is lending money to the market against **collateral** and a reverse repo is the opposite.

Certificate of deposit (Or **CD**.) A security, generally **coupon**-bearing, issued by a bank to borrow money.

Cheapest-to-deliver (Or **CTD**.) The bond which it is most cost-effective for a **futures** seller to deliver to the buyer if required to do so.

Classic repo ▶ *See repo.*

Clean price The price of a bond excluding any **accrued interest**; in most but not all markets, the price quoted and dealt in the market, usually expressed as the clean price of 100 units of the bond's **face value**.

Clearing house Organization through which transactions in a particular instrument are settled.

Collar (Or **cylinder** or **tunnel** or **fence** or **corridor**.) The sale of a **put** (or **call**) **option** and purchase of a call (or put) at different **strikes** – typically both **out-of-the-money** – or the purchase of a **cap** combined with the sale of a **floor**.
▶ *See range forward.*

Collateral Something of value, often of good creditworthiness such as a government bond, given temporarily to a counterparty to enhance a party's creditworthiness.

In a **repo**, the collateral is actually sold temporarily by one party to the other rather than merely lodged with it.

Commercial paper (Or **CP**.) A short-term **security** issued by a company or bank, generally with a zero **coupon**.

Compound interest Interest calculated on the assumption that interest amounts will be received periodically and can be re-invested (usually at the same rate).

Condor The purchase of a **call** (or **put**) (generally **out-of-the-money**) combined with the purchase of another call (or put) at a different **strike** (generally **in-the-money**) and the sale of two calls (or puts) at two different strikes between the first two (generally one in-the-money and one out-of-the-money).

Continuously compounded interest rate An **equivalent interest rate**, where the frequency of **compounding** is infinite (i.e. the period of compounding is infinitesimally short).

Contract for differences A transaction which is cash settled against a reference rate, rather than delivered in full. That is, where a net cash payment is made from one party to the other to reflect the difference between a price or rate fixed at the time of transaction and a reference price or rate determined later, or between two such reference prices or rates.

Conversion factor (Or **price factor**.) For any particular bond **deliverable** into a **bond futures** contract, the number by which the **exchange delivery settlement price** is multiplied, to arrive at the delivery price for that particular bond.

Convexity A measure of the curvature of an investment's price/**yield** relationship, indicating the extent to which its value does not change in direct proportion to yield.

Correlation A measure of the extent to which two things do, or do not, move together.

Corridor ▶ *See collar.*

Cost of carry The difference between the financing cost of holding a position and the interest (or **coupon**) income from the position.

Counter currency ▶ *See variable currency.*

Counterparty risk The risk that a borrower, or a counterparty to a deal, will default on repayment or not deliver its side of the deal.

Coupon The interest payment(s) made by the issuer of a **security** to the owners, based on the coupon rate and **face value**.

Coupon swap An **interest rate swap** in which one leg is fixed-rate and the other is floating-rate.
▶ *See basis swap.*

Covariance A concept linking **correlation** and **variance**, measuring how much two things vary, relative to each other.

Covered interest arbitrage The creation of a borrowing or deposit in one currency by combining a borrowing or deposit in another with a **forward swap**.

Covered option An **option** bought or sold against an existing position.
▶ *See naked option.*

CP ▶ *See commercial paper.*

Credit risk The risk that a borrower, or a counterparty to a deal, or the issuer of a **security**, will default on repayment or not deliver its side of the deal.

Cross-currency repo A **repo** in which the cash and **collateral** are denominated in different currencies.

Cross-rate An exchange rate between any two currencies, neither of which is the US dollar. Also sometimes used for any exchange rate derived from two other exchange rates.

CTD ▶ *See cheapest-to-deliver.*

Cum-dividend When (as is usual) the next **coupon** or other payment due on a **security** will be paid by the issuer to the buyer of the security.
▶ *See ex-dividend.*

Currency risk The risk that an exchange rate movement will adversely affect profitability.

Currency swap An exchange of a series of cashflows in one currency for a series of cashflows in another currency, at agreed intervals over an agreed period.
▶ *See interest rate swap.*

Current yield The **coupon** rate of a bond as a proportion of its **clean price** per 100.
▶ *See yield to maturity, simple yield to maturity.*

Curve fitting Joining a series of known **yields** together to form a **yield curve**.

Customer repo When the US Federal Reserve ('Fed') does a **central bank repo** with the market on behalf of one of its own customers, such as another central bank or supra-national organization.
  ▸ *See system repo.*

Cylinder ▸ *See collar.*

Deferred annuity An **annuity** where the payments are made at the end of each period.

Deliverable bond One of the bonds which is eligible to be delivered by the seller of a **bond futures** contract at the contract's maturity, according to the specifications of that partic-ular contract.

Delta (Δ) The change in the value of an **option** as a proportion of the change in the value of the **underlying**.

Delta neutral An option portfolio with zero **delta**.

Derivative Any financial instrument whose value is derived from another, such as a **forward** foreign exchange rate, a **futures** contract, an **option**, an **interest rate swap** etc. Forward deals to be settled in full are not always called derivatives, however.

Diagonal spread An **option spread** constructed from options with different strikes and dif-ferent maturities.
  ▸ *See spread.*

Directional trade An **option** trade in which the trader expects a move up or down in the price of the **underlying**.

Dirty price The all-in price paid for a bond including any **accrued interest**.

Discount The amount by which one currency is cheaper, in terms of another currency, for **forward** delivery than for spot.
  ▸ *See premium.*

  To discount a future cashflow means to calculate its **present value**.

Discount factor The number by which you need to multiply a future cashflow, in order to calculate its **present value**.

Discount rate An alternative method of market quotation used for certain **securities** (US and UK treasury bills for example), which expresses the income earned on the security as a proportion of the face value of the security received at maturity, rather than as a propor-tion of the amount invested at the beginning.
  ▸ *See yield.*

Diversified A portfolio whose risk is spread so that a fall in the value or creditworthiness of one part of the portfolio is not particularly likely to lead to a fall in the value or credit-worthiness of another part.

Dollar value of a basis point ▸ *See price value of a basis point.*

Dollar value of an 01 ▸ *See price value of a basis point.*

Double knock-in option/Double knock-out option Respectively, a **knock-in option** and a **knock-out option**, with two trigger levels – one above and one below the **underlying** rate at the start – either of which will trigger the cancellation or activation of the option.

Down-and-in option A **knock-in option** where the trigger is lower than the **underlying** rate at the start.

▸ *See up-and-in option, up-and-out option, down-and-out option.*

Down-and-out option A **knock-out option** where the trigger is lower than the **underlying** rate at the start.

▸ *See up-and-in option, down-and-in option, up-and-out option.*

Duration (Or **Macaulay duration**.) The weighted average life of a bond or other series of cashflows, using the **present value** of each cashflow as its weighting.

DV01 ▸ *See price value of a basis point.*

Earnings at risk ▸ *See value at risk.*

EDSP ▸ *See exchange delivery settlement price.*

Effective interest rate An **equivalent interest rate**, where the frequency of **compounding** is annual (i.e. 365 days) and also the interest is calculated on the basis of a 365-day year.

Elasticity The proportional change in the value of an **option** as a proportion of the proportional change in the value of the **underlying**.

End-end A **forward swap** or money-market deal commencing on the last working day of a month and maturing on the last working day of the corresponding month.

Equivalent interest rate The rate which achieves the same total proceeds as another given interest rate (the nominal rate), but assuming a different frequency of **compounding**.

Eurocurrency A currency owned by a non-resident of the country in which the currency is legal tender.

European option An **option** that may be exercised only at **expiry**.

▸ *See American option.*

Exchange delivery settlement price (EDSP) The closing price of a **futures** contract on its last day of trading.

Ex-coupon ▸ *See ex-dividend.*

Ex-dividend (Or **ex-coupon**.) When the next **coupon** or other payment due on a **security** is paid by the issuer to the seller after he has sold it, rather than to the buyer, generally because the transaction is settled after the **record date**.

▸ *See cum-dividend.*

Exercise To require the seller of an **option** to fulfil the underlying transaction.

Exotic option A general term for any complex **option**.

Expiry date The final day on which an **option** can be **exercised**.

Exploding option ▸ *See barrier option.*

Extinguishing option ▸ *See barrier option.*

Extrapolation The process of estimating a price or rate for value on a particular date from other known prices, when the value date required lies outside the period covered by the known prices.

Face value The principal amount of a **security**, generally repaid all at maturity but sometimes repaid in stages, on which the **coupon** amounts are calculated.

Fence ▶ *See collar.*

Fixed rate A borrowing or investment where the interest or coupon paid is fixed at the beginning of the arrangement.
▶ *See floating rate.*

Fixing Setting of a reference rate such as **LIBOR** for determining the settlement amount in a loan or a **contract for differences**.

Floating rate A borrowing or investment where the interest or coupon paid changes throughout the arrangement in line with some reference rate such as **LIBOR**.
▶ *See fixed rate.*

Floating-rate note (Or **FRN**.) **Security** on which the rate of interest payable is refixed and paid in line with market conditions at regular intervals (often each 6 months).

Floor A package of interest rate **options** whereby, at each of a series of future **fixing** dates, if an agreed reference rate such as **LIBOR** is lower than the **strike** rate, the option buyer receives the difference between them, calculated on an agreed **notional** principal amount for the period until the next fixing date.
▶ *See cap, collar.*

Forward A deal for settlement later than the normal settlement date for that particular commodity or instrument.

Forward outright An outright purchase or sale of one currency in exchange for another currency for delivery on a fixed date in the future other than the **spot settlement date**.

Forward rate agreement (Or **FRA**.) An agreement to pay or receive, on an agreed future date, an amount based on the difference between a fixed interest rate agreed at the outset and a reference interest rate actually prevailing on a given future date for a given period.

Forward swap The purchase of one currency against another for settlement on one date, with a simultaneous sale to reverse the transaction on a subsequent settlement date.

Forward with optional exit ▶ *See break forward.*

Forward-forward A cash borrowing or lending or a **forward swap**, which starts on one forward date and ends on another forward date, with the term, amount and rate or price all fixed in advance.

Forward-forward yield curve A **yield curve** showing **zero-coupon yields** against time to maturity for **forward-forward** periods of a particular length, often 1 year.

FRA ▶ *See forward rate agreement.*

FRN ▶ *See floating-rate note.*

Fungible Holdings of **securities** or other instruments which can be combined with an existing holding of the same instrument, so that there is no distinction between the two holdings, which become a single, larger holding of the instrument.

Future value The amount of money which can be achieved at a given date in the future by investing (or borrowing) a given sum of money now at a given interest rate, assuming

compound re-investment (or re-funding) of any interest payments received (or paid) before the end.

Futures contract A deal, traded on a recognized exchange, to buy or sell some financial instrument or commodity for settlement on a future date.

Gamma (Γ) The change in the value of an **option**'s **delta** as a proportion of the change in the value of the **underlying**.

Gamma neutral A portfolio of **options** with zero **gamma**.

GC ▶ *See general collateral.*

General collateral **Collateral** used in a **repo**, **sell/buy-back** or **securities borrowing** transaction which is not considered **special**.

Generic IRS An **interest rate swap** with a standard structure and pricing, as opposed to one whose structure has been adjusted to suit the counterparty's requirements.

Gilt (Or **gilt-edged security**.) A long-term **security** issued by the UK government.

GMRA General Master Repo Agreement, the standard international documentation for transacting **repos**.

Gross redemption yield ▶ *See yield to maturity.*

GRY ▶ *See yield to maturity.*

Haircut Additional **collateral** required by the holder of collateral in a **repo**, **buy/sell-back** or **securities borrowing** transaction, to protect against the possibility of a fall in the collateral's price.
▶ *See margin.*

Hedge Protect against the risks arising from potential movements in exchange rates, interest rates or other variables.
▶ *See arbitrage, speculation.*

Hedge ratio The **face value** of one instrument which must be used to **hedge** another instrument or a portfolio, as a proportion of the face value of the latter.

Historic volatility The actual **volatility** observed using historical data over a particular period.

Holder The purchaser of an **option**.

Horizontal spread (Or **calendar spread**.) An **option** spread constructed from options with the same **strike** but different maturities.
▶ *See spread.*

Immunization The construction of a portfolio of **securities** so as not to be adversely affected by **yield** changes, provided the portfolio is held until a specific time.

Implied ▶ *See implied volatility.*

Implied repo rate For any **deliverable bond** in a **futures** contract, the break-even interest rate at which a purchase of that bond must be funded until delivery of the futures so that, when combined with a sale of the futures, there is no **cash-and-carry arbitrage** possible.

Implied volatility (Or **implied**). The current measure of **volatility** being used by a particular option dealer or by the market in general to calculate **premiums**, i.e. the volatility implied by an option premium.

Index swap   Sometimes the same as a **basis swap**. Otherwise, a swap like an **interest rate swap** where payments on one or both of the legs are based on the value of an index, such as an equity index.

Initial margin ▶ *See margin.*

Instrike   The trigger level in a **knock-in option**.
▶ *See outstrike.*

Interbank   Deals between banks, rather than between banks and customers.

Interest rate guarantee   (Or **IRG**.) Effectively an **option** on a **forward rate agreement**. An IRG can be either a borrower's option (i.e. a **call** on an FRA) or a lender's option (i.e. a **put** on an FRA).

Interest rate swap   (Or **IRS**.) An exchange of one series of interest payments, at agreed intervals over an agreed period, for another series, each based on an agreed **notional** principal amount but with no actual exchange of principal.

Internal rate of return   (Or **IRR**.) The one single interest rate which it is necessary to use when **discounting** a series of **future values** to achieve a given **net present value** or, equivalently, the interest rate which it is necessary to use when discounting a series of future values including an initial cashflow now, to achieve a zero net present value.

Interpolation   The process of estimating a price or rate for value on a particular date by comparing the prices actually quoted for value dates earlier and later than the date required.

In-the-money   An **option** whose **strike** is more advantageous to the option buyer than the current market rate.
▶ *See at-the-money, out-of-the-money.*

Intrinsic value   The difference between the **strike** price and the current market price of an **in-the-money** option (zero for an **out-of-the-money** option).

Investment book ▶ *See banking book.*

Invoicing amount   The amount paid by the buyer if a bond is delivered at maturity of a **bond futures** contract.

IRG ▶ *See interest rate guarantee.*

IRR ▶ *See internal rate of return.*

IRS ▶ *See interest rate swap.*

ISDA   The International Swaps and Derivatives Association.

Iteration   The repetitive mathematical process of estimating the answer to a problem by trying how well this estimate fits the data, adjusting the estimate appropriately and trying again, until the fit is acceptably close.

Kappa (κ) ▶ *See vega.*

Kick-in option ▶ *See reverse knock-in option.*

Kick-out option ▶ *See reverse knock-out option.*

Knock-in option   An **option** which is activated if a trigger level is reached.
▶ *See barrier option, knock-out option.*

Knock-out option An option which is cancelled if a trigger level is reached.
> *See barrier option, knock-in option.*

Lambda (Λ) *See vega.*

Large exposure risk Under the **capital adequacy directives**, the extra risk to be assessed if one particular counterparty accounts for a very large amount of a bank's outstanding transactions.

Lender's option *See interest rate guarantee.*

Leveraged A **speculative** position where the amount of cash which it is necessary to invest is less than the principal amount at risk.

Liability swap An **interest rate swap** or **currency swap** used to change the interest rate exposure and/or the currency exposure of a borrowing.
> *See asset swap.*

LIBID *See LIBOR.*

LIBOR London inter-bank offered rate, the rate at which banks are willing to lend to other banks of top creditworthiness. Generally used to mean both the interest rate at any time, and specifically the **fixing** at a particular time (11:00 a.m.). LIBID is similarly London inter-bank bid rate. LIMEAN is the average between LIBID and LIBOR.

LIMEAN *See LIBOR.*

Liquid An investment easy to sell or a position easy to close out.

Lognormal A **probability distribution** where the logarithm of the data shows a **normal distribution**.

Long A surplus of purchases over sales of a given currency or **asset**, or a situation which gives rise to an organization benefiting from a strengthening of that currency or asset. To a money market dealer, a surplus of borrowings taken in over money lent out.
> *See short.*

Lookback option An **option** whose value at **expiry** depends on the market rate achieved (best, worst, etc.) during the option's life.

Macaulay duration *See duration.*

Manufactured payment A payment from one party to the other in a **repo** or **securities borrowing** transaction, to compensate for a **coupon** or other payment received by the temporary owner of a **security**.

Margin Initial **margin** is collateral placed by one party with a counterparty or clearing house at the time of a deal, against the possibility that the market price will move against the first party, thereby leaving the counterparty with a credit risk. In a repo, initial margin is the same as a **haircut**.

Variation margin is a payment made, or **collateral** transferred, subsequently from one party to the other because the market price of the transaction or of collateral has changed. Variation margin payment is either in effect a settlement of profit/loss (for example in the case of a **futures** contract) or the reduction of credit exposure (for example in the case of a **repo**).

In **gilt** repos, variation margin refers to the fluctuation band or threshold within which the existing collateral's value may vary before further cash or collateral needs to be transferred.

In a loan, margin is the extra interest above a benchmark such as **LIBOR** required by a lender to compensate for the credit risk of that particular borrower.

Margin call A request by one party in a transaction for variation margin to be transferred by the other.
> *See margin.*

Margin ratio In a **repo**, the ratio agreed for the market value of the **collateral** including **hair-cut**, divided by the amount of the cash loan plus accrued interest.
> *See margin.*

Margin transfer Payments of cash or transfers of **securities** to maintain the value of **collateral** in a transaction.
> *See margin.*

Mark to market Revalue a position at current market rates.

Market maker A trader who is prepared to quote two-way prices in a particular instrument.

Market risk (Or **position risk**.) The risk that the market value of a position falls.

Matched book dealer A **market maker** in **repos**.

Matched sale/purchase Same as a **central bank reverse repo** in the case of the Federal Reserve.

Mean ▶ *See arithmetic mean.*

Modified duration The proportional change in the price of a bond or other series of cash-flows, relative to a change in **yield**.
> *See duration.*

Modified following The convention that if a **settlement date** in the future falls on a non-business day, the settlement date will be moved to the next following business day, unless this moves it to the next month, in which case the settlement date is moved back to the last previous business day.

Money market basis The calculation of interest on the basis that there are 360 days in each year but using the actual number of days in the period.

> *See bond basis.*

Monte Carlo simulation Application of a large number of random price changes to a position or portfolio, to assess the risk or probable outcome.

Moosmüller A method for calculating the **yield** of a bond.

Naked option An **option** bought or sold for **speculation**, with no offsetting existing position behind it.
> *See covered option.*

Negative skewness A greater probability of a large downward movement in prices than of a large upward movement.

Net present value (Or **NPV**.) The net total of several **present values** (arising from cashflows at different future dates) added together, some of which may be positive and some negative.

Nominal rate A rate of interest as quoted, rather than the **effective rate** to which it is **equivalent**.

Non-deliverable forward A foreign exchange **forward outright** where, instead of each party delivering the full amount of currency at settlement, there is a single net cash payment to reflect the change between the forward rate transacted and the **spot** rate two working days before settlement.

Normal probability distribution A particular **probability distribution** assumed to prevail in a wide variety of circumstances, including the financial markets.

Notional In a **bond futures** contract, the standardized non-existent bond traded, as opposed to the actual bonds which are **deliverable** at maturity.

> **Contracts for differences** require a notional principal amount on which settlement can be calculated.

NPV ▶ *See net present value.*

Odd date ▶ *See broken date.*

Off-balance-sheet A transaction whose principal amount is not shown on the balance sheet because it is a contingent liability or settled as a **contract for differences**.
> ▶ *See on-balance-sheet.*

Offer The price at which the dealer quoting a price or rate is prepared to sell or lend. The offer price of a foreign exchange quotation is the rate at which he will sell the **base** currency and buy the **variable** currency.

> In a **repo**, the interest rate at which the dealer will lend the **collateral** and borrow the cash.
> ▶ *See bid.*

Off-market A rate which is not the current market rate.

O/N ▶ *See overnight.*

On-balance-sheet A transaction whose principal amount is shown on the balance sheet.
> ▶ *See off-balance-sheet.*

Option The right, without any obligation, to undertake a particular deal.
> ▶ *See call option, put option.*

OTC ▶ *See over-the-counter.*

Out-of-the-money An **option** whose **strike** is less advantageous to the option buyer than the current market rate.
> ▶ *See at-the-money, in-the-money.*

Outright ▶ *See forward outright.*

Outstrike The trigger level in a **knock-out option**.
> ▶ *See instrike.*

Overnight (Or **O/N** or **today/tomorrow**.) A **forward swap** or money market deal from today until the next working day.

Over-the-counter   (Or OTC.) A transaction dealt privately between any two parties, rather than dealt on an exchange.

Own funds ▶ *See capital adequacy ratio.*

Par   In foreign exchange, when the **forward outright** and **spot** exchange rates are equal, the **forward swap** is zero or par.

When the price of a **security** is equal to its **face value**, usually expressed as 100, it is said to be trading at par.

A par swap rate is the current market rate for a fixed-rate **interest rate swap** against LIBOR.

Par yield curve   A curve showing **yield** against time to maturity for theoretical bonds which would be priced at **par** to be consistent with the yields of actual instruments available in the market.

Participation forward   A **forward** deal where, if the **spot** rate at maturity turns out to be more advantageous than the forward rate, the customer receives a share of the better result that he would have had if he had not dealt forward.

Path-dependent option   An **option** where the decision or ability to exercise it – and hence its value – depends not only on the **underlying** price at **expiry**, but also on the path that the price of the underlying has taken during the life of the option.

Perpetual   An **annuity** where the payment stream lasts indefinitely.

Plain vanilla transaction   A straightforward transaction.

Points   The last two decimal places in an exchange rate.

Position risk ▶ *See market risk.*

Premium   The amount by which one currency is more expensive, in terms of another currency, for **forward** delivery than for spot.

▶ *See discount.*

An **option** premium is the amount paid, generally up-front, by the purchaser of the option to the **writer**.

Present value   The amount of money which needs to be invested (or borrowed) now at a given interest rate in order to achieve exactly a given cashflow in the future, assuming **compound** re-investment (or re-funding) of any interest payments received (or paid) before the end.

▶ *See time value of money, future value.*

Price factor ▶ *See conversion factor.*

Price value of a basis point   (Or **PVB** or **dollar value of a basis point** or **dollar value of an 01** or **DV01**.) The price change in an investment arising from a 1 basis point change in **yield**.

▶ *See modified duration.*

Probability distribution   The mathematical description of how probable it is that the value of something is less than or equal to a particular level.

Put option   A deal giving one party the right, without the obligation, to sell an agreed amount of a particular instrument or commodity, at an agreed rate, on or before an agreed future date. The other party has the obligation to buy if so requested by the first party.
▶ *See call option.*

Put/call parity   The theoretical relationship between the value of a **put option** and the value of a **call option** at the same **strike** price.

PVB   ▶ *See price value of a basis point.*

Quasi-coupon date   For **zero-coupon** instruments, the regular date on which a **coupon** payment would be scheduled if there were one.

Quoted currency   ▶ *See variable currency.*

Range forward   A **forward outright** with two forward rates, where settlement takes place at the higher forward rate if the **spot** rate at maturity is higher than that, at the lower forward rate if the spot rate at maturity is lower than that, or at the spot rate at maturity otherwise.
▶ *See collar.*

Rate of discount   The interest rate which has been chosen for calculating a **present value** from a future amount.

Ratio spread   The purchase of a certain number of **calls** (or **puts**) combined with the sale of a different number of calls (or puts).

Record date   A **coupon** or other payment due on a **security** is paid by the issuer to whoever is registered on the record date as being the owner.
▶ *See ex-dividend, cum-dividend.*

Re-investment rate   The rate at which interim interest cashflows can be re-invested – which may or may not be the same as the original investment rate.

Repo   (Or **sale and repurchase agreement** or **RP** or **repurchase agreement** or **classic repo** or **US-style repo**.) A single agreement to sell a bond or other **asset** and buy it back again from the same counterparty for settlement on a later date at an agreed price, equivalent to borrowing money against a loan of **collateral**.
▶ *See reverse repo.*

Repurchase agreement   ▶ *See repo.*

Reverse knock-in option   A **knock-in option** where, at the point of its being triggered, the option would be **in-the-money** rather than **out-of-the-money**.
▶ *See reverse knock-out option.*

Reverse knock-out option   A **knock-out option** where, at the point of its being triggered, the option would be **in-the-money** rather than **out-of-the-money**.
▶ *See reverse knock-in option.*

Reverse repo   (Or **reverse**.) A single agreement to buy a bond or other asset and sell it back again to the same counterparty for settlement on a later date at an agreed price.
▶ *See repo.*

Rho (ρ)   The change in the value of an **option** as a proportion of the change in the interest rate.

Risk asset ratio   A bank's own funds divided by its risk-weighted assets.
▶ *See capital adequacy directives.*

Risk-free rate of return For a given currency, the yield expected on an investment (typically a government security) considered to carry no credit risk.

Risk-reversal The purchase (or sale) of a **call** combined with the sale (or purchase) of a **put** at a lower **strike** (generally transacted with both **out-of-the-money**, at net zero **premium**).

Risk-weighted assets ▶ *See capital adequacy ratio.*

RP ▶ *See repo.*

Running yield ▶ *See current yield.*

Sale and repurchase agreement ▶ *See repo.*

Securities borrowing (Or **stock borrowing.**) A temporary transfer of legal title in a **security** to one party from another, often collateralized by a matching temporary transfer of **assets** or cash in the opposite direction. Securities lending (or stock lending) is the same transaction viewed from the counterparty's point of view.

Securities lending ▶ *See securities borrowing.*

Security A financial asset sold initially for cash by a borrowing organization (the 'issuer') and often tradable in the market.

Sell/buy-back The sale of a bond or other **asset** and the simultaneous purchase of the same asset back again from the same counterparty for settlement on a later date.
   ▶ *See buy/sell-back and repo.*

Settlement date (Or **value date** or **maturity date**.) The date on which a transaction is consummated, i.e. delivery takes place.

Settlement risk The risk that a counterparty defaults during settlement – a particular category of **counterparty risk**.

Short A surplus of sales over purchases of a given currency or **asset**, or a situation which gives rise to an organization benefiting from a weakening of that currency or asset. To a money-market dealer, a surplus of money lent out over borrowings taken in.
   ▶ *See long.*

Short date A foreign exchange **forward swap** or **forward outright** transaction or a money market deposit for settlement less than one month after **spot**.

Simple basis ▶ *See basis.*

Simple interest Interest calculated on the assumption that there is no opportunity to re-invest the interest payments during the life of an investment and thereby earn extra income.

Simple yield to maturity The **coupon** rate of a bond plus the principal gain or loss amortized over the time to maturity, as a proportion of the **clean price** per 100.
   ▶ *See current yield, yield to maturity.*

S/N ▶ *See spot/next.*

Special A bond in particular demand by borrowers in a **reverse repo**, **buy/sell-back** or **securities borrowing** transaction.

Speculation A deal undertaken because the dealer expects prices to move in his favour.
   ▶ *See hedge, arbitrage.*

Spot A deal to be settled on the customary **settlement date** for that particular market. In the foreign exchange market, this is for value in 2 working days' time.

Spot yield curve The **yield curve** showing **zero-coupon yields** against time to maturity.

Spot/next (Or **S/N**.) A **forward swap** or money market deal from **spot** until the next working day.

Spot-a-week (Or **S/W**.) A **forward swap** or money market deal from **spot** until a week later.

Spread A trading strategy in which a trader buys one instrument and sells another, related instrument, with a view to profiting from a change in the price difference between the two: a **futures** spread is the purchase of one futures contract and the sale of another; an **option** spread is the purchase of one **call** (or **put**) and the sale of another.

The difference between the **bid** and **offer** prices in a quotation.

Standard deviation The square root of the **variance** of a series of numbers.

STIR futures and options (Acronym for 'short-term interest rate'.) A **futures** or **option** contract for short-term interest rates, on a recognized futures exchange.

Stock borrowing ▶ *See securities borrowing.*

Stock lending ▶ *See securities borrowing.*

Straddle The purchase of a **call** combined with the purchase of a **put** at the same **strike** (generally purchased with both **at-the-money**).
   ▶ *See strangle.*

Strangle The purchase of a **call** combined with the purchase of a **put** at a lower **strike** (generally purchased with both **out-of-the-money**).
   ▶ *See straddle.*

Strike price/rate (Or **exercise** price.) The price or rate at which the holder of an **option** can insist on the underlying transaction being fulfilled.

Strip (An acronym for **separately traded and registered interest and principal**.) A **zero-coupon security** created by separating each **coupon** payment and principal payment due from a coupon-bearing bond and allowing each cashflow to be traded as a separate zero-coupon bond.

The purchase or sale of a series of consecutive interest rate **futures** contracts or **forward rate agreements**.

S/W ▶ *See spot-a-week.*

Synthetic forward The combination of a purchase (or sale) of a **call option** on an instrument and a sale (or purchase) of a **put option** at the same **strike**, theoretically with the same economic effect as a forward purchase (or sale) of that instrument.

System repo A **central bank repo** by the US Federal Reserve on its own account, in order to adjust the supply of cash in the market, or to signal a change in interest rate policy.
   ▶ *See customer repo.*

Tail The exposure to interest rates over a **forward-forward** period arising from a mismatched position (such as a 2-month borrowing against a 3-month loan).

A **forward** foreign exchange dealer's exposure to **spot** movements.

TED spread The simultaneous purchase/sale of a eurodollar **futures** contract and the sale/purchase of a US **Treasury bill** futures contract.
▸ *See spread.*

Theoretical basis The difference between the theoretical futures price which can be calculated according to the underlying cash market prices and (100 – the current cash interest rate).

Theta (Θ) The change in the value of an **option** as a proportion of the change in time.

Tick The smallest change in price allowed by the exchange for a particular **futures** contract.

Tick value The profit or loss on a **futures** contract arising from a one-tick change in price.

Time bucket In assessing interest rate risk, positions are typically grouped according to maturity; each separate maturity band is called a time bucket.

Time value That part of the **premium** paid for an **option**, over and above its **intrinsic value**.

Time value of money The concept that a future cashflow can be valued as the amount of money which it is necessary to invest now in order to achieve that cashflow in the future.

▸ *See present value, future value.*

T/N ▸ *See tom/next.*

Today/tomorrow ▸ *See overnight.*

Tom/next (Or **T/N** or **rollover**.) A **forward swap** or money market deal from the next working day until the day after.

Top combination An **option** strategy such as a **straddle** sale which has a top limit to its profitability.

Trading book Under the **capital adequacy directives**, those of a bank's outstanding transactions which are not in its **banking book**.

Treasury bill A short-term **security** issued by a government, generally with a zero coupon.

Treasury bond A long-term **security** issued by the US government.

Trigger level ▸ *See barrier option.*

Trigger option ▸ *See barrier option.*

True yield The **yield** which is equivalent to the quoted **discount rate** (for a US or UK **Treasury bill** for example).

Tunnel ▸ *See collar.*

Underlying The instrument or commodity which is being bought or sold in an **option**.

Up-and-in option A **knock-in option** where the trigger is higher than the **underlying** rate at the start.
▸ *See down-and-in option, up-and-out option, down-and-out option.*

Up-and-out option A **knock-out option** where the trigger is higher than the **underlying** rate at the start.
▸ *See up-and-in option, down-and-in option, down-and-out option.*

US-style repo ▸ *See repo.*

Value at risk   (Or **earnings at risk**.) The maximum potential loss which a bank expects to suffer on its positions over a given time period, estimated with a given confidence level.

Value basis   The difference between the actual **futures** price trading in the market and the theoretical futures price which can be calculated according to the underlying cash market prices.

Value date ▶ *See settlement date.*

In some bond markets there can be a difference between the date on which the cash/bond delivery takes place (**settlement date**) and the date to which **accrued coupon** is calculated (value date).

Vanilla ▶ *See plain vanilla transaction.*

VAR ▶ *See value at risk.*

Variable currency   (Or **counter currency** or **quoted currency**.) An exchange rate is quoted as the number of units of one currency (the variable currency) equal to one unit of the other currency (the **base currency**).

Variance   The **arithmetic mean** of all the squares of the differences between a series of numbers and the arithmetic mean of all the numbers.

Variation margin ▶ *See margin.*

Vega   (Or **lambda** (Λ) or **kappa** (κ).) The change in the value of an **option** as a proportion of the change in **volatility**.

Vega neutral   An **option** portfolio with zero **vega**.

Vertical spread   An **option spread** constructed from options with the same maturity but different **strikes**.
▶ *See spread.*

Volatility   The annualized **standard deviation** of the **continuously compounded** rate of return on an instrument. A measure of how much the price fluctuates.

▶ *See historic volatility, implied volatility.*

Modified duration is also known as volatility.

Volatility trade   An **option** strategy in which the trader expects an increase or decrease in **volatility**.
▶ *See directional trade.*

Warrant   An **option**, generally referring to a **call option** on a **security** where the warrant is purchased as part of an investment in another or the same security.

Writer   The seller of an **option**.

Yield   The interest rate which can be earned on an investment, currently quoted by the market or implied by the current market price for the investment.

For a bond, generally the same as **yield to maturity** unless otherwise specified.

Yield curve   A curve plotting **yield** against time to maturity.

Yield to maturity   (Or **YTM** or **yield** or **gross redemption yield** or **GRY**.) The **internal rate of return** arising from the cashflows of an investment. This is the same as the yield necessary to **discount** all the investment's cashflows to a **net present value** equal to its current **dirty price**.

YTM ▶ *See yield to maturity.*

Zero-cost option A combination of **options** bought and sold, such that the **premiums** paid and received net to zero.

Zero-coupon security A **security** that makes no **coupon** payments, paying the investor only the face value at redemption.

Zero-coupon yield The actual or theoretical **yield** earned on an instrument where there are no cashflows other than at the start and at maturity.

A SUMMARY OF DAY/YEAR CONVENTIONS FOR MONEY MARKETS AND GOVERNMENT BOND MARKETS

Instrument	Day/Year Basis	Yield or Discount Rate
Australia		
Money market	ACT/365	Y
Bond (semi-annual coupons)	ACT/ACT	
Austria		
Money market	ACT/360	Y
Bond (annual coupons)	ACT/ACT	
Belgium		
Money market	ACT/360	Y
OLO (annual coupons)	ACT/ACT	
Canada		
Money market	ACT/365	Y
Bond (semi-annual coupons)	ACT/365 (accrued coupon)	
	ACT/ACT (dirty price calculation)	
Denmark		
Money market	ACT/360	Y
Bond (annual coupons)	30(E)/360	
Eire		
Money market	ACT/360	Y
Bond (ann. and semi-ann. coupons)	ACT/ACT[1]	
Finland		
Money market	ACT/360	Y
Bond (annual coupons)	ACT/ACT	
France		
Money market	ACT/360	Y
OAT, BTAN (annual coupons)	ACT/ACT	
Germany		
Money market	ACT/360	Y
Bund, OBL (annual coupons)	ACT/ACT	
Italy		
Money market	ACT/360	Y
BTP (semi-annual coupons)	ACT/ACT	
Japan		
Money market	ACT/365	Y
JGB (semi-annual coupons)	ACT[2]/365	
Netherlands		
Money market	ACT/360	Y
Bond (annual coupons)	ACT/ACT	
Norway		
T-bills	ACT/365[3]	Y
Other money market	ACT/360	Y
Bond (annual coupons)	ACT/365	
Spain		
Money market	ACT/360	Y
Bono (annual coupons)	ACT/ACT	
Sweden		
T-bills	30(E)/360	Y
Other money market	ACT/360	Y
Bond	30(E)/360	
Switzerland		
Money market	ACT/360	Y
Bond (annual coupons)	30(E)/360	

UK

Depo/CD/£CP/T-bill (€)	ACT/365	Y
BA/T-bill (£)	ACT/365	D
Gilt (all semi-annual coupons except for one quarterly)	ACT/ACT	

US

Depo/CD	ACT/360	Y
BA/$CP/T-bill	ACT/360	D
T-bond/note (semi-annual coupons)	ACT/ACT	
Federal agency and corporate bonds	30(A)/360	

Euro (the single 'domestic' currency for the
    European Monetary Union countries)

Money market	ACT/360	Y
Bond	ACT/ACT	

Euromarket (non-domestic markets
generally, regardless of the currency)

Money market	ACT/360 (exceptions using ACT/365 include GBP, GRD, SGD, HKD, MYR, TWD, THB, ZAR)	Y
Eurobond (almost all annual coupons)	ACT/ACT[4]	

Notes
1   Some older bonds still use ACT/365 or 30(E)/360.
2   One day's extra coupon is accrued in the first coupon period.
3   Quoted as an effective (annual equivalent) yield rather than a simple rate.
4   According to the ISMA convention, yields are conventionally quoted on an annual basis, even for
     Eurobonds with semi-annual coupons. Bonds issued before 1999 use 30(E)/360.